Unionist Voices and the Politics of Remembering
the Past in Northern Ireland

*Also by Kirk Simpson*

TRUTH RECOVERY IN NORTHERN IRELAND: Critically Interpreting the Past

# Unionist Voices and the Politics of Remembering the Past in Northern Ireland

Kirk Simpson

*RCUK Post Doctoral Fellow, Transitional Justice Institute, University of Ulster, UK*

WITHDRAWN

First published 2009 by
PALGRAVE MACMILLAN

Palgrave Macmillan in the UK is an imprint of Macmillan Publishers Limited, registered in England, company number 785998, of Houndmills, Basingstoke, Hampshire RG21 6XS.

Palgrave Macmillan in the US is a division of St Martin's Press LLC, 175 Fifth Avenue, New York, NY 10010.

Palgrave Macmillan is the global academic imprint of the above companies and has companies and representatives throughout the world.

Palgrave® and Macmillan® are registered trademarks in the United States, the United Kingdom, Europe and other countries.

ISBN-13: 978-0-230-22414-8 hardback

This book is printed on paper suitable for recycling and made from fully managed and sustained forest sources. Logging, pulping and manufacturing processes are expected to conform to the environmental regulations of the country of origin.

A catalogue record for this book is available from the British Library.

A catalog record for this book is available from the Library of Congress.

10  9  8  7  6  5  4  3  2  1
18  17  16  15  14  13  12  11  10  09

Printed and bound in Great Britain by
CPI Antony Rowe, Chippenham and Eastbourne

*For my Mum, Dulcie, and*
*in loving memory of my Dad, John.*

# Contents

# Acknowledgements

Sincere thanks are due to the following for helping me to write this book:

My colleagues at the Transitional Justice Institute (TJI) at the University of Ulster, Northern Ireland. In particular I would like to thank Professor Colm Campbell for encouraging this research from the beginning; and Catherine Turner, who offered helpful comments and suggestions during discussions about this work. Sincere thanks also to Professor Henry Patterson for all of his advice and support.

Dr Phil Clark of the University of Oxford – a good friend with a terrific sense of humour, a formidable intellect and boundless energy.

John McClure, an Ulsterman abroad, but an excellent friend in every sense whose insights and wit are dispensed in equal measure, and always at much needed moments.

Philip Morton – a man of few words, but who picks them more wisely and astutely than anyone I know. From boy to man, it has quite simply been an honour to count him as my closest and oldest friend and confidante. Philip still is the 'best man'.

The University of Ulster, the Research Councils of the United Kingdom (RCUK) and the British Academy, to whom I offer my most sincere thanks for their support.

All of the staff in the Politics section of Palgrave Press. From the beginning Amy-Lankester-Owen in particular has really believed in this project and supported it in every way she could, for which I am extremely grateful.

Ryan and Keir, my older brothers, who are always supportive and help to remind me of the importance of our relationship, the experiences we have shared, our past and the strong bond that we formed at such a young age. I am very proud to call them both my brothers.

Julia, my sister-in-law and one of my very best friends. It is difficult to put into words how much she means to me. Her advice, patience and consideration are invaluable. She is wise beyond her years and her unconditional love and support is a very rare treasure that I guard carefully. In times of hardship, Julia has a unique ability to raise me up. For that I am forever grateful. She is and always has been an absolute privilege to know.

John and Rosemary Black, my parents-in-law, who have taught me much not only about the past in Northern Ireland, but also about how to conduct myself with integrity, honesty and generosity. They have my love, utmost respect and thanks for their support.

My parents – my mother, Dulcie, and in remembrance of my late father, John – for whom I have immeasurable devotion and love. I have learned more from my parents than from anyone else, or anything else. They made endless sacrifices so that my brothers and I had every chance to pursue our ambitions and our goals, and their constant support and belief in me as a person made this book possible. My Mum in particular gave endlessly of her time to offer insightful, wonderfully informed historical and political analysis – as well as all the countless other loving things she did for me. I could not ask for a better Mum. My Dad trusted in me completely as a boy and as a young man. In our countless late night conversations he made me feel both completely safe and capable of anything. He made me laugh, relax and always achieve perspective. To me, he was absolutely everything that a good Dad could be, and I loved him more than I can ever possibly explain. I miss him more than words can say, but I know that he would have been proud of this work. I owe my parents everything, and this book is dedicated to them.

Janice, my wife. In remembering my own past, I cannot think of a time when Janice was not there by my side, as my girlfriend, my fiancée and my wife, always offering me wise advice and helping me to get me through so much, both good and bad. Janice knows that I can never thank her enough for the constant love and direction she provided me with in times of need. I am totally and continually overwhelmed by her goodness, her kindness, her compassion and her support. Quite simply, I have never met a better person, and never admired someone more than I admire her. More than anyone else, Janice encouraged me to write this book. Despite having written so much, the words to describe how I feel about Janice – and how much gratitude I owe her – continue to elude me. They are beyond expression. She is my inspiration. I am truly blessed to have met her and to have her as my wife.

# List of Abbreviations

| | |
|---|---|
| DUP | Democratic Unionist Party |
| GAA | Gaelic Athletic Association |
| HTR | Healing Through Remembering |
| INLA | Irish National Liberation Army |
| MLA | Member of Legislative Assembly (Northern Ireland Assembly) |
| MP | Member of Parliament (The House of Commons, the lower chamber of the United Kingdom of Great Britain and Northern Ireland Parliament) |
| NGO | Non-Governmental Organisation |
| NICRA | Northern Ireland Civil Rights Association |
| NIO | Northern Ireland Office |
| OIRA | Official Irish Republican Army |
| PIRA | Provisional Irish Republican Army |
| PSNI | Police Service of Northern Ireland |
| RUC | Royal Ulster Constabulary |
| SDLP | Social Democratic and Labour Party |
| TRC | Truth and Reconciliation Commission |
| UDA | Ulster Defence Association |
| UDR | Ulster Defence Regiment |
| UFF | Ulster Freedom Fighters |
| UK | United Kingdom of Great Britain and Northern Ireland |
| UTV | Ulster Television |
| UUP | Ulster Unionist Party |
| UVF | Ulster Volunteer Force |
| UWC | Ulster Workers' Council |

# 1
# Thematic Introduction and Background to the Northern Ireland Conflict

Northern Ireland has entered what is arguably the key phase in its troubled political history – truth recovery and dealing with the legacy of a violent past – yet the void in knowledge and the lack of academic literature with regard to unionist civilians is particularly striking (Simpson, 2008). This book aims to fill that gap. On the basis of new, original and extensive empirical and theoretical research, this book will begin to fill the 'hole' in the academic literature by presenting and offering critical and thematic analysis of previously unheard unionist oral histories and recollections of the conflict, stretching from the earliest iterations of violence in the 1970s to the final atrocities in the mid-1990s. Crucially, in so doing, it offers – for the first time – a reflective explanation of the ways in which unionists conceive of the past in the present post-conflict environment, and thus contributes genuine and necessary 'balance' to the contemporary political debate in Northern Ireland. Truth Recovery and remembering (and consequently mastering) the past in Northern Ireland cannot function successfully without unionist participation, and so the 'unlocking' and symbolic reading of their narratives and remembrance is not only desirable but is also politically and socially imperative (cf. Searle, 1970; Squire, 2005). This book is therefore structured in what is intended to be a new and fresh way that can draw on significant extracts of unionists' oral histories to illustrate core thematic issues regarding the construction of counter-hegemonic discourse and forgotten narratives in Northern Ireland.

In this chapter, it is important to emphasise that I do not attempt to provide a comprehensive overview of the Northern Ireland conflict or Northern Irish history. The limitations of space and the particular objectives of this book prevent me from doing so. In any case, this has not only been done much more often and much more extensively elsewhere (Buckland, 1981; Hennessey, 1997; Bew and Gillespie, 1999; Bew et al., 2001), but it is chiefly a professional historical endeavour, and the inclusion of an abridged version would do comparatively little to fortify the intellectual aims of this project. Additionally, this book is purposely designed to provide an original and somewhat innovative format in which the reader is 'taken through' the conflict – using a unionist lens and original unionist storytelling – from its earliest incarnations in the 1970s until its conclusions and outworkings in the late 1990s and the contemporary period. This is designed to act as a much more direct and relevant way of concentrating on the main thematic issues that are presented, some of which are explained in the remainder of this chapter. This is not to say that the history of Northern Ireland is irrelevant to the analysis of unionist civilians and how they deal with the politics of remembering the past. Rather, as this book progresses the very deliberate objective is to direct the reader episodically through various stages of the conflict. This is a methodologically distinct and – in my estimation – engaging way of introducing the reader to key issues about social and political remembrance in Northern Ireland (cf. Donnan and Simpson, 2007; Simpson, 2007[a]). It encourages the reader to occupy the same 'memory space' as the unionist civilians who are the focus of the book: that is, not only constructing the past in the present, but facing and attempting to experience and imagine the violence as it unfolded, *in the way that unionist civilians did at the time* (cf. Rosenwald and Ochberg, 1992; Antze and Lambek, 1996; Edkins, 2003; Olick, 2003). Including a lengthy examination of the construction and collapse of the Northern Ireland state, and all of the major events leading to the Troubles, would potentially disallow – and most certainly reduce the intellectual efficacy of – this possibility. To fully understand unionist perspectives on the past as they are being composed and recomposed in the post-conflict present, I have deliberately chosen an approach that I believe enables the reader to consider the issues in a way in which the 'rawness' of the surprise and shock that unionist civilians experienced is, at least in some way, transmitted (cf. Felman and Laub, 1992; Caruth, 1995).

This book is not seeking to uncover one unifying objective truth about the Northern Ireland's past. Instead, it is a reflection – indeed, perhaps even a portrait – of a people and the ways in which they recollect the Northern Ireland conflict (cf. Crawford, 1987). In this regard, a detailed historiography would limit the room available for analysis of new, contemporary empirical material, and would also introduce a fundamentally difficult epistemological problem. Deferring to what even the most venerated and respected Irish historians have written on

Northern Ireland and the conflict therein would not constitute a suitably original contribution to knowledge, and nor would it satiate the bold aims of this book. It should be noted that this is not a criticism of Irish historians: quite the reverse. My suggestion for anyone keen to know more about the entire history of the Northern Ireland state and the various factors that contributed to the widespread outbreak of violence in 1969 would be to seek out the seminal work of Patterson (2007) or Townshend (1998), among others, both of which provide a superb and incisive account of a much wider time frame.

However, given the nature of this project, it is my firm belief that simply 'squeezing in' that which would necessarily be a truncated history of a state that is nearly a century old would be both formulaic and unnecessary. It would also infuse this work with a recurrent sub-text that as the author I am seeking to avoid. It is fundamental to this book that everything that unionists have to say about how they were affected by violence in the past is judged on the immediacy of its impact in the contemporary post-conflict context, rather than according to a predetermined template of how the reader *should* understand Irish politics. Thus, in the next section I provide some crucially important introductory 'facts' about how the conflict affected unionists in Northern Ireland, but make no attempt to offer a synopsis of the Northern Ireland conflict in its totality.

## Background – Unionists and the Northern Ireland conflict

Despite the apparent political endgame in Northern Ireland, there is still considerable disagreement as to the most effective and appropriate means of dealing with the past (Bell, 2004). During the protracted 1969–1998 conflict ('The Troubles') in Northern Ireland, Northern Irish unionists (almost exclusively Protestant in composition) sought to maintain Northern Ireland's status as part of the United Kingdom. Anti-state Irish republican paramilitaries (almost exclusively Catholic in composition) were seeking to collapse the Northern Ireland state, end British sovereignty and reunify Ireland, and included most notably the Provisional Irish Republican Army (PIRA) (for an in-depth examination of this group see English, 2003). It is important to note at this point that the conflict was multi-directional, and while figures for unionist casualties are provided in this book, this is not intended in any way to reflect a partisan political position. There is no desire or intention here to act as an academic 'megaphone' for unionism in

Northern Ireland, or to amplify their stance at the expense of republican or nationalist counter-narratives. Rather, this book attempts to underline the importance of acknowledging the existence of unionist stories in the quest to find some meaningful, workable form of dealing with the past in Northern Ireland, and to illuminate the ways in which counter-hegemonic discourse is constructed in a volatile political context. Based on data supplied by the Conflict Archive Service (CAIN, 2009) at the University of Ulster, the conflict was responsible for the deaths of 3075 people. Of this total number, collectively Irish Republican paramilitary groups killed 2055 people. Of these, 980 were Protestants, 446 were Catholics and 629 were not from Northern Ireland (indicating that they were British Army or British security forces not indigenous to Northern Ireland). There remains considerable disagreement among both communities as to the sectarian nature of the Irish republican paramilitary campaign. While republican paramilitaries and their political representatives claimed that Protestants indigenous to Northern Ireland who were also members of the security forces were targeted and attacked for their role as agents of the state (rather than because they were Protestants or unionists), and therefore completely reject the notion of a sectarian conflict (Campbell and Connolly, 2006), many (in particular unionists within Northern Ireland) repudiate this rationale and believe that local Protestant unionist policemen and army members were killed as part of a sectarian, ethnically and politically motivated plot (Dingley, 1998; Parkinson, 1998; Taylor, 1999, 2001).

In a campaign that included assassinations and bomb attacks, Irish republican paramilitaries killed not only British forces, including those from the Ulster Defence Regiment [UDR] (a part-time local British Army reserve unit, largely composed of local Protestants/unionists), and members of the Royal Ulster Constabulary [RUC] (a police force which was 92% Protestant/unionist), but also former RUC members, British police officers, Northern Ireland Prison officers, former Prison officers, and contractors working for the British security services (most notably the Teebane Massacre in 1992, when eight innocent Protestant civilian victims killed by a PIRA bomb); and Protestant and Catholic civilians. This has created enormous tension in the transitional phase in Northern Ireland for unionists as they have struggled to come to terms with the early release of former republican paramilitaries and the electoral, democratic succss of Sinn Fein, which has very close links with the PIRA (and is now the largest Irish republican/nationalist political party in Northern Ireland). It is important to note in the interests of balance that Loyalist paramiltaries, in the same way that that republican paramilitaries thought of Protestant members of the security forces as 'legitimate targets' for assassination, viewed Catholic civilians as 'responsible' for sheltering, aiding or supporting PIRA attacks on Protestants (Dillon, 1989; McDonald and Cusack, 1997). Loyalists thus attacked and killed Catholic civilians; republican and nationalist politicians and political activists; republican paramilitaries; supposed informers; Protestant civilians; and other Loyalist paramilitaries in internal feuds. In a very clear majority of cases – almost 80% according to some estimates (Rolston, 2005) – Loyalist paramilitaries killed Catholic civilians, and not republican activists or republican paramilitaries, despite political and pseudo-military rhetoric that spoke of only attacking members of the republican movement.

This is a crucial issue. The main unionist political parties – the Democratic Unionist Party (DUP) and Ulster Unionist Party (UUP) – repeatedly and consistently condemned Loyalist paramilitary activity, much to the chagrin of those Loyalists who felt that the impassioned speeches of leading unionist politicians had motivated them to act in defence of 'their' community (Bruce, 1994; Taylor, 1999; Crawford, 2003). The tension between Loyalists and unionists (in particular the DUP) is often very pointed, with mainstream unionists totally refuting the idea that Loyalist paramilitaries – who posed and presented themselves as defenders of the Protestant people (McDonald and Cusack, 2004) – were in any way legitimate. For the majority of law-abiding unionists, the 'Crown Forces' (UDR, British Army and RUC) were perfectly viable, legal and valid options for those Protestants who wanted to defend the state against the threat of Irish republican terrorism. Republican critics will of course claim that collusion between the security services and Loyalist paramilitaries renders this claim somewhat obsolete (cf. Sluka, 1999; Jamieson and McEvoy, 2005), but on the basis of the evidence of this book, that notion can be repelled. Almost without exception, the unionists in this book with whom I spoke articulated no support – tacit, active or otherwise – for state-sponsored assassinations of PIRA members or Catholic civilians via Loyalist terrorist proxy. I have no reason to doubt the sincerity of these sentiments. While in some cases such views were the product of staunch refusal to contemplate the very idea of collusion (i.e. some unionists believe it was extremely isolated if it happened at all, and that the collusion 'agenda' of part of a republican propaganda campaign to discredit the army and police), for the most part they were calculated considerations and genuine expressions of disdain for the notion that the British state or its security forces might have involved themselves – at a collective and institutionalised level – in a 'dirty war' with republicans and Loyalists (Dillon, 1991). For unionists in this research, this was regarded not only as morally objectionable, but also as 'stooping to the level' of terrorists, which they regarded as contemptuous.

Although the armed conflict in Northern Ireland has now apparently ended, the political lessons of other violent societies in transition have demonstrated that the past should be confronted, and that all narratives must be voiced and heard, or liminal groups like unionists will be forced into subterranean social and cultural quarantine, re-stigmatised and objectified, and ultimately forgotten, as has happened in a range of other contexts – notably Argentina, Spain, Germany and Chile, where governments which attempted to 'lock down' the past at the point of transition, or to face it in a highly technocratic fashion, are now having to deal with the ramifications of its excavation by victims decades later (Jackson, 2002; Wilson, 2003; Humphrey, 2005; Simpson, 2007[b]). Dealing with the past in Northern Ireland is arguably in a position of crisis. Despite the self-congratulatory mood that has followed the restoration of devolved, power-sharing government in the Province, and the co-operation between erstwhile political enemies the DUP and Sinn Fein, my research with 'ordinary' unionist civilians and victims has revealed that many are struggling to reconcile their remembrance of the conflict with the political and economic dynamics and imperatives and outworkings of the post-settlement phase. This is despite the fact that the principle of consent – that there will be no change in Northern Ireland's status as a constituent part of the United Kingdom without the consent of the majority of Northern Ireland's citizens – has been recognised by the Irish Republic, which has abandoned its territorial claim on Northern Ireland – and enshrined in law as a consequence of the Northern Ireland Act of 1998 (NIO, 1998). That the British have presented themselves as 'independent facilitators' in negotiating an end to a conflict in which they themselves were both key political protagonists and combatants, and which took place in their sovereign territory (Cunningham, 2001; Dixon, 2001), has created much distrust and anger among the unionist community in Northern Ireland (Patterson, 2007; Simpson, 2008). If unionists cannot be persuaded to become involved in a process of truth recovery even by their own local political 'leaders', comparatively uninformed attempts by the British government – to which unionists pledge conditional allegiance – to master the past and to solidify peace in Northern Ireland will in all likelihood have significantly reduced prospects of success (Bruce, 2007). This has been evidenced in some of the ways in which recent British administrations have framed the idea of commemoration, dealing with the past and truth recovery – the extremely expensive and protracted Saville Inquiry into Bloody Sunday for example (http://www.bloody-sunday-inquiry.org.uk), and the concomitant but ridiculous (and offensive) notion that a public inquiry into the murder of Billy Wright, a convicted Loyalist paramilitary (Anderson, 2004), would somehow compensate law-abiding unionist civilians who despised Wright and what he stood for (http://www.billywrightinquiry.org). This inquiry mode of dealing with the past has been perceived by the unionists with whom I have conducted research as congruent with an Irish republican agenda and has met with deep cynicism and opprobrium.

## Dealing with the past in Northern Ireland – A brief overview

As part of the truth recovery process in Northern Ireland – as piecemeal and fractured as it has been – unionists have suffered from having 'no voice', and no opportunity to tell their stories. It might have been expected that the architects of the Belfast Agreement of 1998 would have provided more substantial mechanisms for dealing with the past than has actually been the case. Regretfully, despite unionist victims' lengthy search for truth (which stretches back to the very first incidences of political violence of the conflict), in the ensuing years there has been little done to comprehensively addressing the history of the Troubles or offer unionists a platform for commemoration with which they feel comfortable (i.e. one which, as they perceive it, is not manipulated by Irish republicans). The appointment of Mrs Bertha McDougall as Interim Victims' Commissioner in 2005 was a comparatively recent example of poor policy-making in this regard. Generally welcomed by unionists, in 2006, the Northern Ireland High Court upheld a judicial review application challenging her appointment. The judge in the case, Lord Justice Girvan, asserted that the decision to make Mrs McDougall Interim Victims' Commissioner had been 'motivated by improper purpose', implying strongly that it was a strategic political concession to unionists (and in particular the DUP) by the then British Secretary of State Peter Hain MP. Mrs McDougall's husband served in the RUC during the Troubles and was assassinated by Irish republican paramilitaries, and as such the republican community questioned her suitability for the role. In a further judgement delivered in January 2007 Lord Justice Girvan held that her post of Interim Victims' Commissioner had formally come to an end on the 5 December 2006.

The Interim Commissioner's final report, 'Support for Victims and Survivors: Addressing the Human Legacy', was completed and made available to the public in January 2007, but crucially the report was issued in Mrs McDougall's own name and did not receive the support of the Northern Ireland Office (NIO). This was regarded as a blow to unionists, who having garnered some level of confidence from McDougall's appointment again felt that republicans had succeeded in ensuring that unionist history would not have a fair hearing – even by the British Government – and that a situation would be engineered in which republicans could continue to historically legitimise their 'armed struggle' and elide unionist biographies of suffering. Mrs McDougall has since been replaced by a panel of four Victims' Commissioners (somewhat ludicrously, she has been re-appointed as one of these four commissioners), at much greater expense to the tax-payer, and according to the respondents in my research, with less chance of accessing unionist history. The four posts were created as the product of a bipartisan agreement between the DUP and Sinn Fein.

In addition to McDougall, the identities of the other three commissioners are: Mike Nesbitt (a former local television news journalist); Brendan McAllister of Mediation Northern Ireland; and perhaps most controversially – certainly for unionists – Patricia MacBride, whose brother was a member of the PIRA and who was shot and killed by the Special Air Service (SAS), an elite unit of the British Army. Unionists were infuriated in January 2008 when the newly created panel of commissioners issued a statement that stated that MacBride's brother was an 'IRA Volunteer' who was 'killed on active service'. I was carrying out informal interviews with a group of unionists in a rural area of the Province the day that news broke, and they were outraged. Many unionists steadfastly refuse to recognise the PIRA as 'volunteers' – preferring instead that they be referred to as criminals or terrorists (or even both). The notion that they were 'killed on active service' is for many unionists – not least those with whom I was speaking – total anathema and further evidence that there is some sort of master plan to legitimise the PIRA campaign as a 'just war'. As one respondent, a male farmer in his early 50s, said to me:

> Killed on active service? Is that meant to be a joke? Are we meant to accept that? This just shows you what we've been saying to you all along – they set up these groups and we think at last we maybe have a chance to get our story across and then they go and appoint someone as a commissioner for victims who is not only connected

to a dead IRA terrorist, but someone who seems proud of it!! An IRA 'volunteer'? Sure what does that mean? What did he volunteer for? To murder innocent Protestants? Active service, that's an insult! This just is more of the same thing they've always done you know? Sinn Fein, the British Government and the Irish Government, and now even the DUP! They cook up these schemes to make sure they keep hold of power but they don't want to know what really happened to innocent unionists during the Troubles. That wouldn't sit easily with the nice wee picture of peace they're trying to create so they can sit up there at Stormont in their nice suits and have their big cars. We'll be forgotten again.

Although the DUP backed the appointments of the four commissioners, there has since been internal wrangling between it and Sinn Fein over the form of legislation that will be used in the Northern Ireland Assembly to formally create the posts. More interestingly, a single unionist campaigner, Michelle Williamson – whose parents were killed by the PIRA in the Shankill Road Bombing of 1993 (which resulted in the deaths of nine Protestant civilians, among them a teenage girl) – challenged the appointment of the commissioners in the Belfast High Court in March 2008 and won the right to apply for a judicial review. In January 2008, the Northern Ireland Executive set aside 36 million pounds for 'issues relating to the past'. In July 2008, it then announced that almost 3 million pounds of that money would be allocated directly to groups working with victims and survivors. DUP First Minister Peter Robinson claimed that this was a clear message to all victims and survivors that their needs are a priority for the devolved government. Deputy First Minister Martin McGuiness of Sinn Fein – who has confessed to being a one-time member of the PIRA in Londonderry – also backed this sentiment. Flooding the Victims' Sector (which is the current governmental and political lexicon) with this money might seem benevolent and approximating a 'solution', but the major problem for Robinson's core constituency of unionist voters was that in offering this package he and his party made no distinction between the diametrically opposed views of those whom unionists would consider 'victims' of the conflict and those whom Sinn Fein and the PIRA would consider to be victims. This ambiguity has been fairly typical of the awkward machinations of the devolved regime. The lack of a clear boundary line between those innocent civilians who were victimised and those who perpetrated acts of terror represents a major problem not only for unionist politicians, but also for the process of remembering the past (Dawson, 2003; Margalit, 2004; Ricoeur, 2004; Donnan, 2005; Olick, 2007).

Prior to the appointment of the four Victims' Commissioners, in 2007 the British Government created an Independent Consultative Group to examine the 'legacy of the past'. The Group was composed of a curious mix of people, and was male-dominated. Its members were: Lord Eames (former Church of Ireland primate and co-chair); Denis Bradley (former vice-chairman of the Policing Board and co-chair); Jarlath Burns (former Gaelic Athletic Association [GAA] captain of Armagh county); Presbyterian Minster Reverend Lesley Carroll; Willie John McBride (former captain of the British and Irish Lions rugby union team); James Mackey (a former philosophy lecturer); Elaine Moore (a drugs and alcohol counsellor); and David Porter (director of the Centre for Contemporary Christianity in Ireland). Ex-President of Finland Martti Ahtisaari (who was part of the decommissioning team appointed by the British Government to inspect the destruction of PIRA weapons in Northern Ireland) and South African lawyer Brian Curran (who has experience in Northern Ireland as a former chairman of the Parades Commission) served as international advisors to the Group.

On the basis of my research, however, there is a definite fear – among unionist civilians in particular – that the Group would continue to essentialise victims and conduct its enquiries according to a collective memory paradigm, and that it would subscribe to a republican-led version of history. Objections were raised by unionist individuals at every meeting I observed, in particular regarding the possibility of amnesty for those terrorists on the run or who wanted to 'trade' freedom for a version of truth about unsolved crimes. The co-chair of the Group, Denis Bradley, has since announced that amnesty has been firmly ruled out by the Group. Despite this, unionists remain sceptical, and have been criticised very publicly by one of the most strident and high profile of unionist victims' groups, Families Acting for Innocent Relatives (FAIR), which commented publicly on its Web site that it was with 'utter and total disgust that the victims see another quango set up to look into how to deal with Victims' past'. FAIR added that it wanted to send a 'clear message to these quangos and government not to even consider trying to enforce a political arrangement that suits them onto the victims' (www.victims.org.uk/news.html). It is salient to note though that the sentiments of FAIR, in my research experience, are not echoed by the majority of unionists. It is very difficult to estimate how representative FAIR is of the wide spectrum of people traumatised by paramilitary violence in the Protestant community. One might suggest, despite its high profile, that the weak showing of support for FAIR's leader and spokesperson in local and national elections indicates that although it sometimes portrays itself as the predominant voice of unionist victims in Northern Ireland, such claims are exaggerated and inaccurate.

Sitting in the audience in 2008 I listened to people making public submissions to the Independent Consultative Group on the Past, as it moved around Northern Ireland for a series of public hearings. I was struck by the impassioned texture and tone of the discourse, particularly in so-called unionist towns. In my considerable research experience with them as a group and as individuals, it has always been apparent that unionists are in some way desperate to tell their stories, but are concurrently extremely concerned that in so doing they will be unwittingly co-opted into a process that will 'manufacture' a synthetic, sanitised version of history that they feel would be loaded in favour of Irish nationalists and republicans. Based on my substantial empirical analysis, unionists stress the importance of their own biographies of suffering and the public re-telling of their experiences, which they feel – rightly or wrongly – have been hitherto 'erased' or 'ignored'. Unionists *can be persuaded* to participate in the politics of remembering the past, but they are anxious about the possibility of being written 'out' of history (cf. Trouillot, 1995), and as noted are also firmly opposed to forms of moral relativism in which perpetrators of political violence would be afforded equal status with victims. Although unionist participation in dealing with the past might appear highly conditional, it is still nonetheless feasible, but only if stories – such as those that are provided in this book – are disseminated publicly and widely, so that 'hidden histories' become more widely known, both internally to Northern Ireland and within the rest of the United Kingdom. History, and the writing of history, is the key to securing ultimate victory in any conflict. According to the long-held maxim, history is written by the victors. It comes as no surprise then, that as the Independent Consultative Group on the Past (more commonly and hereafter referred to as 'Eames-Bradley') moves towards its conclusions unionists are beginning to realise that a version of 'their history' must at least be heard, if not universally validated.

The suggestion, however, that the various iterations of state-sanctioned remembrance for fallen police officers or soldiers of the UDR or regular British Army have offered unionists a viable way to externalise their grief is unfortunately – at least in relation to the many, many unionist civilians murdered by Irish republican terrorists in gun and bomb attacks – totally erroneous (cf. Mitscherlich and Mitscherlich, 1975). Even allowing for the fact that 'official' state memory in the form of memorial gardens or ceremonial parades – allied to pitiful compensation packages – might have satiated the grief of the relatives of police officers and soldiers, this still did nothing for ordinary unionists who were murdered by paramilitaries, or who experienced the murder of innocent civilians vicariously. The idea that state-designed or state-sponsored commemoration allowed an outlet for widespread unionist sadness and despair is – on the basis of my research – simply not the case; and the articulation of that argument is predicated upon the notion that all unionists 'are the same'. This is a fundamental underestimation that is routinely made by British politicians and policymakers and which is fortified by a process of republican-led 'othering' of unionists. There have been initiatives in Northern Ireland that have earnestly tried to involve a cross-section of the community in commemorative activity, but their efficacy and their appeal to people who were victims of attacks that were three decades ago is less certain. Most notable among the non-governmental initiatives that have been attempted has been the work of the Healing Through Remembering Group (HTR). HTR is a cross-community organisation based in Northern Ireland that was formally created in 2001. It draws not only on the work of academics but also on the work of victims, victims' groups, political actors, the general public and other Non-Governmental Organisations (NGOs). It has endeavoured to create a myriad of ways in which victims of violence can find strategies for dealing with the past, including commemorative strategies and storytelling processes. Although it has gained significant academic and policy credibility, many unionists have remained deeply cynical – and in many cases angry – about what they view as HTR's attempt to impose false moral equivalence between victims and perpetrators. The point to note here is that irrespective of macro-level processes – and these are often thought to have hidden or overt political agendas, depending on which political party one listens to – both the British and Irish Governments have failed to implement a project of truth recovery in Northern Ireland which has been unquestionably victim-centred and critical in its texture and its objectives, and which has won the confidence of unionists.

## Unionist civilians – Forgotten victims

A key issue to address in this book therefore is the way in which I have conceptualised the term 'victim'. Clearly, commemoration and remembrance in deeply divided societies is highly contested (cf. Gillis, 1996;

Jarman, 1997; Huyssen, 2003), and there is ostensibly little or no neu-
tral social or cultural space in Northern Ireland in which a definition
of 'innocent victims' can easily be agreed upon (Lundy and McGovern,
2001; Switzer, 2007). Consequently, even perpetrators of heinous acts of
political violence have made spurious claims to innocence – that they
were forced to participate in paramilitary activity because of political
circumstance, or socialisation or peer pressure, for example. My position on this is clear, as has been outlined in my other work (Simpson,
2007[a]; Simpson, 2007[b]; Simpson, 2009). Using a morally normative
framework, it is my contention that the identification of innocent victims of the conflict is, at least in one sense, not at all problematic. If
we disaggregate civilians – both Protestant and Catholic – from those
who were active or past members of the British security services or
members of Irish or Loyalist paramilitary organizations, the picture is
much clearer. The argument postulated by some Irish republican terrorists that during the 'Troubles' *no unionist* could be 'innocent' as they
implicitly supported the Union and the state apparatus that enforced
its supposed injustices (Taylor, P., 1997; English, 2003), is expedient
and specious structuralism. It serves only as a lamentably weak rationalization of evil wrongdoing that resulted in the murder of civilians,
and should not be accepted as legitimate in any society grappling with
a violent past (Borradori, 2004). This book condemns illegal political
violence outright from wherever it came. It was absolutely, irreducibly
wrong and unacceptable. Additionally, for unionists, the PIRA's claim
that it waged a non-sectarian 'liberation struggle' in Northern Ireland
was rendered absurd by its attacks on civilians with no connections
to the state security forces (Dingley, 1998). As the focus of this book
is those ordinary unionist civilians – some of whom were directly victimised by Irish republican terrorism, and others who experienced the
victimisation of members of 'their community' vicariously – it is so that
the analysis will predominantly focus on atrocities carried out by Irish
republican paramilitaries. This book does not attempt to underscore or
venerate the legal legitimacy of the British security services, or to condone the morally repugnant activities of Loyalist paramilitaries on the
basis of their misshapen and sectarian rationale. Rather, there is a conscious decision to disaggregate and uncouple *ordinary unionist civilians*
from other sections of the unionist community, to pre-empt criticism of
this book as one that is simply seeking to perpetuate the so-called hierarchy of victimhood in Northern Ireland (cf. Bell, C., 2003). While it is the
case, for the most part, that 'ordinary' unionists also view those Protestant men and women in the RUC and the UDR who were murdered

by Irish republican (and Loyalist) paramilitaries as innocent victims –
a viewpoint republicans do not share – this is not a philosophically
or morally justifiable reason to peripheralise ordinary unionist civilians' history of suffering, especially in relation to the numerous cases
described in this book, which accounted for the deaths of many innocent Protestant civilians who had no connection to the conflict or the
security forces, other than having the misfortune to be the victims of
callous attacks by violent terrorists; and also the many unionist people who felt victimised by a PIRA terrorist campaign that they believed
targeted ordinary Protestant unionists, their towns and their businesses.

In this book I have deliberately chosen not to focus on the testimony
of former or current Loyalist paramilitaries, or that of serving British
Crown forces (police or Army), as this has been done very capably elsewhere, and was never the intention of this research (see, for example,
Nelson, 1984; Potter, 2001; Crawford, 2003; McDonald and Cusack,
2004; Wharton, 2008). Instead, this book is about mainstream unionist civilians – a group hitherto comparatively unexplored (with notable
exceptions including Dudley-Edwards, 1999; McKay, 2000; and Bruce,
2007). In particular I interviewed those who would usually be considered 'ordinary' unionist people with no formal political, paramilitary or
military affiliation, and who are all too often factored out of academic
analysis. They were drawn from a political community of whom the
DUP – now the largest political party in Northern Ireland – and the UUP
would be representative. Part of the *raison d'etre* of this book is the focus
for the first time on the importance of accessing unionist remembrance
and its manifestation as counter-hegemonic discourse; the discordance
of such discourse with the contemporary trajectory of 'dealing with the
past' which many unionists feel have involved political and tactical
sidesteps designed to outmanoeuvre them; and ensuring some form of
successful truth recovery in Northern Ireland. The book is constructed
on the basis of very extensive fieldwork – in particular in-depth concentrated ethnographic and theoretical research with unionists from
2006 to 2008. As someone indigenous to Northern Ireland, it has been
an academic privilege to be able to embed myself within the unionist community. It has meant that very long-term ethnography – at
least in terms of participant and non-participant observation – has
been comparatively straightforward (though of course not without its
methodological challenges, which I discuss throughout). I often, though
by no means always, learned more from detailed field-notes made during or after informal conversations, chats and reactions to events as they
unfolded than from semi-structured interviews in which interviewees

have 'prepared' themselves and felt that they had to stick to a particular 'script'. It is important to stress, however, that none of this work was in any way clandestine. Anyone with whom I spent time in the union-ist community was aware that my research was building towards this book, and ethically it was also always important to me as a scholar to make that clear. The exploitation of research respondents, in any field, is indisputably reprehensible and part of an anti-intellectual project and agenda. In this case, it would also have been to run the risk of re-traumatising people who had experienced unimaginable sorrow during a protracted conflict.

The ethnographic dimensions of this work enabled me to build a very clear picture of the unionist community in the contemporary political and social context. It was, in many ways, the 'fine grain' of unionism in its quotidian arena. The more 'formal' aspects of the work such as pre-arranged semi-structured or unstructured one-on-one interviewing – in which people were able not only to articulate their views on issues of obvious political currency but also to narrate their worldview and expe-rience of the Troubles – provided me with what were extremely stark, emotionally potent, poignant and at times provocative and evocative stories and memories of the past. Being able to locate these stories within a detailed ethnographic framework allowed me almost unprecedented access to those who feel that they have so often been forgotten – the ordinary unionist people of Northern Ireland. Serious efforts were also made during this research to ensure gender and age balance by con-tacting prospective female and younger interviewees utilising a variety of largely Protestant social networks. Although the interviews were, in the end, male-dominated, very significant contributions were made by female and younger respondents. In some instances, female respondents were my first point of contact – but were often quite resistant to articu-lating political views, or would defer, asking me to speak instead to their husbands or sons. In this regard, Northern Ireland is still quite a patriar-chal society. The research was also spread geographically, and an attempt was made to balance it between rural and metropolitan areas, and ensure that it was not Belfast-centric, though of course given the amount of violence in Belfast, especially in the early years of the conflict, that was not always possible. Many of the 'formal' interviews lasted for 2 hours or more; informal conversations often just as long or longer. Respon-dents were, if possible, interviewed in their homes. Some interviews were recorded, and some were not. In the case of those that were not, very detailed notes were made by me *in situ*. Some respondents feared being 'on tape' and being identified by terrorists as a consequence. If recording a respondent was likely to inhibit their candour, I made a methodological decision to make detailed notes instead. With long-term experience 'in the field' of short-hand note making I was confident that this – though clearly never quite as accurate as the verbatim nature of taped interviews – would more than adequately capture the necessary detail.

Previous analyses of unionism in Northern Ireland which have concentrated on the security services, Loyalist paramilitaries or evangelical Protestants – as worthy and as necessary as such studies have been in their own right – have often been misunderstood as representative of the entire Northern Irish unionist community (cf. Ryder, 2001; Bruce, 2004; Lister and Jordan, 2004; Mitchell, 2005; Ganiel, 2006; Bruce, 2007). This has factored out the potential for understanding the deep complexities of the attitudes of the unionist population in Northern Ireland, which are to an extent investigated in this book. Furthermore, relative to political developments in Northern Ireland, much of the literature is becoming rapidly outdated. This is potentially catastrophic in terms of the potential for dealing effectively with the past, which, subsequent to the revitalisation of devolved government and the agreement between the DUP and Sinn Fein to power share, has arguably become the most pressing issue in the post-conflict context (Simpson, 2007[a]; Simpson, 2009). This book seeks to move away from static assumptions and categorisations, and to illuminate differing cultural perspectives in a conflicted society. There is also an attempt to provide an examination of the social processes by which specific socio-political and social memory 'norms' and narratives have become established and embedded in the unionist community, and how or why this has become discordant with the pervasive imperatives of post-conflict political reconstruction in transitional Northern Ireland (cf. Abell et al., 2004; Andrews et al., 2004).

It is important to note, however, that this book is not a hagiography of the unionist community. Recognising my own methodological subjectivity in this process, it is imperative to preserve the credibility of this data by maintaining a dispassionate and detached tone. Many people on both sides of the community in Northern Ireland suffered greatly during the conflict (Simpson, 2007[b]). Anyone who has read my other published work, including my previous book (Simpson, 2009), will be aware that I have advocated the introduction of Habermasian directed morally normative frameworks, dialogically based and controlled, in order to allow for communicative rationality and the force of better argument to prevail in the creation of an agreed history of Northern

Ireland (Habermas, 1984; 1990; 1996). In the course of that work, I identified the need to prioritise the human rights of victims, in particular
those who were civilians. I made no apology for that stance, and my
view now is the same as it was then. Indeed, part of the motivation
for this book was to apply that theoretical model to the case of unionist
civilians, not least because they have often been unfairly and egregiously
stigmatised as the casual agents of the conflict. More importantly, their
voices have not been heard. What is it in Northern Ireland that prevents
policymakers and competing political factions from drawing a moral
bottom line in terms of what was indisputably and irreducibly wrong –
that is, political violence? That is the question that ordinary unionists
have often asked me, and struggled to rationalise, and it is one that I
attempt to explore in this book.

## Thematic focus

Crucially, therefore, this book aims to stimulate constructive discussion
and awareness among the *entire community* in Northern Ireland of what
have been hitherto (and irrespective of the level of their legitimacy or
'truthfulness') 'hidden unionist narratives' of the conflict in Northern
Ireland. This difficult and unsettling interrogation and interpretation
of the conflict from a comparatively unknown perspective is central
to the prospects for critically examining the past in Northern Ireland.
This book attempts to disentangle the nuances of unionist identity and
social memory, and is based on a scholarly examination of new empirical material in the contemporary context that theorises unionism as a
distinct but not monolithic political and social creed that cannot be
simplistically restricted or reductively defined by either religious fer-
vour or extra-legal paramilitary involvement. Rather, having tracked,
observed and interviewed 'ordinary' unionist civilians who were unin-
volved in the conflict (i.e., those who were not active members of the
security forces or Loyalist paramilitary groups) – some of whom were
directly victims of violence, others who experienced structural victimisation, and those who experienced a sense of hurt and bereavement
vicariously – this book will show that unionist civilians, like many other
victims of terrorist violence throughout the world, have had enormous
difficulty in coming to terms with their loss both as a community and
as individuals (Das et al., 2001; Hastrup, 2003). In remembering 'their'
past, and having their previously silenced voices heard, unionists are
now attempting to move out of the epistemological and ontological
straightjacket of the collective memory paradigm to which they have

largely been consigned, and begin to critically engage with the past and with their political opponents (cf. Jackson, 2002). This is crucial in any transitional society that is seeking to cement the foundation stones of democracy and equality. Escaping manufactured, distorted master narratives that essentialise and falsely homogenise unionists as 'all the same' is fundamental to the prospects for any sort of durable pace in Northern Ireland (cf. Rae, 2002). In this case, the 'othering' of unionists has involved stereotyping of them on a relatively (though by no means completely) harmless basis as members, or at least supporters, of the Orange Order (cf. Dudley-Edwards, 1999; Patterson and Kauffmann, 2007). On a much more insidious and dangerous level though, it has encouraged ethnic division and the portrayal of ordinary unionist civilians as tacit or even active supporters of Loyalist paramilitarism; as intolerant religious bigots unwilling to compromise; or as those who constructed, supported, manned and maintained the apparatus of a state that purposely discriminated against Catholics (Farrell, 1980; McGarry and O'Leary, 2004). Even allowing for the possibility that one could gather information to suggest that any of those things were or are definitely the case, it is to reduce the argument to the absurd to impose this negative characterisation upon *an entire community*. This book intends to debunk these myths and caricatures, not only because the vast majority of unionists with whom I conducted research would find such a description (and its explicit value system) abhorrent, but also because such unconsidered attitudes only give credence to those extremists who refuse to relinquish their grip on the past.

The fascists who once took it upon themselves to patrol Northern Ireland's streets during the Troubles with rifles and bombs now try to police the ways in which the past is constructed. For those who seek genuine peace in Northern Ireland, the re-telling of unionist stories is central to the prospects for democratic durability. My research with unionists has confirmed for me that it is the case, as I have argued elsewhere (Simpson, 2007[a]), that dialogue and storytelling within and between communities is the key to effective truth recovery. Those who wish to exclude the right of individuals to offer a version of their past concentrate only on the negative aspects of unionism, seeking to draw sinister parallels between the unionist community and other oppressive groups throughout the world. In 2005, even the much-venerated President of the Irish Republic Mary McAleese compared unionists' supposed hatred of Catholics to the Nazis' hatred of Jews (although she later apologised). Every drip of this preposterous propaganda – ordinary unionists enlisted in the British Army and fought bravely and with the utmost dedication against Nazism and its allies in every corner of the globe from 1939 to 1945, and Belfast was flattened by the *Lutwaffe* – corrodes the willingness and confidence of unionists to retell their accounts of the past. In a society that is supposedly shared, unionists feel isolated, and this – allied to the devastating effects of terrorist violence – are key reasons why their stories have been hidden (cf. Humphrey, 2002). It is a vicious circle, and by allowing themselves to be discouraged by historical and political exclusionists, ordinary unionists have contributed to their own position of powerlessness (cf. Phelps, 2004). Hence, there is the recurring tension between wanting to speak and not wanting to speak (Donnan, 2005). The notion that tragedy – especially that which was brought about by acts of terrorist violence – can somehow exemplify the resilience of the human spirit was one that unionists in Northern Ireland were in many ways keen to uphold, chiefly to demonstrate to the PIRA that they would 'not be broken'. This defiance inhibited unionist voices from being heard. However, the cessation of the conflict in 1998 witnessed something of an emotional disintegration. Many unionists began, for the first time, to tentatively self-identify as victims (Simpson and Donnan, 2006). This, for many, was an unnecessary admission of weakness, incongruent with the proud history of the Protestant tradition and the ostensibly successful defence of the Union against republican terrorism. Yet it was as if the stress – for some at least – of bearing such an unmanageable load for so long had finally taken its toll. There have been varying responses to the aforementioned tension between speaking and not speaking, indicating a fragmentation of worldviews and of needs, but also some very important commonality in terms of how unionists narrate and seek to remember their past (cf. Bal, 1999). This book investigates how many unionists have begun to create mini and even micro stories that rationalise the conflict and, in extreme circumstances, can be used to somehow explain their suffering (cf. Crossley, 2000). With the passing of time, the victims of terrorism are mourned with an often increased sense of poignancy. How and where those micro stories are told – and re-told, as if the suffering might somehow be crushed by narration – are fitted into an overall picture of a 'community', often erroneously assumed to be collective and the same (but actually composed of many different elements) is especially intriguing. Some people have attempted, by telling *their* stories (often stories that *belong to victims*), to master trauma and its attendant psychological difficulties, sometimes via vaguely defined paths of what is loosely termed 'reconciliation' (Humphrey, 2005). The notion of 'working together' with the 'other side' – however poorly defined this concept might be – is argued by some to be the only answer. Others, as is evidenced by some of the extracts in this book – both ordinary civilians who were not directly affected and victims – have rebuffed the idea of looking back at the conflict and trying to make sense of it at all. Many more, however, feel that the conflict makes sense only in terms of a historical framework in which they, as the innocent, were persecuted by wrongdoers (cf. Margalit, 2004). For them, the mourning must never end. It is a moral duty. Those who suffered must never be forgotten. Their enduring sadness is often tinged with anger, hurt and an overbearing sense of futility. What was it all for? How can stories of devastation be re-told in a way that can possibly change the outcome, and ameliorate the pain?

For the majority of unionists, as I have discovered during extensive analysis, notions of the conflict remain for the most part '*as was*'. They view the PIRA as a terrorist organisation that perpetrated vicious and illegal crimes. This is not to suggest that unionists cannot cope with the political reality of peace and the difficult negotiations and compromises with the PIRA that this required. However, they are suspicious of the attempts of Irish republicans – in their new-found political guise – to take, control and command the terrain of social and political memory in Northern Ireland: indeed, unionists view this as integral to how the PIRA and its allies might retrospectively legitimise the 'armed struggle' which was responsible for the deaths of over 2000 people. For reasons partly unknown, though, the inner sanctum of the Republican Movement has recently altered its strategy. Almost immediately prior to the PIRA announcement that it would have nothing to say to the Eames-Bradley in 2008, Martin McGuiness, the Sinn Fein Deputy First Minister of Northern Ireland and alleged one-time commander of the Londonderry brigade of the PIRA, appeared on RTE Radio in the Irish Republic to 'firm up' his credentials as a symbolic figure of physical force Irish Republicanism. He relayed his view that, if he could, he would have shot every British soldier in Londonderry following the unlawful killing of innocent Catholic civilians by the Parachute Regiment of the British Army on Bloody Sunday in 1972 (which is the subject of an ongoing, long-term, high-profile and high-cost public inquiry). This was unusually patent political manoeuvring by McGuiness, and a seemingly crass attempt to shore up support among disaffected republican 'hardliners'.

It nonetheless set the scene for the PIRA's rejection of the Eames-Bradley project, and Irish republicans, for the first time in the peace process, found themselves out on something of a political limb. As I have written previously and continue to outline in this book, it has long been the fear within unionism that republicans would win the 'conflict about the conflict', and set about erasing unionist history completely. This was, and still is, a legitimate fear. Logically, for the PIRA to admit to its culpability in murder and bombings in Northern Ireland would potentially irredeemably – in the post-9/11 climate at least – undermine its hitherto successful efforts to present its activities as part of a 'just war' (cf. Walzer, 2006); for example: the forced abductions, torture and assassinations of security force personnel, commercial bombings, and most notably the murders of Protestant civilians. None of these events sit easily within the defining parameters of what Irish republicans presented as a non-sectarian 'anti-colonial struggle' against the British political Establishment and its sovereignty in Northern Ireland. Having long despaired of the seemingly unstoppably programmatic nature of the republican agenda for political change, there is new – but cautious and extremely fragile – optimism among unionists with whom I have been conducting research that there might finally be a platform upon which they can begin to tell their stories. This positive attitude is heavily tempered with well-worn cynicism and the bitter legacy and experience of being ignored in the past (Parkinson, 1998; 2001). However, having shown itself prepared to engage with Eames-Bradley, an initiative which the international community has largely backed, and which has the support of the government of the Irish Republic, the unionist community has at last been presented with an opportunity to begin to articulate 'its history'. Unionists are slowly beginning to feel that they have a slight chance to capitalise on this opportunity, and there is increasing confidence that they might be able to demonstrate to the watching world that they are in fact a community willing to confront the past. They know, however, that this requires them to emerge from their long-held position of metaphorical hiding, and to somehow invest some form of trust in the political process by daring to narrate their stories (cf. Bar-On, 1999; Caruth, 1996). Perhaps for the first time, all is now seemingly 'up for grabs' in the political endgame in Northern Ireland. This, in part, explains why I was fortunate enough to speak to many unionists and to gather their stories and present them in this book. Previously, the silence of unionists was arguably almost impenetrable, even for researchers indigenous to Northern Ireland.

Acknowledging all of that, this book also presents some harrowing tales of people who were the targets of the most horrific attacks, and that is a core part of unionist history that the British and Irish governments, Sinn Fein and the international community now have to accept. They cannot encourage unionist storytelling only to then attempt to 'rinse' or decontaminate the process of its less desirable and more graphic elements – especially those which do not chime with the exigencies of an expedient, rapid political and cultural transition. In this book, I therefore make every effort to include as much 'raw' data as possible. This is often extremely upsetting – accounts of violent attacks in which innocent civilians were brutally murdered are bound to invite despair and sadness. To protect the feelings and the anonymity of all who contributed, all respondents are afforded a simple one-name alias. In this book, I cite examples of grotesque terrorist assaults – Bloody Friday in 1972; the Kingsmills Massacre of 1976; The La Mon Hotel Bombing of 1978; the Enniskillen Bombing of 1987; and the Shankill Road bombing of 1993. Kingsmills aside (an attack in which ten men were machine gunned to death), these were all random attacks on Protestant-unionist civilians using devastating and indiscriminate explosive devices. In total, these attacks alone accounted for the deaths of 48 innocent Protestant civilians, including a number of children and old age pensioners; they also affected people in both urban and rural areas. These are high-profile and comparatively prominent examples of suffering that figure large in unionist thought and remembrance, but there are numerous other examples of similar incidences contained in this book. An example of this is the so-called economic or commercial bombing of Protestant towns throughout the conflict which became a spearhead of PIRA strategy throughout the 1980s and 1990s, which spread fear, panic and devastation among the inhabitants of those areas. The sophisticated bomb-making capacity of the PIRA added to its mystique and its fearsome reputation, and it struck deep fear into the hearts and minds of unionists throughout the conflict (Oppenheimer, 2008). One need only to look at the panic caused by Islamic terrorism and its chosen *modus operandi* of using high-impact explosive devices in heavily populated areas of Western Europe and North America to recognise how deeply this affects the psyche of individual civilians in otherwise stable contemporary democracies.

As is discussed throughout this book, the beginning of the conflict in the 1970s in Northern Ireland in many ways seemed more 'fierce' to unionists, partially because of the 'newness' of the violence and the expectation or hope that it might cease (and statistically because it was the decade in which there were the most casualties), but the 1980s was a decade of hopelessness for the Protestant community, when any political, social or cultural attempt they made to talk – even to one another – about the conflict became almost impossible. It was beginning of the PIRA 'long war', a twin-track strategy that involved electoral politics by

Irish republicans (Moloney, 2007) – in the form of Sinn Fein – while the armed wing of the movement, the PIRA, simultaneously carried out a campaign of continued violence (it should be noted that membership of the two organisations often overlapped). Sometimes – though by no means always – issuing coded but often inadequate and elliptical warnings by telephone, the PIRA set about attempting to rip the heart out of many Protestant towns with car bombs. The aim was threefold: to cause fear, panic and mayhem among the residents of those areas; to demoralise unionist civilians by wrecking their businesses, often beyond repair, and making Northern Ireland economically unviable and unattractive to prospective investors; and to push successive British administrations into committing more money and personnel into trying to 'contain the uncontainable', notably random explosive attacks (Harnden, 1999; Coogan, 2002). Absurdly, this strategy played well among some naïve and sympathetic international audiences. Shamefully, this included elements of the self-styled revolutionary 'vanguard' of the British and European intellectual left, whose outdated grasp of Marxist politics and rationale both agitated and sponsored generations of student fantasists who became bent on overthrowing or attacking people whom they viewed as 'colonialists' (Ferguson, 2006). This was not just in relation to Northern Ireland – such spurious rhetoric had contributed to the emergence of other sinister terrorist groups throughout the world, including the 'Red Brigades' and 'Baader-Meinhof' (Burleigh, 2008). 'Ireland for the Irish' – or at least, a particularistic Catholic and Gaelic form of Irishness – was a cry routinely used to attack Protestant unionists indigenous to Northern Ireland, but this was unthinking and crass sociological sloganising at its worst, all too often vocalised by ignorant and naïve bourgeois students at top English universities desperate to ascertain fashionable proletarian credentials (Beattie, 2004). In juvenile episodes of self-loathing, financially privileged youths set about the kind of empty placard waving and chanting that was an embarrassment to the rich tradition of British socialism. Anyone acquainted with the nuances of Irish history instantly recognised and dismissed such vacuous trash with the contempt it deserved. Irish republicans articulated a more sophisticated version of this often paradoxical liberation struggle – claiming that they were pursuing a legitimate 'war' against forces of British occupation – but their rationale was also largely nugatory. The PIRA campaign of violence was ostensibly predicated on the right of the Irish people to self-determination, as evidenced in the parliamentary election results of 1918 (Foster, 1990; English, 2007). Even discounting the fact that Sinn Fein had limited success in what now constitutes Northern Ireland in that election (19% of the total vote compared with 56.2% for unionists), its cry for the realisation of an independent democratic socialist republic that valued the rights of all of its citizens, Protestant and Catholic alike, was founded on the outcomes of a contest that was over 50 years old by the time the Troubles began, and in which the electoral franchise had been comparatively limited to men over 21 years old and women over 30 years old. To 'wage war' (to use the PIRA euphemism for terrorism) using a half-century-old 'unilateral mandate' was more than faintly ludicrous, and northern republican rhetoric from 1970 onwards of ejecting 'the British presence in Ireland' (unionists for the most part hold British passports and consider themselves British, so presumably were not excused from this purge) was in no way congruent with the inclusive socialist utopia republicans reportedly desired. Furthermore, a murderous campaign of political violence that spanned three decades, and the reality of an increasingly prosperous – and decidedly capitalist – 26 county Irish Republic whose government repudiated PIRA terror weakened the potency of such arguments considerably.

However, because 'commercial' bombings lacked the apparent viciousness of gun attacks and murder, the PIRA was able to attempt to portray huge, devastating explosions as 'victimless' and as a calculated strike against the British infrastructure in Northern Ireland. This, for unionist civilians, was atrocious mendacity. Those fortunate enough not to get caught in the blasts – and there were notable examples when supposed 'adequate warnings' were anything but, not least at Enniskillen in 1987 and in the bomb attacks in Lower Donegall Street in Belfast in 1972 when six people were killed, three of whom were Protestant civilians (this is discussed in more detail in Chapter 2) – were forced to sift through the detritus of businesses, many of which were the sole family income and that had been handed down through generations. Onlookers felt disempowered, evermore threatened by the apparent attempt at some form of 'ethnocide' by the PIRA, and shattered psychologically by the rubble, dust and destruction. As they began picking through the detritus of 'their towns', unionists told me that they felt increasingly that it was not safe to venture out, and that it was particularly not safe to let their children out. Leisure and recreational activities were severely curtailed, even though many unionists attempted to portray an image of being unshaken (this is discussed in much more detail in Chapter 5). Even as the PIRA talked peace, in July 1993 – just over one year before their first ceasefire – they carried out the largest car bomb attack of the entire campaign, destroying the centre of Newtownards, a Protestant satellite town of Belfast with an enormous 1500lb device. Fortunately, there were no casualties, but the damage to local churches, eateries and businesses was untold. This attack followed on from two large car bomb assaults on nearby Bangor, another Protestant satellite town of Northern Ireland (only a short distance from Newtownards). In October 1992 the PIRA exploded a 200lb bomb in Bangor. Just as the town and its inhabitants, which had escaped the worst excesses of the Troubles – and where a lot of unionists seeking to escape the violence of Belfast had fled – the PIRA carried out another, larger attack in March 1993, using a huge 500lb bomb. Both attacks were in the Main Street, the economic hub of a small town that at that time was almost totally reliant on personally owned businesses. Four members of the RUC were seriously injured in the second attack, with the cost of the damage estimated at a staggering 2 million pounds. The second attack also came 5 days after the then British Secretary of State, Patrick Mayhew, had delivered a speech in the town. Unionists civilians believed this was a deliberate tactic by the PIRA to 'bring the war' to what were otherwise comparatively stable Protestant areas, and according to my research there were rumours and fears that the PIRA was going to 'step up' its campaign and being to target unionist civilians in a very deliberate sectarian fashion. Despite all this, floods of money and weapons poured in from sources as diverse as the elements of the Irish Diaspora in the United States of America and the militant revolutionary forces of the despotic Colonel Gaddaffi in Libya. It was not surprising then that unionists felt that to even attempt to 'take their story' beyond the constricting boundaries of the category into which they had been objectified ('oppressors') was pointless. Additionally, despite self-identifying as a community with the utmost resolve, the attritional effects of attacks against civilians via bomb attacks on their towns in the 1980s and early 1990s not only witnessed, I argue on the basis of evidential empirical material, a decrease in unionist civil and political strength, but also contributed to perhaps the most curious and complex period of history and remembrance for unionists in the present post-conflict phase. The attacks mentioned – and many more besides – became a totemic symbol of the conflict in Northern Ireland for unionists, and they persisted right up until the first PIRA ceasefire. Terrorist bomb attacks strike at civilian populations when they are at their most vulnerable and often at their most unsuspecting (Burleigh, 2007). They contravene all known moral codes, and are usually condemned, at least rhetorically, in international law and by politicians (Walzer, 2006). They are extremely callous and cowardly in both planning and deed, and for unionists the carefully crafted attempts by republicans to retrospectively rationalise them or legitimise them as part of a 'necessary' struggle against 'legitimate targets' are ethically offensive. It has also often proved an insuperable barrier in unionist attempts to present their view of what happened and to subsequently engage in a shared process of publicly remembering the past.

The politics of remembering the past in Northern Ireland, as part of an expedient attempt to erase and elide unsavoury incidents during the conflict, have thus far translated to unionists that I have conducted research with an apparently firm instruction: that those whose recollection of the past is not consonant with the synthetic version offered by the current political elites should remain silent. This is surely not a way to better understand unionists, or to build a democratic society with any notion of shared values. This is not to suggest that the mere presentation of unionists' memories in this book is an indication of their veracity. Rather, it is a clear need to redress the imbalance that unionists feel in terms of remembering the past by allowing the marginalised an opportunity to narrate their stories; and for these stories to be theorised in such a way that they can be located within a social memory paradigm that can help determine a better political and social situation not just for unionists, but for everyone in Northern Ireland.

Much writing on Northern Ireland is de-legitimised because it is regarded as an academic megaphone for a particular set of partisan political views. This is not the intention of this book. Northern Ireland certainly poses as having reached a stage of political maturity whereby it is able to withstand critically reflective analyses, especially ones that challenge the myth-making enterprises of those perpetrators of violence who committed unspeakable acts of violence (cf. Bell, D., 2003). The challenge now is finding out whether this is actually the case. Presenting, analysing and theorising unionist narratives of the conflict are one viable way of doing that. Without the exposure of the ways ordinary unionists feel about the past – given that they are, after all, the majority community in Northern Ireland – attempts to forge new beginnings will be mere 'doublespeak', a cynical and expedient political cover for the triumph of one version of history over another (Wilson, 2003). Offering unionist civilians' accounts of the past is not a zero-sum game for Irish republicanism. Unionists can gain from being permitted to share their views without it necessarily being regarded as a 'victory' for them at the expense of everyone else in Northern Ireland. There has to be a candid review and acknowledgement of the wrongs that were done; and how and why they have led to the need for a peace process and mechanisms for dealing with the past. If such a project topples or destabilises newly created administrative structures, it would suggest strongly that the new elitist political dispensation is so weak that it has been predicated upon a particularist, manufactured version of history which has disallowed the insertion of unionist storytelling, and which cannot tolerate dissent.

There is no reason for me to pre-empt criticism of this work by pandering to those whose agenda is such that they would never want unionist history to emerge in any case or in any form. No apology is required – or in my view expected – for interrogating in depth the contemporary ways in which unionists in Northern Ireland attempt to remember and master the past. As the renowned philosopher A.C. Grayling (2007: 274) has so eloquently written: 'It is an obvious comment that only if a civilisation looks at itself frankly and accepts what it sees, it can hope to learn from the exercise, and progress in the right way and direction thereafter.' In this context, and to re-iterate, this book asks Northern Irish society if it is ready to look at itself and accept what it sees – namely, that among a violent and often sectarian maelstrom in which wrongs were committed on all sides, a systematic campaign of terrorist violence was nevertheless perpetrated by the PIRA between the years 1971 and 1998, and that this resulted in the murder and deaths of many innocent Protestant civilians. If it is, then as this book will demonstrate, unionists are now in a position where many feel that while 'justice' might have eluded them, the right to an apology and to the truth has not (cf. Tavuchis, 1991; Ricoeur, 2004). Consequently, many unionists – but by no means all – feel ready to tell their stories, to reflect on their suffering, and to try to remember what happened to them during the conflict. The politics of this process must be fashioned in such a way that this not only tolerated, but encouraged. This book attempts to offer a new and different angle on truth recovery, historical representation and transitional justice in Northern Ireland, one that is viewed through the prism of a group that now perceives itself to be marginalised. It is based on new and original empirical research, at a period in the history of Northern Ireland when the need for scholarly presentation and critical analysis of unionist perspectives in Northern Ireland in regard to remembering and mastering the past has never been more urgent.

## Moral judgement?

This book, as discussed, is an attempt to fill a huge gap in the available literature on Northern Ireland, truth recovery and remembering the past. By its very nature – that is, in uncovering and exposing unionist stories of the conflict in Northern Ireland – it runs the risk of being dismissed as merely seeking to frame moral polemics about the political or cultural righteousness of various actors during the conflict. As I have stated clearly, however, this book has more serious objectives, not least the presentation of stories of a group that has hitherto been marginalised in the 'memory project' of truth recovery in a transitional context. A form of 'memoricide' has taken place, in which distorted versions of the past have been taken as templates for sketching shallow, partisan and 'flattened out' stories about Northern Ireland, and which in their own way – by act of excluding or falsely 'othering' one side of the community – reduce the prospects for Northern Irish society and the international community to exercise any form of realistic and objective judgement about what took place. It would have been a much simpler and undoubtedly contentious endeavour to make this book some kind of moral disquisition in which the *acts of violence rather than their consequences for unionists and how they remember the past* was the main focus. I cannot avoid – and in fact I make considerable allowance for – the right to apply a morally normative framework. There is no 'hidden subjectivity' here. As in my other work (Simpson, 2007[a]; Simpson, 2007[b]; Simpson, 2008; Simpson, 2009) I condemn political violence from wherever it came absolutely. Additionally, as noted, for unionists, the PIRA's claim that it waged a non-sectarian 'liberation struggle' in Northern Ireland is rendered absurd by its attacks on innocent civilians. As the focus of this book is about how ordinary unionist civilians remember the past and the ways in which they have been silenced, it is so that any moral evaluation will predominantly focus on atrocities carried out by Irish republican paramilitaries.

As the author, I acknowledge that the conflict in Northern Ireland has played out in extremely complex and subtle ways, and that the lack of unionist cognisance of the experiences of Irish nationalists and republicans is a contributing factor to the way in which those same unionists frame their own remembrance and their moral assessments of the Troubles, but my aim here is not to provide an analysis of republicanism or nationalism. It is unionism that this book examines. Where possible I try to let – while avoiding the pitfalls and perils of methodological naïvety – the voices to 'speak for themselves'. This is the crucial oral history dimension of this work, and it is perhaps never more important than in the section of the book that deals with some of the more unspeakable PIRA attacks upon innocent unionist civilians, such as the La Mon House Hotel bombing of 1978. It is incumbent upon me as an author of a work that seeks to make a serious intellectual contribution to the debate on remembering the past in Northern Ireland not only to offer a theoretical space in which unionist narratives can be located – and tether this to the way in which the politics of recalling the past have taken shape in the post-conflict environment – but also to provide a philosophical evaluation of the conflict. To pretend otherwise would be disingenuous in the extreme, and would negatively taint the worthiness of this project. As an academic, I am tasked with identifying and writing about the social phenomena that the legacy of violence has created among a population with whom I have considerable ethnographic experience. In my case, this is not only professional ethnographic experience, but as someone indigenous to Northern Ireland, *unconscious personal* ethnographic experience. As intellectuals, we are also – at least in my view (and the view of many other serious commentators like Jurgen Habermas) – impelled to offer scholarly commentary and analysis that goes beyond abrogating moral responsibility (by attributing all viewpoints to respondents, for example). It is arguably our right and our duty in studying a population – *any population* – that has been victimised by violence to weave a moral position into the fabric of our investigations and our analyses, not least because to erase this approach would be to deliberately elide aspects of that population's worldview. Gun attacks and assassinations, torture, kidnapping, robbery, car bombs, brutal assaults, indiscriminate bomb attacks on Protestant towns, the deliberate destruction of economic and social infrastructure, and the murder of Protestant civilians: these are all deeply uncomfortable aspects of what has often euphemistically been called 'dealing with the past'. Any attempt to implant or insert unionists' recollections into the received history of Northern Ireland can easily and perniciously be misinterpreted and misrepresented as an attempt to create a false political and ideologically motivated paradigm of memory that is concerned only with justifying the unionist position. I repudiate this notion entirely, and this book will hopefully demonstrate that reflecting critically – as a society – on the past fundamentally requires that *all sections of the community* are included; and that furthermore memory is not a collective, static bloc, but rather a fluid, heterogeneous and changing process that requires historical contextualisation, and which is often highly individuated (cf. Scarry, 1985; Hass, 1998). Where this involves unionist stories in which the condemnation of immoral and illegal acts of political violence features largely, the respondents in this study – and my subsequent analysis of their discourse – does and cannot shirk from addressing difficult, awkward and uncomfortable questions that might deeply upset the established orthodoxy of how the politics of remembering the past are currently being devised in Northern Ireland. It was undeniably something of a struggle to decide whether or not to let the potency of some of the stories herein act as a lone marker of the suffering that the unionist community endured, but this book – unlike my other work – is not just about victims who were directly affected by violence. It is about a community that feels, rightly or wrongly, that it has been misunderstood. It is about a community that feels it has no voice. It is about a community that is in the process of struggling to find coherent ways of recollecting and articulating the past. It is about a community that feels its culture and its identity are being eradicated. It is about a community that is frightened, anxious and unsure. None of this is to deny the suffering experienced on all sides during the conflict in Northern Ireland, and I cannot stress that point more forcefully.

## The politics of remembering the past – Figurations of memory

Unionist figurations, configurations and reconfigurations of memory are a central tenet of this book. As noted above, any research that attempts to simply elevate the suffering of one community over the other would be, in my view, an entirely pointless exercise and would contribute little or nothing to the meaningful debate that is required in relation to remembering the past in Northern Ireland. Acknowledging that, this research does not attempt to suggest that the suffering of innocent unionist civilians was or is any worse than the suffering of innocent nationalist civilians. However, unionists are the focus of this book – and crucially, they perceive themselves to be a marginalised group with no voice, and no say on how the history of the past is written. Even in the aftermath of the conflict, this silence and the stifling of individual and collective memory have added to a sense of continuing victimhood. For a long time, 'stoicism' and a sense of duty characterised unionist attitudes to the past, which many viewed as having been 'shattered' by the effects of violence (Phelps, 2004; Donnan and Simpson, 2007). For unionists, rebuilding their capacity to storytell and narrate their experiences, as I have written elsewhere in relation to all victims of violence in Northern Ireland and beyond, requires that they are not erroneously othered by misinformed commentators, and that the atomised agony of each person is viewed just as importantly as the devastation of high-profile incidents (Torpey, 2003; Simpson, 2007[b]). There are the forgotten *even among the forgotten*. Researching unionism, I was intrigued to discover how their memories, and the contestation over memory and historical terrain in Northern Ireland, might be cognisant of these subtleties and nuances – the tension between the *seemingly unaffected* (perhaps most notably the 'younger generation' of unionists who have little or no memory of the Troubles) and the despairing victim, for example. Are unionists simply seeking to impose a morally righteous version of their history? Is it the case that many are not interested, content to let the unprecedented economic regeneration, witnessed by a topographic transformation on Belfast's skyline that was unthinkable a decade ago, continue apace without interference from the relics of the past (cf. Huyssen, 2003)? Or are they lost and afraid, marooned in an existential morass, searching for untraceable explanations of the irrational events and atrocities that at worst robbed them of a loved one, or at the very least denied them some kind of normal environment in which to work and raise a family? All of these are crucial questions, and as such it is important to try and analyse whether or not this unionist memory is a heavily individualised, fragmented phenomenon; or if there are narrative tropes and foundation stones of identity that hold unionist civilians together, which bind them, and which are not simply 'collective memory' but the product of processual *collectivisied* memory (Halbwachs, 1992).

To some extent, as noted, there are also generational differences at play. The conflict persisted for so long that 'the Troubles' cannot be treated in any examination as a single period of time. It is a transcendental phenomenon. In the course of this book, therefore, I make every effort to analyse unionists' narratives within this context, and to take stock of how they have changed and evolved from the early 1970s to the contemporary political environment. This is particularly the case in Chapter 6. It is not simply terrorist atrocities that are of interest, but rather how unionists have managed to cope with their long-term aftereffects and psychological and emotional reverberations (Cappelletto, 2003), and the ways in which they have presented or even created (not only externally but also internally) a picture of themselves as a unified people, at least in terms of the cultural characteristics of bravery and stoicism. The bickering between factional unionist politicians has made any notion of macro-level unity a chimera (Walker, 2004), but only what unionist civilians term 'outsiders' judge the unionist community on the basis of what its politicians do or say.

Regrettably, the suggestion that there could be potential amnesty for perpetrators of political violence as an inducement for their participation in any truth recovery process has begun to consume and distort unionist thought, and so it is that a consideration of amnesty and the sociology of apology are necessary in this book (Tavuchis, 1991; Zur,

1994). Such suggestions have had the negative effect of re-entrenching unionist views and encouraging them to retreat to a familiar, voice-less position of widespread distrust and fear. Having gradually emerged from behind their traditional cultural 'wall of silence' in recent years (Donnan, 2005; Donnan and Simpson, 2007), the mere hint of 'trad-ing' freedom for truth has solidified feelings of extreme trepidation. Recently, there has been much debate about whether or not the PIRA conducted a 'war' in Northern Ireland. It is not my intention to pro-vide an answer to that question in this book, although in assessing unionist stories it would be naïve to suggest that some evaluation of this claim will not be made, especially in regard to the morally norma-tive framework to which I adhere. What I can say, though, is that the majority of the unionist community with whom I have spoken reject the notion of a 'just' PIRA war outright. It is perhaps salient to note that if the PIRA actually did believe that it had the *jus ad bellum* for 'war' in Northern Ireland (the just cause), its behaviour that evening demonstrated beyond reasonable doubt that on occasions it lacked the requisite *jus in bello* (just conduct during the war) to be regarded, cer-tainly by unionists, as a legitimate fighting force. Based on extensive interviewing and observation, I can also say that the suggestion that unionists refuse to face the past is quite simply wrong. Why then does such confusion remain? Why, among the voices demanding 'truth' and 'justice', does the silence from 'ordinary' unionists seem almost deaf-ening? Admittedly, a minority of unionist victims' groups have made their case strongly, but it is very difficult to measure how representa-tive they are of the wider unionist population. Many commentators and politicians have also suggested that the so-called and aforemen-tioned unionist hierarchy of victimhood is the main sticking point in implementing a truth recovery process in Northern Ireland. While it is the case, for the most part, that 'ordinary' unionists view those Protes-tant civilians, and those men and women in the RUC and the UDR who were murdered by Irish republican (and Loyalist) paramilitaries, as morally superior to perpetrators of illegal political violence, *this is not the major stumbling block* and it is not a philosophically justifiable reason to continue to eliminate unionist history.

To re-iterate, the main problem – having witnessed the anger and resentment of unionists first hand, and having interviewed and listened to scores of 'ordinary' mainstream unionist civilians – is that unionists now fear that 'their history' is in danger of being erased by the way in which the politics of remembering the past in Northern Ireland have been conducted. Many unionists with whom I conducted this research are still convinced that there is a concentrated effort to 'blame' unionists for the conflict and to 'demonise' those unionists who were killed during the Troubles (cf. Irwin-Zarecka, 1994). One of the most difficult and unsettling aspects of this process for unionists is the idea that Protestant and Catholic civilian victims of the conflict – 'all of the lost souls' as one unionist put it to me during my research – will be 'forever forgotten'. For unionists, truth recovery is now linked to the fundamental importance of history. Widows, husbands, siblings, sons and daughters – indeed all those who yearn for a dead loved one – are terrified that their stories will be ignored and that no monuments to their community will be erected. This is now *the key issue* for many unionists. Their silence and reluctance to get involved in dealing with the past to this point is a political and moral decision, because they want – first and foremost – an acknowledgement, admission and apology by the IRA that their campaign of terror was totally unjustifiable and wrong. Unionist victims and civilians have told me that they will not participate in a process that they believe will destroy their cherished individual and collective memories. For many, such memories are all that they have left. Yet an overwhelming number of those with whom I have spoken hope that some method of facing the past can be found that will reassure them that they will not be 'wiped out' of history, and that their sacrifice – in defence of their community, their identity and their culture – was not wasted. This is not a complete rejection of confronting the legacy of the conflict in Northern Ireland. Encouragingly, therefore, unionists are not opposed to dealing with the past as an idea. Rather, they are afraid that in its current form, it will result in the creation of a distorted version of history that they feel they cannot support. Lacking clear leadership at the top political level, unionists in the course of my research have issued a clear and loud call to the British and Irish Governments, and all those who desire lasting peace in Northern Ireland, to help bring silenced unionist voices in from the political wilderness, and to 'remember all the lost souls'. The politics of remembering the past in Northern Ireland, beyond the political posturing and the setting up of various independent groups, must therefore engage with precisely these sorts of uncomfortable questions. Only that way can people ensure, together and across communities, that there will never be more sectarian atrocities. It is clear, therefore, that there is much to learn about unionism and how unionist civilians in Northern Ireland remember the past. In the next six chapters, I hope to move towards addressing some of these questions.

# 2
## 'They started it': Unionists, Memory and Subjectivist Constructions of the Political 'Other'

### Introduction

In the hundreds of formal and informal qualitative interviews with unionist civilians that I have conducted, various iterations of the sentiment 'they started it' – meaning that Irish republicans initiated the conflict in Northern Ireland – have been extremely common. In ethnic conflicts throughout the world, such a process of socio-cultural and political 'othering' is far from unusual (cf. Daniel, 1996; Das et al., 2000). In Northern Ireland, I found that such a view has greatly infused unionists' perceptions of the past, in part transcending temporal, spatial and class boundaries. In this research, it was also evident that there was a trans-generational effect of this over-simplified narrative trope. Younger members of the unionist community who were born in the 1970s and 1980s, and who have no memory of how the conflict began, often retreat unthinkingly to this discourse and position of argumentation (cf. White, 1987).

This chapter therefore begins a long and thematic exposition of unionist narratives to a wider audience by focussing on the testimony of those old enough to recall the period 1969–1971 in detail. As noted in the previous chapter, it is crucial to tread carefully so as to avoid the perils and pitfalls of epistemological or methodological naiveté. This is particularly the case given that the aim of this work is not to 'prove' the superiority of unionists stories of the past – at least not in the sense of imbuing them with some extra quality that will allow unionism to gain the upper hand in the ludic political games of an increasingly enigmatic political and legal transition in Northern Ireland (Simpson, 2009). Nonetheless, I firmly rebut the notion that the forgotten voices of ordinary civilians cannot and should not be allowed to be heard (cf. Ankersmit, 2002; Edkins, 2003; West, 2003). Within the bounds of reason – which unionist civilians innocent of any wrongdoing most certainly are – the right to speak, to articulate versions of the past and to be acknowledged are human rights that should be underscored in the post-conflict phase (Rotberg and Thompson, 2000; Wilson, 2001). The unique nature of the narrative material that I have collected over an extended period of time demands to be analysed in its totality, not only because of its potency and originality, but because it shines a far more illuminating spotlight on the nature of the contemporary unionist condition and the ways in which they frame and construct the past (and the ethnic and political other) than any contrived hermeneutic enterprise using more limited data possibly could. It also contributes necessary balance in terms of the recomposition and reconfiguration of the past that is necessary if unionists are ever to be persuaded to participate in any process of truth recovery (Olick, 2007). In that sense, these voices *have to speak for themselves* (Luckmann and Berger, 1991).

Besides the 'impact effect' upon the reader, which communicates an authentic feeling of unionists' worldviews, any attempt to shroud this valuable data in a miasma of author-led interpretation would serve only to lead the reader away from a deeper understanding of unionists and the past. For that reason, and to the best of my ability, I have included as much data in its original form as space limitations permit. This is not to say that I reject the 'interpretive turn' in social science or that I do not stress the importance of figurations of memory (Boyarin, 1995; Rossington and Whitehead, 2007); nor do I seek to claim that the presentation of these oral histories simply validates their veracity. Later in the book I make strenuous efforts to address the symbolic and political importance of these untold stories (cf. Terdiman, 1993; Torpey, 2003). This is especially the case with regard to the complex intersection between subjective unionist truths and the restrictive political and legal modalities of transition in Northern Ireland, which seem to disallow their articulation – not least in the persistent marginalisation of unionist memory both past and present. The new regime in Northern Ireland – at least as far as unionists are concerned – appears to fear the potentially destabilising effects of unionist storytelling. Even erstwhile unionist firebrands from the DUP, who at one time vowed to 'smash Sinn Fein', appear to have traded power for morality (cf. Habermas, 1996). Proponents of the new devolved political arrangements bathe in the luxuries afforded to them by realpolitik, while the liminal, who carry stories of loss and suffering, are regarded as dangerous contaminants, unrecognisable relics of a bygone age in which unionist politicians' rhetoric fanned the flames of conflict (Bruce, 2007; Patterson, 2007). For many ordinary unionist civilians, this explains why they feel that they have been forced into peripheral social and political space, on occasion ignored even by those who claim to represent them. Within this chapter, where it is relevant and thematically consistent, I attempt to contextualise and theorise some of the articulations of these respondents, comparing and contrasting their stories of the past and identifying key moral issues which have become the foundation stones of individual and collective unionist memory in the present (cf. Bal, 1999; Cubitt, 2007).

Yet the intention here is not to re-politicise the Northern Ireland debate in a depressingly familiar and ubiquitous manner. I do not use these narratives instrumentally to advocate unionism as a superior creed, or to make grand claims that the history of unionist civilians as they tell it themselves necessarily constitutes a positivistic, objective measure of the reality or history of the conflict. Neither do I seek to elevate unionism above republicanism as a more legitimate set of political and cultural beliefs, although the assertion that ordinary unionist civilians – as law-abiding supporters of democratic politicians in a democratic state – have more moral credibility than those who sponsored, supported or engaged in physical force illegal terrorism (republican or Loyalist) is one that is made in this book emphatically and without reservation. As noted in the introductory chapter, it is fundamentally important that in order to understand the unionist worldview, one must be acquainted with the 'moral bottom line' that underpins the way in which many unionists perceive the conflict and the past (Habermas, 1984; Ricoeur, 2004). Unionist civilians – who were undoubtedly worthy, from any perspective, of the status of non-combatant immunity during the conflict in Northern Ireland (Walzer, 2006) – were not afforded that right by Irish republican (and in other cases) Loyalist terrorists (Taylor, 1999). That is an irreducible, non-erasable facet of the political and social past in Northern Ireland. To ignore this and to try instead to manipulate unionist narratives to fit into an ideological straitjacket that encourages facile relativistic, structuralist explanations for what was an egregiously vicious and protracted campaign of violence would be to abrogate the intellectual responsibility to morally condemn terrorism (Burleigh, 2007). Contextualising unionist narratives – and in particular how they relate to subjectivist memory formation and sometimes misinformed caricatures of ethnic and political rivals – is undoubtedly important, but to smother this empirical material in a cloak of elliptical and esoteric, even tangential, theory would remove the academic punch and purpose of this book.

To over-theorise the narratives would strip them of their power, and would also cohere with the self-righteous voices of many terrorist 'converts', who in their new-found guise of champions of peace now have the audacity to preach to those people who were victimised by the euphemistically named 'armed struggle' about the virtues of 'moving on' (cf. Adams, 2001; 2004). For many unionists, this is part of an Irish republican project masterplan to reshape the past in a malformed way that deviates greatly from how unionists recall it, and which elides any hint or hope of instituting a historical moral framework for judging and remembering the past (cf. Borneman, 1997). For those with whom I spoke, the notion of 'moving on' with such undue and unseemly rapidity is utter anathema – a crude attempt by an uneasy alliance of power elites to force unionist history into unending oblivion (Augé, 2004).

In Chapter 6 and the conclusion, I will return in considerable depth to these moral and social frameworks of analysis, but between here and there, I invite the reader to digest and inspect unionist narratives for themselves. I implore those who have hitherto been unaware of the nature and texture of unionist memory to search for it among the first-person historical accounts that are offered as part of this book. The reader must feel free to critique these extracts if they find them unreasonable or implausible. The raw data presented here is not finessed and theorised in way that leads ineluctably to a particular and predetermined conclusion. There are no *a priori* assumptions about what each individual reader might make of these accounts; there is also no attempt to use theory to disfigure the past or to hide a partisan position. There is simply an honest commitment to provide the data in much the same form as it was collected, and to make an original contribution to knowledge of the past in Northern Ireland by offering a selection of previously unheard stories.

## A brief methodological note

Acknowledging all of the factors that have been discussed in both the opening chapter of this book, and the introduction to this particular section of the book, it is pertinent to note that in the ensuing chapters – most notably, 2, 3, 4 and 5 – there will not be a consistent rehearsal or continued elucidation of the method that has been utilised in this research. I trust that my objectives and my methodological apparatus have been sufficiently explained in the previous chapter. In this book,

I have made a conscious decision to provide a platform for unknown unionist stories. In the following chapters therefore, I turn my attention fully to allowing those voices to be heard. From Chapter 6 onwards, and particularly in the conclusion, I will re-visit these narratives and analyse their meaning in terms of the politics of remembering the past in Northern Ireland. Wrestling 'out loud' with ways of 'ethnography-ing' this data along the way (Taylor, S., 2001; O'Reilly, 2004), however, is something of a waste of important space, and vacillating between integrated interpretive analyses and chunks of data devoid of scholarly scrutiny would render this book ineffectual in terms of its overall inten-tion. Those works which in my view have best presented the narratives of the forgotten have contextualised the salient issues and then in the main trusted their respondents and their data to convey the power and meaning of their stories (cf. Appy, 2006). It is this path that I intend to pursue.

## 'They started it' – 1969–1971

In the years 1969–1971, the unionist population in Northern Ireland was adjusting to an almost earth-shattering change in society, politics and culture (Tonge, 1999; Mulholland, 2002). For so long the unwit-ting and unconscious custodians of a state with a large in-built Catholic minority that from its inception was opposed to its very existence (Hughes, 1994), the beginnings of the conflict and the concomitant attribution of blame were and are core elements of how unionists remember and reconstruct the past. A reading of the selected histories that are provided below – which are designed where possible to reflect gender and spatial differences – reveals much commonality, not least the widely held belief that Irish republicans had long been agitating for what they regarded as 'revolutionary change', and which eventually manifested itself – for these unionist respondents – as blatant sectari-anism and bloody murder. In the extracts that follow, I have attempted to provide a wide-ranging set of views. These range from those of the long suspicious 'praetorian guard' of religiously observant provincial unionist farmers to the somewhat more cosmopolitan, educated young men and women who were full of hopes and dreams as they set off for university hoping to change the world – or at least escape their part of it – but who were cruelly exposed as ill-informed ingénues, tar-geted by thugs and bullies because of the ethnic and political badge which was pinned upon them, often against their will. These oral histo-ries demonstrate the ways in which unionists access and possess social memory in the post-conflict phase. The absence of the 'airing' of these narratives outside a limited unionist audience for over three decades means that unionists have not only subjectively constructed imagined versions of the political and ethnic 'other' based on limited and often damaging experiences, but crucially have also been the victims of ethnic and political stereotyping that was deleterious to their interests as long ago as 1969, if not before (Donnan and Simpson, 2007). This latter point is in defiance of the received and predominant Irish republican revolutionary narrative (English, 2007), but the tolerance of counter-hegemonic discourse is fundamental to the prospects of effective politics of memory in Northern Ireland. This chapter deals with the events of 1969–1971, widely regarded as the 'beginning' of the modern Northern Ireland conflict.

As evidenced in the narratives below, some unionists now talk of how naïve assumptions about the conflict and their role in it were destroyed very early on. Alternatively, the more cynically minded respondents have reconfigured their own personal recollections of the eruption of IRA terrorist violence as proof of their long-held fear and suspicion that Irish republicans were always preparing to attack the state, and its unionist population. As republican terrorists emerged in Belfast, Londonderry, Armagh and Tyrone, unionists cast their minds back to a more stable time when things (at least for them) 'made sense'. A natural outworking of this cultural and political thought process was a search for who was responsible for inducing such unwelcome chaos. The result – for the majority of unionists with whom I spoke – was the identification of Irish republicans as chief antagonists. Unionists believed that republicans had long awaited the opportunity to systematically and purposefully set about 'wrecking' Northern Ireland. For the vast majority of unionists with whom I conducted this research, pre-1969 remains a protective and collective psychological redoubt in which Catholics and Protestants co-existed peacefully and in a friendly manner. Post-1969, however, is regarded as a nadir, when innocent civilians began to find themselves at the epicentre of a protracted conflict they could not control. The phantasmagorical notion of peaceful and stable pre-Troubles Northern Ireland is a cornerstone of unionist memory. This rather conveniently overlooks episodic sectarian pogroms on both sides; but more pertinently the earlier IRA border campaign of 1956–1962 in which six RUC officers were murdered and 32 were wounded. Despite how recent the border campaign had been, it made little impact beyond the immediate rural border locales in which it unfolded, and was not widely regarded as a serious threat to the security of the state because the IRA had issued direct instructions that there was to be no paramilitary activity in Belfast (English, 2003). Additionally, Eamonn De Valera's Fianna Fáil government in the Irish Republic had adopted an extremely tough policy in 1957 of internment without trial of all suspected IRA members (Moloney, 2007). While during the 1969–1998 Troubles the PIRA would often evade arrest and imprisonment by fleeing across the border where they enjoyed apparent impunity, no such luxury had been afforded to them during the border campaign, which ended in 1962 as an undisputed failure. Therefore, many of the narratives that unfold in this chapter reflect a sense of extreme disruption and surprise, and register a variety of emotions in a variety of tones, from indignation to shock, from anger and resentment to enervation, and from initial optimism to utter dismay at the perceived attempt by Irish republicans to irreparably fracture unionist communal solidarity by mercilessly attacking the very fabric of unionist culture in a way they had never done before. It is worth re-stating for the purposes of clarity that all of the respondents whose testimony is included in this book have been given a one-name alias. Their age and a broad indication of where they resided (by city or county) is included to give the reader an indication of how old they were when the atrocities took place, and the geographical spread of the violence. It is extremely important to note that this is potentially complex, however, especially in relation to the early phase of the Troubles. Although many respondents describe events in Belfast, many have since moved away. No other biographical detail is provided in order to protect their anonymity.

**('Ray', 66, County Tyrone)**

They'll tell you in Belfast – even unionists, you know – that it all started there. But it didn't. You can't believe that. Republicans were agitating down here in Tyrone from the 1950s, if not before. But we had peace. It was a stable place. Don't you forget the IRA border campaign in the mid 50s. We had to deal with that violence until they gave up and went home in '62. Beaten they were! We were back to normality. And this supposedly bigoted unionist government up at Stormont? What did they do? Pardoned those IRA boys – probably the same ones was [*sic*] able to come back 10 years later and start it all over again, and kill our neighbours – the barbarity of them, they even cut people open with knives and all sorts. But I tell you, this was a peaceful wee part of the world until your boy Currie, that nationalist, and all his lot, the SDLP – and then the civil rights movement which we all knew was just an excuse for the IRA – came along and wrecked it. They wrecked it! Shouting about unfair housing and discrimination. What about us? We were farming people. We worked hard to get what we had, and no-one ever gave it to us. That's what republicans never understood about Protestant people in Northern Ireland. They talk about the Orange state. That's a lot of rubbish. The so called Orange state never gave me anything, I built my own house from nothing! With my own hands! I never even had running water for years! It was about 1968 or 1969 they started marching from here to Coalisland, as I remember, giving Protestants dog's abuse along the way, calling us black bastards, Orange f-ers and all sorts. I bet you never got told that in your history classes did you? Oh aye – black this, orange that – awful it was! We are churchgoing people and that sort of language, there's never any call for it – that was the type of them though. Now we get told there were Protestants were in that movement. Lot of nonsense! I was never against a Roman Catholic getting his rights, and I had many Roman Catholic friends, but there was [sic] no Protestants round here involved in that lousy rabble. Sure it was no time later after marches down here that they were shooting people up there in Londonderry and in Belfast. It was just an excuse.

They never wanted Northern Ireland and I'm sorry to say, a lot of them never wanted a Protestant about the place. And they still don't. That's why they'll never listen to us. Throwing petrol bombs, blowing the main streets up, shooting police officers, murdering them in cold blood. It was all downhill from that moment on. That was it. That started it, and to me it's never ended. A lot of people in this community thought it would be over quickly you know? That the British wouldn't stand for this sort of thing – murderers planting bombs and forcing people off their land, to get our land – Protestant land, at a cheap price. But they did. And they paid the price. Or we paid the price. Certainly, certainly, we paid the price very dearly in the unionist community when they started their terrorism.

('Gina', 56, Coleraine, County Londonderry)

They started it. You need to have lived up in Londonderry in 1969 and 1970 to know that, to know what it was like. It was absolutely desperate. Chaos. My father owned a shop in the town centre, and before that everything had been okay you know? I would go so far as to even say it was good. Business was good, things were going well, and we got on with out Roman Catholic neighbours. I never sensed trouble. But by 1970 it ended up that we just couldn't even get to the shop, there was that much trouble on, and then of course they started the 'Battle of the Bogside', as they now call it. Well, once that happened, my father's business, especially with him being a Protestant, it had no chance. It was a struggle for him to even get to his work, and he wasn't a young man or in the best of health. The yobs would come down and throw petrol bombs and rocks and anything they could get their hands on. My father's windows were shattered time and again, his stock was damaged, he was threatened himself personally to get out of the city. But we weren't going to be rattled that easily. As far as we were concerned this was just an unruly mob, but looking back we were very naïve. They had it very well planned and every PR trap they set for our people we just walked into it. The RUC was that badly stretched, and even the B Specials, that they had to call for the British Army. Even that didn't work. 'Free Derry' they called it. What a joke. There was nothing free about it for Protestants. It was August 1969. When that happened, I remember I was getting ready to go to university in Belfast, and my father said to my mother 'that's the end of it now'. I was shocked. My father was a stern man, a good man, a good Protestant – I never thought he would give up you know? He had his church, his shop, he had lived in the city all his days. But he saw the writing on the wall. We lived on the city side and it wasn't long before that became impossible. We would get threatened and get abused, even on the bus or out and about, language I wouldn't ever repeat. You just didn't feel safe you know? Not at all safe. There were rumours all the time they were going to shoot the Protestant businessmen in the city. If they could effectively take control of nearly half a city, right under the noses of the government, what could we do? The IRA they used that – they used that tactic, to drive ordinary good law abiding Protestant people out of Londonderry. They didn't want our sort, or our culture, or our religion, it was obvious. They used all these boys, boys who never went to their work nor wanted a job, to come out and riot – day after day after day and night after night.

How were you supposed to run a business in the middle of that? You couldn't even walk about your own city, in the United Kingdom in the 1960s! These boys would come out and throw rocks and petrol bombs to lure the British Army in, and that's when the IRA would then start firing their guns you know? This was by about 1971 that this had happened. I was down in Belfast studying – and it was not much better there let me tell you that much – but when I came home that summer in 1971 my father had put up with it for nearly two years. Then as he was coming home one night two boys came out of the side street and said to him 'don't you come back into this town you black 'f-er' or you'll not get out of it', or words to that effect. Now my father reported that to the RUC, but nothing was ever done. He was very upset and he had a very bad turn, he had to go to the hospital. He never really got over that. That was the defining moment for me, for my family. That was when it all changed, certainly as I remember it. A lot of Protestants will tell you the same. They were threatening to shoot him, there is no doubt about it in my mind. What else would that mean? If they could shoot the British Army, they could shoot my father. And as I said to you, my family lived on that side of the river too. Well, by 1972, like the thousands of other Protestants who left, we moved out of Londonderry, all the way over here to a safe place. We thought about going to the Waterside, because a lot of Protestants went there, but my parents were fairly elderly by then and my big sister, it was her that made them think sensibly. She told them to get to a Protestant town, a safe place you know? So that's where we went.

Londonderry? I don't miss it, and I'm not ashamed to say I wouldn't be in any hurry to go back next or near it. They nearly ruined my family financially, and they showed us that they were determined to start a campaign to drive Protestants out of Northern Ireland. That is my view – they started it up around here and the saddest thing is it got a lot worse. A lot of police and army men were killed, and innocent Protestants just trying to go about their work. I'm glad we got out. I only regret sometimes that we never left Northern Ireland altogether. But that's that they wanted isn't it? So we stuck it out – only now to be practically, what would you say, force fed a version of the past which is totally made up! All those poor families who lost people, they have no say. We were lucky by comparison – yes, my father lost his business, and I still maintain his health deteriorated badly because he had to retire and that shop had been his whole life, but he wasn't killed and no-one in the family got hurt. I turned on the BBC there the other month and they had a programme on, it was celebrating 'The Battle of the Bogside'. Celebrating it! It was disgusting. All these ones who had agitated, caused I don't know how much damage and hurt, destroyed relationships between the Protestant and Roman Catholic people, they are on the TV like they were war heroes or something! That's what we are up against. When is our story going to be told? I don't think the BBC will be putting on any programmes about the bravery of the ordinary decent Protestant people who tried to stick it out and go about their business while those hooligans and murderers tore the heart out of the city. I tried to ring the BBC to complain, to get on the radio, but they never put me on the air. So, for me, they started it. I'm not even sure it's over. It will be over when they get their version of history just right, so the whole world accepts it, and I'd say they're fairly close to that now. But we are still here, and we will keep telling our truth, no matter what they say or do.

**('Jackie', 49, Belfast)**

I recall as a wee fella of about ten really starting to notice the tension you know? We lived on the Shankill, which for anybody that doesn't know is right by the Falls Road, and in them [*sic*] days there were no peace lines. Night after night there was shouting and rioting and the police used to come up and try to get in the middle of it. It was them I felt sorry for at times. I mean, there's this story that McGuiness and Adams and all the Provies [PIRA] spout now that the RUC couldn't cope with the riots in '69 and that they victimised Catholics and everything. But they got fairly stuck into the Protestant people on the Shankill too and other Protestant unionist areas of West Belfast during that time – at least, into anyone breaking the law, as it should be. Of course that's not part of the history now. Just washed out of it all. That's not what my kids are taught at school. All they get is Catholics' civil rights, Bombay Street, the Battle of the Bogside. What about the Protestant people forced out of their homes up at New Barnsley, off the Crumlin Road in Hooker Street, kicked and spat on as they left, their furniture burned, beaten with sticks? The people up in Londonderry and down in Armagh and Fermanagh who were forced out in their thousands! What about the unionist community that was under threat for thirty years and more from these murderers? What about all the people we lost? For too long unionists have been sitting back, ashamed you know? Believing all that about how the Troubles started, that we were to blame. The simple fact is there was a lot of tension between Protestants and Catholics, nobody can deny that. But that's no excuse for going out and bombing and killing people for three decades. How many lives did the IRA take? And for what? To me, they started it, and they decided when to finish it. The unionist community did its best, it put up its best defence like, but at the end of the day by the time the ceasefires came everyone was relieved – it was at breaking point. The IRA was murdering anyone at that stage, even builders working on police stations, boys just trying to earn a corn. You couldn't go anywhere. And not one year before they decided to call it off, they killed nine people up this road. It's a brave man up here would find it in his heart to forgive them for that. It really is. I know that fella that lost his wife is on the TV saying we have to move on and all that, but when is that story even told? Have you heard a lot about it? Why has there been no enquiry into that Shankill bomb? Then we had Gerry Adams walking along carrying the bomber's coffin – the guy who did it – Adams was carrying his coffin! That was it for me. So, to me if you want my view they started it, and they finished it. The ordinary unionist people – not the Loyalists, because what they done [sic] in retaliation was every bit as bad – the ordinary unionist people, we were out of steam. Now there's not too many will tell you that or admit to it – we're proud people and no-one likes to say the Provies were getting to us. Stalemate I think the British called it, but that was a lot of bullshit. At the start they caught us on the backfoot and at the end we were still there, because basically your ordinary unionist wouldn't resort to making people drive bombs into police stations or blowing up towns, and our defenders were the police and the Army who had their hands tied behind their back by the British government who were too scared of what the Yanks would say if they got stuck into the IRA. They were playing by rules, by the law, but the Provies weren't. It's like in Vietnam or somewhere, and you seen [sic] what happened there. There was only so much more we could take you know, or at least that's how I felt living on the interface of it. I don't know if republicans felt like that too, there's a lot of talk that the Loyalists had put the frighteners on them by the early 90s – Mad Dog Adair and all that crew – going after their top boys, but you'd have to ask them about that and I wouldn't condone it even if it were true. All I know is although in a weird way you got used to it, you couldn't even go to your work in peace. I started work in 1977 and I had to go in and out of republican areas. From day one I never felt safe. 20 years of that? Yeah, no doubt in my mind, they started it, but that's not the history we get is it? So, the chances of our voices being heard? It doesn't strike me it's happened before and so I have to say to you, I'll not lie, I don't think they'll want to hear them now. How would it be if Adams had to sit down and explain why he carried the coffin of a man who murdered nine innocent people? Or why, as my granda used to say, he started the whole thing in the first place blowing our city to bits? I hope, I really hope, we get to a situation where we do get a chance to tell our stories. There's a lot of hurt on this road – hurt about what we went through, hurt that we got blamed and called mobs and rioters who started it, hurt for all the ordinary decent lawful people we lost, and hurt that everyone thinks we're all just paramilitaries or supporters of them, and that's the last thing we are. There's decent law abiding folk up here – churchgoing people – and all's they've ever wanted is to provide for their families and get on with things in peace, not threatened by republicans everywhere they went. That's what I want the world to know – it wasn't bigoted unionist thugs on this road that started it, it was gunmen and bombers that never wanted us here in the first place. They started it, and they finished it.

**('Gerald', 46, Comber, County Down)**

Oh, that's a tough one. It's strange. Who started it? I think my perspective is coloured not so much by my own experience at the time – to be honest as a young boy and in a town not directly affected my memory of the outbreak is not that great – but by my experience later on, and not here, but in England. It was 1980 and I had just done my A Levels and was off to Liverpool University. I was really excited, you know, first son in the family to go to university. Anyway, I was all kitted out, got the Liverpool ferry – no cheap flights in those days – and I arrived in my digs. It was a culture shock. Not only did I realise I probably wasn't British after all – at least, not the way we thought of it back home, but I was studying history and I got in with a crowd and we all thought we were fairly rebellious. There were the usual Che Guevara posters, you know, all that crap. Then it came to the spring of '81, and there was this lunchtime meeting organised 'Support the Hunger Strikers'. I'm embarrassed to say I went along, I didn't know what it was about! That's the truth. No clue. I rang home and all that and you saw the news the odd time but as a first year undergraduate politics back in Northern Ireland was kind of the last thing on my mind. Anyway, we got to this packed hall and I recognised one of these guys I knocked about with. As I got to the door he said 'You're not welcome'. I laughed – I thought he was kidding me on. Then this long haired guy – I'd never seen him before – he was English, a Londoner I think from memory, anyway he barged over and said 'This meeting isn't for your sort'. I looked at my pal and he said 'Ireland for the Irish'. I couldn't believe my ears. What was that supposed to mean? Another guy from our group, he was less confrontational and he came over and said 'Gerald you should just leave this one and go home'. I was no hero. The atmosphere was awful and there was lots of chanting and swearing. So I said okay. As I walked away I passed three lads I studied with – one of them I would have considered maybe not a good friend, but a fairly close pal. He shouted after me 'Yeah, away you go, it was you Protestant bastards started all this anyway ... you're a dirty Hun, get out of Ireland'. Now, the only time I'd heard Hun used was to describe Nazis in war comics! Honestly, I'd no clue what that meant, but I got the gist. The irony was I was out of Ireland, I was in bloody Liverpool! The hunger strikes were a real cause celebre round that time.

When Sands died it was worse, I was persona non grata. It certainly stripped me of my champagne socialist credentials. I had been so naïve! I thought I was as British as the next man, that in England I'd get a fair deal. I'd gone through school in the 70s in Northern Ireland, through all the bombing and murdering, and here I had escaped to my 'mother-land'. What a joke that was. I was hated for a time, I really was. It never occurred to me that the English, of all people, would think that the unionist community started the Troubles. I got home for my summer break and I relayed the story to my parents. They wore a knowing a look. My Dad just said to me 'Son, 50 years from now, even ten years from now, that's what they'll say. They'll forget what happened to Protestants. They'll forget what the IRA is doing. You mark my words. Now keep your head down and when you're done get yourself away somewhere where all this doesn't matter, but don't be so naïve that you think unionists won't get the blame for this whole sorry mess'. It was prescient, you know? We did get the blame.

And I made history my career, teaching and studying it. From that year on I was determined to find out 'what really did happen?' For a while I think I thought that 'my people' if I can use that expression, were to blame. A bit of self-hate. But as time progressed and the IRA atrocities got worse, and as I looked back through the history books I knew it was more complicated than that. I'm convinced we didn't start it – I swung so far to the right at one point I used to be completely of the view that 'they started it'. I would row with people in seminars, in bars, anywhere. I even considered becoming a unionist politician. But in the end it just tired me out. It was, it still, is, exhausting, and futile. I realised – all ethnic conflicts are complex. There was a lot of anger and resentment there, and a whole lot of factors contributed to the Troubles starting. But for me, the continuance was the responsibility and the fault of the IRA. My view has not changed on that. 'They' – if you mean Catholics or nationalists – no more started it unilaterally than we did. But republicans kept it up. And they murdered innocent people for decades. And I cast my mind back to what my Dad said to me and I think 'he was right'. You have it now that the accepted history is just the same as that long haired bully shouted at me in Liverpool all those years ago, that unionists were culpable for the conflict. But we weren't. At least not on our own. But that's not what people want to hear. The narrative is much more straightforward if you have 'Protestant bigots oppressed helpless Catholics and then ran a state that perpetuated the conflict'. It's nonsense, but it's predominant. Will our voices be heard over that? I'm not so sure. I wish they would. I wish that idiot, wherever he is now, could hear ordinary decent Protestant unionist folk tell their stories, about their suffering, about what happened to them, about their loss and sorrow. He might shut his mouth then.

**('Glen', 56, Belfast)**

The problem might be we never really got to know Catholics before the Troubles started. I never knew that many. I had a notion in my mind you know, and it wasn't like it was bad. We just didn't really mix, but there was no hatred there, not from me anyway. But after the Provies [PIRA] formed, we didn't want to know them. You couldn't trust anyone, not one of them, that's how you felt – trust someone from the other side and you'd get a bullet in your back. Young people now don't understand what Belfast was all about then. It was a dangerous place. If it wasn't the Provies trying to bump you off, it was maniacs in the UVF saying you were a tout [informer] or a sympathiser or something if you even knew a Catholic! You couldn't even go out at night. To me, though – at that time, as a teenager, republicans started it. And to me, now, as an older man, they still started it. I'm not going to bend just because no-one wants to hear the truth. Burntollet Bridge, the Battle of the Bogside, that's all we hear. Alright, there was some wrongs done there, nobody denies that, it could have been handled better, but that's well known. Does that excuse them blowing the heart out of our city? Does that excuse them, cowards that they were, planting bombs and running off, or shooting cops in the back of the head? There was a fella lived round our way, I think my Dad knew him. A nice man, he never meant anyone any harm. He had the misfortune to witness the IRA robbing a bus – and let's not forget in those days they were burning buses, thieving and looting, it was just criminality, opportunism at its worst. They found out where he lived, turned up, and murdered him, shot him dead. So you tell me, or that man's family, why a cowardly bastard walked up to him at his own front door, he was still only a relatively young man for fuck's sake, and shot him in the head? No chance to defend himself. An innocent civilian! Is that not starting something? I tell you, if that's not starting something I don't know what is. You can talk until you are blue in the face about how it takes two sides and all of that, but I'm old enough to remember – yes, the RUC handled it badly, but republicans wanted to destroy our wee country and they had a plan to do it. Civil rights marches, the IRA, the PIRA, the INLA. They're all the same. I don't know any of them and I'm not ashamed to say I don't want to know any of them. I accept the new thing up at Stormont, I do.

I want peace, but I want truth too. I want acknowledgement. I accept it because it's taken me thirty years to even get some wee bit of peace in my own mind. I know a lot of parents went to their graves broken by what happened to their kids. I'll talk to whoever wants to talk about the past, I'll let them know who started it, and who continued it. But they don't want that. If they ask me, I'm ready. I want to put republicans on the spot. But they'll say to me 'you have no rights, unionists started it'. It's this, what do they call it, 'hierarchy of victimhood'? That's a lot of shit. I'm a victim. People in my community lost brothers, fathers and sons, men out just trying to maintain law and order. Were they part of the 'British war machine'? A UDR reservist earning a few quid trying to defend democracy? Ask republicans that. The IRA started it, but they never won it, not with guns anyway. The big worry now is they might win it with their words, the way they try to rub out our history, but they never beat us with guns. Their ones can't stand that, can't stand to admit they started a battle they couldn't win. Unionists are proud people, and the vast majority as far as I am concerned did nothing wrong. They went about their business, or tried to, and they got murdered by terrorists. But they never started it, and they never gave up either. And they still won't. They might want to drown out our voices but now we've started telling our stories we'll keep telling them. We have to, for all our people who got killed by those people.

('Ricky', 62, Belfast)

Now that's a hard question – do I think the other side started it? Well, the only thing I can think of is two fellas – just Protestant civilians – one of them I sort of knew as a matter of fact, he wasn't a great friend like but I would have known him from round about you know – the IRA shot the both of them when they were out on the Crumlin Road in 1970. Where is that in the history? Who has told their story? Where are the monuments to them? Where is their voice? As I recall, there was even a wee fella of 18 they shot that day, near the end of June 1970 it was. And a lot more over in East Belfast. Tragic. Now I don't know, they say it was riots and all that, but this guy I knew, he was no rioter. No way. Shooting Prods [Protestants] was the PIRA just making its name, just when they were coming on to the stage. They put it out that it was Prods rioting, or what they would call interface violence now, and that is the accepted history, but what excuse is that? Any time Catholics were out demonstrating, it was justified, you know, it was 'legitimate grievances' against the state and the oppressive unionists, and if the peelers [police] got waded into them, even just with gas or batons or whatever they were calling for inquiries and saying how it showed the world Northern Ireland was a police state. They still are. We just go on with it.

Now, don't get me wrong, all innocent civilians have to be protected – but that has to include unionists as well surely? They might say in 1970 those Protestant fellas were out and they were asking for trouble, but they were innocent civilians, executed by IRA gunmen. Just executed. So who started it? To me the answer is fairly obvious. The thing is, it's so long ago, it seems like a lifetime ago, but for those people's families, why do they have to have their story wiped out – why are they blamed for starting the whole thing? And what did the Provies [PIRA] have to gain from just shooting Prods anyway? They say they were defending their areas, I say they were cold blooded assassins. And it wasn't just Belfast – a couple of months later those two poor fellas, was one of them was called Donaldson I think, only a young guy, the two RUC men, lured into Crossmaglen by these people all smiling at them, giving them the whole 'there's no trouble down here', you know all that? Then they get to a car and its booby trapped – blows them both to bits. I've a mate in south Armagh and he thinks in Belfast we never cared about what was happening down there but we did. Or that we think it only started in Belfast, but I know full well it was going on all over the place.

To me, there's no moral, what would you call it, no moral equation that says RUC men are equal to IRA terrorists. But now, that's what it is and we get told we have to accept that, like we're the white South Africans of the whole thing you know? Now I'm not related to anyone in the police or the Army, so I've no axe to grind, but these guys Eames and Bradley have to get their heads out of the clouds and realise the unionist people all felt victimised whenever the IRA killed the police, because the police were just people – mostly Protestants and unionists – trying to do a job to protect everyone. The IRA says it killed them because they were state agents or crap like that, but we felt – we still feel – it's because they were Prods and unionists. It was sectarian, right from the start. Wasn't it convenient for the IRA that all the cops they killed were Prods and unionists? So for me they started it both ways – they came out on the streets of our city shooting and firing at the army, at the police, at passers by. They robbed and thieved and burned and destroyed, they tried to goad the unionist people on to the streets, then they shot them stone dead – in North Belfast, in East Belfast, in West Belfast, you name it. And all that time they were ruthlessly targeting the RUC and the UDR, usually when they were off duty cos they were fucking cowards, if you'll excuse my language. It's because they knew that struck right at the heart of the unionist community. It didn't stop us though. We're proud people. The more RUC men they shot, the more the RUC doubled their efforts to catch them. And we supported that. We supported the RUC going after Loyalist paramilitaries too, but that gets forgotten. Now, because I say I believe that the policemen they killed at the start of the Troubles were every bit as innocent as the ordinary Protestants they killed, I'm not allowed a voice. I can't say 'I felt like a victim because my people were being killed'. It's a nonsense. So yes, they started it, but they couldn't beat us. Not in the end. Except now, they're winning politically, no doubt about that, for all the reasons I've just told you. We can't mourn our dead or write our history, they won't let us. They started it and they'll probably end it, and that is just the way they like it.

**('James', 54, County Down)**

Living down here in a safe place in those days, it was a world away. Some people, even as early as 1968, had seen the way Belfast was going and they'd got out. We'd created our own wee world down here. Yes, it was and still is a majority Protestant town but that's not the reason there's no bad feeling, I don't think. There was no discrimination here, and I can tell you for certain that unionists here in this town did not start the Troubles – though it cuts me deeply when I think of all the people from this town and from all over Northern Ireland that were killed by the IRA during the Troubles. It does, it cuts me deeply. I'm saddened, so saddened. Just because we were 15 miles removed from it didn't mean we didn't understand what was going on. It was still our country. It was still only up the road. We felt like the victims every time a policeman or an Army patrol was ambushed or killed, or a business was blown up. These were our people, this was our country. Our world was shattered. We were going along nicely and then it started – Londonderry, Tyrone, Armagh, Belfast. At first it was the rioting and then the Provisionals emerged, and they were serious operators. There was just no messing with them. They came along and for me, they were just totally determined to kill Protestants. Now you might think that's a controversial statement, because the received history has it that they wanted to fight the British Army, and if Protestants were in the police or Army that's why they were shot, it wasn't sectarianism. But let me tell you this wee story, and you can make up your own mind.

I went to Queen's University in September 1971. I was 18. The IRA were upping the ante that year – bombs, rioting, shooting, killing. And

1972, I don't need to tell you, was worse. This was my first real experience of the Troubles. I had to watch where I went, to whom I spoke,
even the people I would have chummed about with. But, at 18, even
with soldiers on the streets and bomb warnings and all that, you're still
18 you know? You think you're invincible. I befriended a couple of guys
anyway and we were all studying English literature at that time. I loved
books, just loved them, and my plan was to teach English after I graduated. One afternoon, myself and these two friends went to a bar quite
near the university for a drink. It was pleasant enough to begin with.
They were country fellas – from down round near the border, I'm not
exactly sure where. Anyway, we were chatting and for some reason, the
atmosphere changed right away. This one boy, I think he was called
Sean, he said to me, totally out of the blue: 'Your Dad is a policeman
isn't that right?' It wasn't at all right – my Dad was a civil servant and
had been all his working days. I said, 'No he's a civil servant actually'.
They looked at me suspiciously. The other one – I think his name was
Gerard but I couldn't swear to it – he said 'What do you think of all this,
the IRA killing the police and the Army?' Not knowing the terrain so to
speak, and coming from a town where that question would have elicited
a uniform response – i.e. 'it's dreadful', I said 'It's absolutely terrible, very
sad indeed'.

But this Gerard character, he got quite angry at that. He said 'Oh you
think so?' I said yes again, that they were only men out doing a job;
that they had families and what was to happen to their wives and kids
if their husband or father was shot? And this other fella, Sean, who had
been fairly quiet to this point, he swung round – he had a mean stare
in his eye, I remember this as freshly as the day it happened – he said
'Fuck their families, they're all going to get it too. Our day will come.
The Brits are going home and you'll be going home with them unless
you're not careful, you Protestant bastard'. Well I wasn't the fighting
type and I was stunned to say the least. I think I tried to make some sort
of rational argument, muttered something, but these guys were having a
fair amount to drink and things had got a bit sinister. In the meantime,
a crowd of lads had come in that they knew and I didn't know at all,
and I tried to make my excuses and leave. But the Gerard guy, he said,
almost taunting me: 'Sure why don't you stay King Billy' – that's what
he called me, to mock me – 'and come back to a party we're having.
Sure we can talk about this some more'. Then he shouted over to this
crowd of lads 'Our mate here thinks the RUC are alright'. And one of
them – I'd never even met him before – he leant over and he said 'You
should watch your back then you Orange fucker'. I grabbed my coat and

made for the door, and as I was going out I just felt a big crack. The next thing I knew I was on the ground and my shirt was covered in blood. I don't know who hit me, but someone had thumped me right in the face. Lucky for me, a barman got up to intervene and he helped me out. There were people kicking at me, I think, even girls, it was frenzied. He got me out the door and he said to me: 'What the hell are you doing in here? Don't you know republicans drink in here?' Obviously I didn't! I was crying – I was only a young lad – and this man got me down to the train station and I got home.

I got in the door and my Mum started to cry. She said 'My goodness what on earth has happened?' It honestly took me half an hour to convince my parents – they were still in what I call the 'Unionists Bubble' – I'd just been assaulted for being a Protestant, or for just expressing support for the police. They asked me time and again 'What did you say wrong, who did you aggravate?' We went to the hospital and it turned out my nose was very badly broken, I had five stitches right over my cheekbone and I had a bad concussion. I never reported it to the university. They wouldn't have done anything even then. The scariest thing of all is that was the 15th October 1971. When we read the newspapers the next day it turned out the PIRA had shot two RUC men that very same day, probably the same time I was having what I thought was a friendly drink with these guys. One of those policemen was only a young guy, not much older than me. I can only imagine what might have happened if I had gone to the 'party'. So, I don't know if that story proves one way or another who started it, but as far as my experience of the Troubles goes, they did. I came from a town where there was none of that, and I walked right into a situation – I'd only been there a month – where there were people I'd never met, never done any harm, assaulting me and practically baying for my blood. And into the bargain they were killing Protestant policemen, who I maintain to this day were still decent folk trying to an honest job to keep the peace.

I was quite depressed for a while and I missed a whole term's classes. They didn't call it depression then, I was off because of my injuries you know, but I was scared and I didn't go out, not even in my own town. There were more British Army being killed and policemen and then in '72 they started killing just about everyone in the unionist community. I dropped out of Queen's the next term and I went to Oxford University the next year. I was glad to get away, and it was only a month or so after Bloody Friday I left. That made my mind up that I had done the right thing. I graduated and stayed in England for a while, but the lure of here, I don't know. My family was here and I felt like republicans had pushed me out, both directly and indirectly, so I came back. It's my home. They started a conflict to drive us out, and if we all had taken the easy route, and stayed away, then thugs like those guys who hit me – and I've reason to believe more than one of them did because I'm sure I was knocked out – would have won. They probably went on to become IRA killers. Violence would have triumphed. It might yet. These stories are so little known – I mean, before telling you, I've only ever told about four or five people that tale. But it's crucial, the more I think about it, to make sure we do tell them. We need our voices heard.

**('Chris', 54, County Down)**

For me, it really hit home in June 1970. That's when I thought 'these people want us off this island altogether'. Oh aye, 1970 – June it was. I remember that. It was bad at that time alright. I was living in about 5 miles away from East Belfast, and we worried it was going to spread down here. I remember – I was about 16 at the time – lots of my relatives were round that Friday afternoon. They would come on a Friday night and we would get a chippie [chips] you know? It came on the TV that your woman Devlin had been arrested again and they were rioting up in Londonderry. A lot of my family were from up round East Belfast and they were saying 'it's going to get worse before it gets better, the IRA are taking it up a level'. They said they had heard the IRA was going to try and lure a lot of unionists out on to the streets by firing from the Short Strand into Protestant areas. I don't know how the events there unfolded, I really don't. I wasn't there and I'm sure there are a lot of different views depending on what your politics are. But the facts remain – they killed two innocent Protestant civilians and injured a lot more using an IRA sniper shooting from inside a Roman Catholic Church! Now how is that right in any way? They'll say the police wouldn't defend their area against loyalist mobs and all that... who knows, maybe that's true. But to me it's much more likely, knowing how well the republicans have played this whole thing for nearly 40 years that they set a bear trap and the unionists just walked right into it. The point is this – those families of the Protestants killed, who ever remembers them? Who even remembers the names of the victims who were murdered? And the bigger point in all of it is: the IRA made it part of their mythology, you know, defending a Catholic Church from Protestants. And the world just bought it! It didn't matter that it wasn't true. It didn't matter our community was weeping for our dead, five

Protestants across Belfast alone that weekend. We had been cast in the role of the villains and we're still cast in that role today in my opinion, but what use is that to anyone? If unionists were in the wrong they'll admit it, if only to get at the truth. What the world outside here, even republicans, don't understand is that we can admit – though they accuse us of being self-righteous – that there might well have been Protestants out up to no good, or thinking in their own minds they were defending their own areas. But that gives no one the right to execute them! And we all felt that. The start of the Troubles was strange. As time went on, it became easier to say – 'well alright the IRA killed a UVF man and he was a terrorist too and we can't sympathise because we condemn all violence no matter where it comes from', but at the start, all hell had just broken loose. No-one knew what was going on. Protestants were just as frightened as Catholics, if not more so. The B Specials had gone, the police had been disarmed. A way of life, a culture of a generation, had just been wiped out because the British were too scared to take on law breakers and thugs in Londonderry. The unionist people were threatened and frightened by what I view as no more than republican gangsters, and if some young boys went out on the streets then to me, even if they were involved in disturbances, or if they were attacking Catholic areas – and I personally very much doubt the majority of them were – we trusted that the RUC would arrest them, and they would be punished. We accepted that – in fact we wanted it. No-one in my family or the people I knew wanted loyalists who were using violence to be claiming to be representing Protestantism or unionism. Protestants in Northern Ireland are church-goers. We respect the law. Our tradition of upholding the law goes back centuries, and if there were idiots attacking people they needed to be brought into line. But that was the job of the law and of the security forces! For a terrorist sniper – I mean, even in real war that's the lowest of the low – to shoot two men from a hidden position, stone cold dead. That's unforgivable in so many ways, and every unionist in Northern Ireland felt that, I'm sure. They say it was a gun battle with Loyalist paramilitaries, but neither of those men that were killed were Loyalist paramilitaries. The IRA also said it was defending Catholics because Protestants were coming to put them out of their houses, but I don't believe that for a second. This was the IRA – now that they were the Provisionals – taking it up a gear and whether you were police, army, out on the street, whatever – if you were a unionist, then no matter what they were coming for you. And they showed that not much longer because only a year or two later they were blowing innocent Prods to bits on the streets of Belfast, and they carried that on for years, decades! I wouldn't say I lapse too easily into that explanation of 'they started it', because it depends what you mean by 'they'. But we felt at that time, and I certainly feel on reflection, that the IRA started it and they must have had some level of support from the people in those areas in which they were operating. To me, that's baffling, and I just can't understand it. They must have really hated us. But we're not allowed to say that, because that's not what is in the history books now. I mean, Eames and Bradley, do they even want to think about 1970? Someone needs to, because there's families there still missing a son or a brother, and there's a whole unionist community feeling that unless the whole story is told, the exercise is totally pointless.

### ('Des', 60, County Antrim)

Well my overriding memory of the start of the Troubles was when the IRA started to come out on the streets, it must have been 1971 I suppose, because I remember I still lived in Belfast. They patrolled the areas like big men, you know, tough guys in hoods with guns and sticks. You have to understand at that time there were huge demographic changes round that part of Belfast where I grew up. Anyway, my father had died when I was young and it was my Uncle who'd really brought me up, you know, like been a Dad to me? When my Auntie passed away, he wasn't able to cope on his own. So the family, we'd made a decision to put him in a home, you know, for his own good? His health was really going down-hill and he'd had a visit one night from this pack of yobs, republicans, telling him to move out of his house or they'd burn it down. So that's the context, you know? That was the sort of people you were dealing with. Threatening an old man, a widower. Anyway, to get to the home where my Uncle was I took a route up through a part of North Belfast I'd known all my life – it was just the quickest way from my work. And on Wednesdays, I picked up my wee mate Sammy. Sammy was head-ing up that way to go to his church, he was a great one for taking the Boys' Brigade and all that, even with all the violence going on. So this one night we came upon this IRA patrol. They stopped the car and the guy asked me for my ID and where I was going and why. I was rightly frightened – he had a gun you know? The only ID I has on me was my passport, which was a British one of course, so I handed it over. So this IRA man, he walks away with it to talk to this other IRA guy, and he came back and he said 'You'd better find another way to get where you're going, you Orange so and so – no Brits allowed up here'. I said to him 'What do you mean Brit? I'm from only down the road, I need to get up to see my family'. He said to me, really aggressively 'Listen you, if you don't turn the car round and get out of here you'll not be seeing any of your family again. You're a Brit and you're not welcome in this area.' I said 'How am I a Brit? I've lived here all my life'. He says 'Well youse [*sic*], all of youse are Brits, and you'll not be here much longer. You can't stop the march of history, we're getting you out of Ireland, all of you'. So I went to turn the car round and he shouted 'Hey! Hold on. Who is your mate?' Because you know wee Sammy, he'd said nothing the whole time – I think they'd hardly noticed him. But he had a crew cut hair style, short like, you know, and that was very uncommon in those days. Only soldiers had that haircut. This guy shouted to the other IRA man 'We've a soldier here!' I panicked. I tried to spin the car round, but they stopped us. The guy rushed over to Sammy's side of the car and he pulled him out on to the side of the road and said 'Show us your ID you wee f-er'. Wee Sammy, though, he was brave as a lion, he says to him 'No I don't have any'. This IRA thug, he said 'You're in a lot of trouble then aren't you?'

Sammy said to him 'Why don't you leave us alone in peace? We're only a couple of ordinary people going about our business, we're no threat to you'. This IRA man, he was furious then. He started going on, saying all of us [Protestants] were a threat and they had to go, and that Sammy had better keep his mouth shut. And then he just lost it, he thumped Sammy with the butt of a big bat he had, and then he kicked him over and over again when he fell. All I could do was watch, and this IRA boy, he gave Sammy a really good going over. It was sickening. He kept shouting 'You're a peeler, you're a soldier! Admit it you wee bastard!' Sammy said nothing. Lucky for us the Army, they were coming up the road on their own patrol. That saved us. I'm convinced of it. The IRA boys scarpered. The Army arrived and this English chap, he said 'What's happened here?' So I told him, and he said – 'You're a very silly young man – these people are vicious scum and if you come up here again we can't guarantee your safety.' But they never offered Sammy medical help or anything. That's how much they cared or protected the unionist people of Belfast.

I drove back the other way, all the way over to the City Hospital, into a safe area you know? They had to admit Sammy for a good while. He had a hairline fracture of the skull, a broken jaw and a broken leg. I went up to see him and I recall I said to him 'Why did you not just give the boy your ID?' And he said to me 'Don't you get it? It didn't matter to them. They knew we were a couple of Protestants and they were going to duff us up no matter what. I wasn't going to let some bully terrorise me'. But he was never the same after that, something of the light about him went out you know? He had to stay at home for months to recover and his workplace, they were very good to him but eventually they couldn't hold his job open for him. The whole thing, it made me decide to get out of Belfast, move away out here, start again, but Sammy felt humiliated. He'd been stripped of his dignity. I remember he told me 'We can't let these people continue what they've started, or they'll kill thousands of us. We have to defend the law, do what's right and proper'. The next year he joined the RUC. I'm convinced if they'd never beaten him that night though, he'd have stayed in his job – he was a salesman, and a good one too – and come through it. But only a few years later, Sammy got caught up in a republican ambush. He'd only been in the RUC three years as far as I remember. But that was it for him, I mean he was totally traumatised, he had to drop out of the police and he ended up in a psychiatric ward for a very long time. He was unrecognisable. I went to visit him and that, you know, a good few times, but he barely spoke. He was on all these tablets and he was really skinny and terrible looking. It was heartbreaking. There's not a day goes by I don't think about that. What if I had taken us another route that night? And still I feel so sad – what was the point of it? They started a conflict with all of us in the Protestant community, but for me they started something with Sammy that night that led to him being like that, and I find that hard to forgive, I really do. When that happened to him he had been going steady with a lovely wee girl and he was getting ready to get married, but that all feel apart when he had to go into the hospital with his breakdown. When I saw him, when he was in the police before he had to retire, he would tell me how hard the job was but he was determined to make Northern Ireland a better place for everyone you know? I'm sure there are lots of stories like that. How one episode of being a victim like that changed someone's whole life...he was only 27 when he left the police, but that was it, he was totally washed up. Just a boy. My son is older than that now. His parents went to their graves broken people because Sammy never got out of his depression, and he had 3 or 4 more nervous breakdowns you know, really bad ones? And all I can think about is that guy saying to me that we couldn't stop the march of history. It was such a strange thing to say, and it always stuck in my memory. He was right. We couldn't stop it, or them. They terrorised us for 30 years. And now we can't stop them writing history, and writing it in a way that the likes of wee Sammy – and all the hurt that caused in the unionist community – gets forgotten.

('Duncan', 60, Belfast)

Sinn Fein and all their cronies, they all have these wee phrases 'truth recovery', 'dealing with the past', all that usual trash they trot out. You ask me if it was worse in the beginning. I'm not going to speak for all the unionist people of Northern Ireland, but I will tell you this. And this might give you an idea of what we were trying to deal with in those early days. Not that it got much better. This is what we had to adjust to. Constant patrols – they could have been Army, RUC, UDR, UVF, IRA – you never knew. Gun battles up and down your road. Extortion. Bombs in the middle of our city centre. Businesses destroyed. Families ruined. But this, and this is the worst thing I recall from that time. It was coming up to Christmas in '71, and we were starting to think – despite the chaos all around us, as we lived in north Belfast at that time – about doing a bit of shopping for people for their Christmas presents. We thought about jumping on a bus into town but it was a Saturday and at that time, that was when the IRA liked to plant bombs. So we nipped over to the Shankill – it's not what it is today, it was thriving then. You didn't have your big retail stores, all that, you went to local shops and you got the best of stuff too. The place was bustling. I suppose if you were a unionist you felt a bit safer doing your shopping there than taking a chance in the centre of the town, although people did their best to keep things normal. It was important to us to show the IRA, and the British, that they wouldn't wreck Belfast or Northern Ireland, and that we were not going to be scared away. Anyway, I suppose this sort of answers the question if it was worse or not at the start. You know, now, the slightest thing and people are in, they hide in their houses, they don't venture out. Then, I don't know if it was foolishness or that Ulster Protestant grit and determination, but we had to try and make things normal. We had two wee boys, both under 5. How do you explain to them that Santa wouldn't come because terrorists were blowing up the city? We had to do the shopping, it made us all the more determined to make Christmas special for the kids.

So we took a bus over to the Shankill. To all intents and purposes, I suppose that was our normal. We didn't think of ourselves as depressed, or what the young ones now would say. We got on with it. The kids needed a Christmas box and that was all there was too it. There was a bit of defiance too – the IRA wouldn't stop us providing for our family, and I think unionists everywhere felt like that. We were chatting about what we might get the boys, and then we realised we'd left the house without any money. I was furious. We went all the way back and we were rowing and shouting. Then, even from where we were, which must have been over a mile away, I heard an almighty thud. I knew straight away it was a bomb. Even by then, you'd grown used to what a bomb sounded like. By the time we got home and got the radio on we were trying to find out what had happened. And then we heard. Four people killed in a furniture shop by the IRA. That to me, is something that should never be forgotten, ever. One of the victims as I remember was a Catholic man. But the sickening thing – and this to me I might say it was worse in the beginning, though 22 years later they would do the same thing – was that the bomb killed not only a pensioner, but two wee babies, one of them not even one year old. My wife and me, we thought of our own boys, we thought about what was going on around us, and we realised – maybe for the first time – just how bad it was. That could have been our kids. We had two boys, one was four, and was one was only 2. One of the children that died in that bomb was only 2. I didn't sleep for weeks. Our Christmas was a wash out, though we did our best to try and make it special. How do you get over something like that? The pain I felt, just a member of the unionist community, how would that compare to the pain and suffering the relatives of those wee babies must have felt? I wonder if those people ever got over that. Are they to be told now their stories don't matter? The young people now, even people who recall what it was like in the 80s or 90s, they can never know what it feels like to have tried and dealt with things like that in the early days of the conflict.

# 3
# 'It was worse in the beginning' Recalling the Adjustment to Political Violence

If the period from 1969 to 1971 was 'year zero' in terms of how unionists framed the 'before and after' of the Northern Ireland conflict (and also the 'before' and 'after' of how they constructed perceptions of the ethnic 'other'), then the period from 1971 to 1975 represented the political and social apocalypse that many in the Protestant community had claimed to have foreseen since the first murmurs of discontent by Northern Ireland Civil Rights Association (NICRA) in the 1960s. Others however – even though they had sniffed the pungent breeze of sustained violent conflagration – were taken aback by the sheer scale of terrorist activity in this period. The year 1972 was, statistically, the worst year of the Troubles. There were almost 2000 explosions and nearly 10,000 reported incidences of shooting. Between 1972 and 1975, 365 Protestants were killed, many of whom served in the RUC or the UDR (CAIN, 2009). The Provisional Irish Republican Army (PIRA) began a dedicated campaign of attacking and murdering state security personnel, both in Northern Ireland and in England (Coogan, 2002; Alonso, 2006). Scotland and Wales remained largely unharmed and untouched (apart from the sacrifices of the men from Welsh and Scottish British Army regiments sent to try and restore law and order to an increasingly anarchic part of the UK). There are unlikely anecdotal explanations given for this – the existence of some notional 'pan-Celtic' alliance for example, an assumption most likely predicated upon the loose ties and small weapons exchanges between various incarnations of the IRA and a minority of Welsh nationalists; and the existence of a large cohort of ex-patriot and self-identifying 'Irish' republicans in Glasgow, who regularly chanted their support for the PIRA at the home of Celtic Football Club (and in some cases continue to do so – it was widely reported in all of the UK press in March 2008 that Union of European Football Associations

[UEFA], the governing body of European football, was investigating sectarian and pro-IRA songs that were sung by Celtic fans during a game against Barcelona in Spain, after footage of the chanting was posted on the Internet). The more likely explanation, however, is that the easiest ways to get to England undetected were predominantly through the ferry routes from Dublin to Holyhead in Wales, and from Larne to Stranraer in Scotland. Members of the PIRA are reputed to have dubbed this their 'Ho Chi Minh trail', in reference to the system of roads and rivers that ran through Cambodia and Laos which was used by the North Vietnamese regime to supply manpower and materiel to the Viet Cong in South Vietnam during the Vietnam War.

In any case, during the latter part of this period the PIRA recognised that England could be a much more strategically valuable target than Belfast, not only because it was the largest country in the UK, but also because attacks there would demand the sort of international media coverage that assassinations and bombings in Northern Ireland could not and, the PIRA calculated, pressurise the British government into responding with a political solution that was more favourable to Irish republicanism (Taylor, P., 1997). Once upon the British mainland – either in Scotland or Wales – the explosives and terrorist personnel required to detonate it were relatively easily transported, resulting in attacks such as the dastardly pub bombings in Guildford and Birmingham, though in some cases terrorist 'cells' had been planted in the targeted areas some months before, demonstrating the PIRA's fastidious commitment to wreaking maximum havoc (McGladdery, 2006). The PIRA estimated that an attack in England was likely to provoke the British public to question its commitment to defending Northern Ireland's unionists much more than ten attacks in Belfast ever could, and thus force the British government into withdrawal from the Province (Moloney, 2007). However, during this period they also continued indiscriminate bomb attacks and shootings of innocent civilians in Northern Ireland (English, 2003). In both of these endeavours, they were highly effective. British Army deaths during this period numbered 223, although by 1975 the introduction of more stringent security measures and better training, allied to a succession of PIRA truces (in both 1974 and 1975) – which were founded upon the mistaken political misapprehension that the British were about to withdraw immediately from Northern Ireland (Neumann, 2003) – meant a great reduction in British Army casualty totals, from 105 in 1972 to 15 by 1975 (Taylor, P., 2001). RUC deaths, however, remained fairly constant during the same time frame, with a marginal reduction from 16 in 1972 to 11 in 1975 (but an aggregate for the period of 14). This seemed to indicate to unionists that the IRA's often brutal and cowardly murder of local police officers – rationalised by republican terrorists as assaults upon those who wore the 'uniform of the British state' – was in fact clear and undeniable manifestation of republicans' sectarian loathing for Protestants (Dingley, 1998). It was also suggested by many unionists in this research that such 'routine' and localised executions simply did not figure largely for republicans in the macro-level political negotiations with the British government. They argued that killing RUC officers during this period was important for the PIRA in that it maintained the campaign of attrition designed to make Northern Ireland ungovernable, and that it also satiated the hunger for violence among the more extreme elements of the republican movement whose passionate hatred of the RUC was well known. By keeping extremists content and demonstrating a continued commitment to waging 'war' within Northern Ireland, the PIRA negated the possibility of any further internal IRA splits as had been the case in 1969–1970 (though they could not prevent the rise of the Irish National Liberation Army [INLA]) (Sluka, 1989; Holland and McDonald, 1994). This programme of violence had one further benefit for republicans: it kept unionist civilians in a permanent state of fear and anxiety. Unfortunate as it is to say, based on how the British Government responded to casualties in Northern Ireland, the PIRA was probably correct in its belief that the deaths of RUC officers in Northern Ireland would not evoke anything like the frenzied political activity by the British as did a comparatively small number of serious bomb attacks on civilians in England.

Given its status as a home battalion of the British Army (which had many part-time members), the UDR – and those local Protestants who joined it – were also ruthlessly targeted by the PIRA, though again better training, greater awareness of the terrorist threat and the alteration of PIRA strategy during the period 1974–1975 witnessed a drop-off in deaths from 25 in 1972 to 6 by 1975 (Ryder, 1989; Potter, 2001). There would, however, be a dramatic upward leap in UDR killings in the following two years as the PIRA dispensed with its truce and its 'Eire Nua' (New Ireland) programme. Feeling that it had been 'cheated' by the British Government into believing there would be imminent and radical change in Northern Ireland, the PIRA began its 'long war' (Patterson, 2007). It re-mobilised its murder gangs, who by 1975 found direct military encounters with the British Army much more problematic than the systematic and very often extremely brutal assassination of mostly off-duty UDR men, usually at their homes or places of work, or via the detonation of remote control or booby trap bombs. The year 1972 was also the year of the Claudy Bomb Attacks (when nine civilians, five Protestant and four Catholics were killed by three car bombs in a remote County Londonderry village), Bloody Friday (which is discussed in more detail in the next chapter) and the Donegall Street Bombing in Belfast. From Claudy to Ballymoney, from Belfast to south Armagh (Harndnen, 1999), and especially in public houses and shops of Protestant West Belfast, the PIRA brought its 'war' to the streets of Northern Ireland. For a brief period, it sensed 'military' victory, and the unionist people – though they speak of their characteristic defiance which is an important part of how they retrospectively self-identify – feared the worst, especially when a hitherto unthinkable détente was reached with the Irish government and northern nationalists in the form of the 1973 Sunningdale Agreement (cf. Dixon, 2001). When the chances of a rapid victory by violent means seemed increasingly unlikely, however, the PIRA reformed its tactics. It conditioned itself, its members and its supporters for a protracted programme of political murder and violence allied to political mobilisation that would result in the continuance of the conflict for another 20 years (Oppenheimer, 2008).

## Unionist civilians and State Security Forces

I have already problematised the issue of how one goes about defining Protestant or unionist casualties in the conflict and how this book is intended to reflect the physical, psychological and emotional damage done to ordinary, non-involved unionist civilians who had no direct affiliation with the security services (cf. Edkins, 2003). This is not to disregard, however, the devastating impact that consistent PIRA killings of security force personnel had upon sections of the unionist population, who as previously noted regarded the RUC and the UDR men and women who were murdered during the Troubles as innocent victims. Consequently, and unsurprisingly, the narratives presented in this chapter sometimes refer to incidents in which members of the security forces were attacked and killed. This is a reflection of the phenomenon that I have identified as *vicarious victimisation* of the unionist community. Unionists do not acknowledge – as the PIRA claims to have done – the demarcation between the Protestant unionist who worked, for example, as mechanic by day and patrolled the streets of a Northern Irish town as a UDR part-time soldier or RUC reservist by night. To unionists in this research, these victims were Protestants and unionists first and foremost, and the rationale offered by the PIRA – that they wore the uniform of a colonial power whom republicans were seeking to oust via a legitimate war – has been dismissed with contempt by the vast majority of unionists in Northern Ireland with whom I have spoken. For the most part, though, the stories in this chapter focus less on the particulars of single traumatic episodes and more on the effects of increasing violence upon a range of unionist civilians, and how this trend impacted negatively upon the unionist community's confidence and feelings of safety. The callous bomb attacks that claimed the lives of non-combatant civilians feature in these histories because they negate the logic of a just liberation struggle as articulated by the PIRA, and thus unionists feel empowered to assume the moral high ground in their recollections of the past. These testimonies also show how the concept of victimhood among unionists began to emerge, and consequently how rapidly it morphed from a collective sense of vocalised tragedy into powerless, privatised, internalised discourse (Simpson, 2007[b]). This, arguably, was because of unionists' cultural predisposition for a loathing of self-pity, and also in part because of oppositional identity formation (Mitchell, 2003; 2005). If nationalists and republicans were claiming to be victims of the conflict, unionists did not want to be *like them* (Donnan, 2005). Rather, in adherence with the traditions of a creed that demanded steadfastness and courage in the face of adversity – as at the Somme, Ypres, Dunkirk and Normandy, all iconic representations of Ulster Protestants' vainglorious war efforts (Graham and Shirlow, 2002; Switzer, 2007) – unionists configured their attitudes to the violence in a very traditional Ulster Protestant way (Beattie, 1992). Conscious victims of the conflict became victims in denial, and unionists began to force their public cries of grief underground for the purposes of sending a message to the PIRA: we will not be beaten. As such, when they recollect the past, for unionists the notion that it was worse in the beginning, while empirically true in terms of the statistics for killings and possibly accurate in terms of the 'newness' and frequency of the violence, is much less illuminative of the nature of unionist victimhood. The following narrative extracts highlight all of these issues, not least the claim that whatever the circumstances, the Protestant unionist people of Northern Ireland were intent on remaining proud, defiant and determined to defeat terrorism (even if this silence was to their detriment). This self-constructed idealised stoicism, however much it aided the unionist cause in maintaining the viability of Northern Ireland, and eventually securing its constitutional status in 1998 as part of the Belfast Agreement, masked deep individual and collective despair (Donnan and Simpson, 2007; Dawson, 2007). In so many ways therefore, while it 'was worse in the beginning', unionists' claims that they successfully 'adapted' to 25 more years of terrorist attacks demands more interrogation than has hitherto been the case. The traces of sorrow, angst and fear continue to greatly influence the worldview of unionists in the contemporary period, and are among the reasons why they are so reluctant to 'open up' and publicly engage in the politics of remembering the past.

Indeed, even allowing for the possibility that things might have been worse in the beginning in no way assuages the legacy of awfulness that still pervades the consciousness of those who experienced violent victimisation either directly or indirectly. Posing as the rallying cry of the heroic and long-standing defenders of a proud political and cultural tradition, this expression of Protestant memory in Northern Ireland – in more than one case – actually reveals a sadness intrinsic to contemporary unionism. It is the articulation of a sense of suffocating historical melancholia; of being forced to adapt to a life in which danger is ever-present; to marry, to work and to try to raise a family in a conflict zone, with all of the attendant worries that brings; suspecting or fearing that all are targets for paramilitaries simply because of political beliefs, ethnicity or religion, or because they 'were in the wrong place at the wrong time'. The nefarious activities of PIRA terrorists and their escalation of the conflict denied unionist civilians the basic privileges of normal democratic existence to which they were entitled (cf. Alonso, 2006). These were freedoms that unionists long argued were won by their ancestors in Belgian ditches, and in battles with Fascists on the shores and in the cities of occupied Europe during the First and Second World Wars (Orr, 2008). Compared with horrific genocides of the twentieth century, not least the Holocaust, unionists' experiences during the Northern Ireland Troubles might seem trifling (cf. Hinton, 2002; Miller and Tougaw, 2003). To view unionist suffering as trivial, however, is the grave error of all those who never had to endure the cruel uncertainty of political, social and cultural victimisation in Northern Ireland during that period. Stripped of normality, unionists *had to adjust*, but it does not mean they wanted to; and as a community it does not mean that even despite their ostensibly defiant and proud stance, many were not aching inside, either from their own loss and suffering, from a deep desire for peace, or from the continued fear that their culture was under attack and would be destroyed (cf. Robben and Suarez-Orozoco, 2008). Every PIRA bomb attack, every paramilitary shooting and every death – and some were more tragic and memorable than others – left an empty space somewhere – that of a husband, a son, a brother, a cousin, a sister, a neighbour or a friend. The searing pain of loss reverberated far beyond the immediate families of those in the unionist community who were murdered. Though some attempted to numb the wounds of collective and individual grief and loss with recourse to their strong Protestant faith, this research has shown that there were many in the unionist community who believed that they were not spared the effects of vicarious victimisation, and the stories that are provided below attempt to convey that to the reader.

### ('Michael', 61, Belfast)

It's funny thinking back to that time – not funny, like, amusing – but funny that everything, for the media anyway, seemed to be centred on Belfast and Londonderry. To us – and a lot of Catholics and republicans might take issue with this – it came as a surprise, when it came. I really mean that – that level of violence anyway. We knew they were never really happy with Northern Ireland, but our thinking was they had the Irish Republic and the Protestants down there had no easy time of it; and we didn't think they hated us, ordinary Prods you know? Thinking about it maybe we did feel that the country belonged to us. But was that so bad? Should we not have had pride in our city? Belfast was our city, my city, everyone's city. Northern Ireland was my country but did that mean it didn't belong to Catholics? No, not at all. I had Catholic friends, Catholic work mates, and they were quite happy at that time until the IRA turned up and stirred it all up. But we have it now that there were these 'pogroms', that Protestants all around Northern Ireland were burning Catholics out of their houses. The IRA – and that was even before it split – used that as propaganda, and the Provos have used it ever since – 'no more Bombay Streets'. That's a lot of bollocks, total nonsense. What about the Protestants, the ordinary unionist people as you might call them, who were burned out of their houses? My cousin lived in a very hot [dangerous] part of West Belfast at that time. He called me on the phone one day and he said: 'Can you get me a loan of your work van today?' I had to check with the boss, but he was good about it, he knew what a state we were in. That was a Saturday morning – by Saturday night we had all of my brother's gear, and he had 3 wee girls at the time, in the back of a van and away down to Uncle's house in the country. That's how bad it was for us. The IRA, they were taking pot shots with high powered rifles at anything that moved! Gun battles, day and night. Petrol bombs, rioting, they were at it on their side every night. They didn't care less about civilians. In fact to those boys, probably the more Prods they killed the better. But did the press report that we were the victims of that? Of course not, it didn't suit their agenda, and it still doesn't. Is it in the history books? It was wild in those days. I was in north Belfast but if anything it was getting worse there too. The British Army had arrived in '69 and that, to me, was a bit of a shock. We were happy enough that our own police could do the job and take these fellas down you know? When we saw those ones on the Falls Road giving the soldiers tea and buns and all that we thought 'oh oh, this is it, they're going to hand us over to the Free State' [Irish Republic]. That fear was always there in our community. But it didn't take long for the IRA to use the Army as a target. A lot of young men, good men – some of them only boys – they were murdered by terrorists for no reason other than they had been given a job to do to try and control the situation over here.

I suppose then if you mean between 1972 and 1975, things had changed in terms of how we started to think of ourselves. We had been saying to the British especially 'we are the victims here, what are you going to do about it?' But they weren't listening. Not interested! Just like now, same as always. Even when the IRA really took it to them on the mainland they seemed more sickened by the violence, and more ready to get out of Northern Ireland, than suddenly realising what we were going through every day – every day we were getting it – and trying to do all they could to stop it. So in a way we started to give up saying we were the victims, because what good did it do? All it did was give the British government another way out, and it made the IRA think they were winning. But we weren't going to be shifted. I laugh because outsiders just do not understand that unionist people are not going to be shoved out of their own land. I heard some people say to me way back then 'this is it, I'm away, no more' but very few left the Province altogether. It was their home. A lot of people left Belfast, I don't deny that – myself included. But that there was a decision I never regretted. The sectarianism in that area against Prods got worse all the time and you just didn't know where was safe. I suppose there was some sense too of 'let them have it if they want it so badly'. Of course, the British did everything they could to undermine us – they took the guns off the cops for a while [RUC], that was the worst thing. The Provos were targeting cops left, right and centre, and a lot of time luring them into gun battles. What were the RUC supposed to do? Hit them with sticks? They even moaned about plastic bullets! It was a nonsense and it was no surprise they had to go back on it. The violence was new in those days, and it was more raw, like a wound, you know, or a sore? But we thought it would end quickly. We thought at first the British would come in and crush it, and that the world would know we were the ones who were on the wrong end of it. We should have known better! We were proud people. It wasn't us that asked the British Army to come and rescue us. Don't forget that. It was the nationalists that asked for them, and then they spent the best part of 30 years trying to assassinate them. Then we heard republicans cry and whine all the time – every night they were on the TV – that they were victims of discrimination, and we didn't want to be like them to be honest. Every IRA man that was shot all we got in the paper was 'he was just out minding his own business and the police shot him for no reason'. I mean, I'm not saying that in some cases the Army or whatever might have over-reacted, but that was the same old lies they came out with, even when a few days later they would give these guys full IRA funerals with the guns and all.

So it was bad then, for sure, and I think from what I know I think it was '72 was the worst year. But to say it was worse than the rest of the Troubles, and worse than what each innocent family went through, that there is an insult to all those people who suffered right up until 1994. Families who had relatives murdered, or even the people who felt they were just denied the opportunity to just have a normal time of it. But in terms of the streets of Belfast between '72 and '75, it was ridiculous. The Army had got tea and buns for about a week from republicans, as I told you, and then they got their arses shot off. The Provos had split from the Stickies [Official IRA] and so they were shooting at each other, then the Loyalists emerged – the UDA and the UVF – and everywhere round about where we lived you had people standing in the road – cops, soldiers, UDA, IRA – you just didn't know. My decision to get out of it – and I suppose the reason I think you could label me a victim though no-one has ever acknowledged my right to be called that – is something that happened to me in 1972. I was driving up home and I got flagged down. Then came this tap on the window, you know? This patrol had waved me down, up in West Belfast. I was on my way home from work, and it was dark, really dark. I got out of the car, nervously, but it worried me straight away because of the voice of this guy – he had a thick Belfast accent, he wasn't in army dress. His face was covered, and it all seemed just wrong you know? Just didn't seem right. When I got up close and saw he was just in dark clothes and like a scarf over his face, I knew it was either the UDA or the IRA. So this guy he says to me: 'Where are you going?' So I says 'Home'. He said: 'Where's that?' Now, that was the question in Belfast in those days you just did not want to be asked. Where did you live? Everyone knew if you gave an address – and I lived just off the Shankill at that time – it could be one that meant you got the bullet. And as I tried to think of somewhere, because by now I was convinced this was the IRA, anywhere that wouldn't mark me out as a Prod, all I could hear was the rattle of gunfire in the background. It was unreal. We couldn't have been more than a half a mile away. I was nearly sick with fear. Crack crack crack, and it was getting closer. This voice from behind a car shouted, and now this is from memory 'For fuck's sake Seamus' – it might not have been Seamus, as I say it was a long time ago but it was a name that was definitely Irish republican you know – 'let's get the fuck out of here, the Brits are only up the road'. He was wetting himself.

This one, the leader, he had me by the arm now – he leant over and he said 'You are one lucky bastard. This is a mobile patrol of the Irish Republican Army and you were about to be placed under arrest and interrogated for collaborating with known enemies of the Irish people'. Now those words I remember, that's exactly what he said. I thought, at the same time, how bloody stupid he sounded, like he was in a comic book, and yet how sinister this character was. I mean, arrested? We all knew what that meant. They were going to take me and put a bullet in my head and dump me down an entry. As for collaborating with ene- mies of the Irish people, I think he'd watched too many war movies, though I shouldn't joke about it because I was scared at the time make no mistake. At that time my boss was part-time in the UDR. He had been a B man [B Special] and because I worked for him – trying to earn a few bob – that was probably enough reason for them to pull me and if that machine gun hadn't gone off wherever it was they probably would have shot me. My cousin was in the RUC too. Or maybe they just set out to shoot a Prod that night. I don't know. Anyway, they climbed into their car and this guy says 'You should leave Belfast, you Orange bas- tard, you'll not be so lucky next time'. This other one, a wee fella, he shouted 'crack him anyway he's seen us now'. But they sped off. Just then it dawned on me they had only left me because this gun battle was going on, and as I say it couldn't have been far away. As I headed home I was in total shock. To make matters worse, as I got up the road where I lived another patrol waved me down – this time it was obviously the British Army, probably where the gunfire was coming from. They didn't know the territory at all in those days. So I stopped the motor again and this young lad asked for all my details. He was a bit nervous and this arrogant officer came marching over, and he shouted at me 'Who are you? Where are you going? What are you doing in this area at this time?' I told him I lived there and that I'd just been stopped by the IRA and threatened at gunpoint. You know what he said to me? 'Well you're a bloody idiot driving around here'. I fucking lived there!! He was an arrogant bastard. So in the beginning, that was the sort of totally abnormal situation you had to get used to. I said to him 'Should I report it to the police?' He started to walk away and he said, casually, 'You can do what you like, just get out of my way'. I laugh now when we have this tale of the conflict that the British Army – especially in those days – were all on our side. In West and North Belfast they didn't know where they were, and half the time they were too busy fighting gun battles to do anything else. Unionist civilians living up round there were a pain the arse for them at that time, in my view, because they didn't know the streets and they never could tell who was out to get them.

I got home – I was just married at that time – and I said to my wife what had happened. Well, the two of us never slept a wink that night, or for about a week after. We wanted to start a family and the final straw was trying to get home one night not that long after and the bullets were literally whizzing by the car, there were people on the footpath huddled on the ground like in a film or something – IRA at one end of the road, the British at the other. I came in and I said 'get the house on the market, we're getting out of here'. We took wild stick off the neighbours, that we didn't have the bottle for it you know, we were giving up to the IRA? I couldn't have cared less. This was '72 or '73, and by that time a good school friend of mine had been seriously injured in a bomb on a pub on the Shankill Road where I would have had a pint the odd time. When I looked at the car the next day, there was a bullet mark on it. Right down the driver's side. When I saw that I knew I was making the right decision. My wife, her family were all here, or I would have gone right out of here, to Canada or somewhere, but we moved out to a wee town about 20 miles away, and we've stayed there ever since. It wasn't easy getting out – no one wanted our house in that area then, but I'll always think of Belfast as somewhere that was my city, and that was taken away from me. Maybe if we'd stuck it out a few more years it might have got better, but I think we made the right decision. But we never left Northern Ireland, and that was the main thing. We adjusted to the violence, and we had to because we still went to Belfast quite regularly to see family and friends. But looking back, really, how do you ever adjust to that? Was it worse then? As I said to you, in ways, because it was so new, but in other ways, no, because you didn't realise it would go on for so long. The ordinary Protestant unionist people of Northern Ireland were incredible. They took a total pounding – from terrorists, from the media, bombs and bullets flying, and they hung in there. Those first few years of the Troubles were just beyond the comprehension of

people who weren't there. I was very depressed for a long time after that
you know. I think I'm not a direct victim, but I was what you would call
victimised by the circumstances and by those people that I'm quite sure
would happily have killed me if they had decided to, and never had any
remorse about it. I still struggle with that now, nearly 40 years on. We
never really talked about it – it's not our way to do that you know? Our
fear was a private thing, but now we realise that if we want republicans
to stop trying to re-write history we have to tell our stories, we have to
tell people what happened to us.

**('Keith', 62, Belfast)**

Did we get used to it? Did we feel like victims? Yes and yes, I suppose.
I suppose if you measure it like that, yeah. But we had over 30 years'
worth of this to put up with. But 72–75 was bad, no doubt about it. The
Four Step Inn bombing – you know about that do you? Two innocent
unionists killed, one of them was quite a young man. You don't hear
much about that now do you? The IRA never had the guts to claim that.
We hear all about Bloody Sunday, that thing just goes on and on and
on, and that there was lots of IRA truces and so on in that time. That's
not how I remember it. For me in that same period we were totally
under siege. Under siege! The RUC and the Army just couldn't cope.
You tried to keep you wits about you and carry on as normal and the
strangest thing is, that became your normality. That was just the way it
was. Gun battles, no-warning bombs, friends and colleagues murdered.
The stupid thing is we thought at the start it would end, it would be
stopped quickly. We had no idea. So looking back it was worse, like,
with just how bad it was with everything that was happening, and you
thought 'these gangsters are giving one of the world's best armies the
run around – how can that be?' And they were, there is no argument.
The British troops used to stop you on the Shankill Road with maps
and ask you how to get to certain places. They knew by then they were
safe in our area, but they didn't always give us an easy time either. It
was ridiculous, but probably worse for them. There was no let up during
that time. It was constant. But you tried to get on with it. Ulster unionist people, Ulster Protestant people, whatever you want to call them,
they are resilient, they didn't want to be victims – they were put in that
situation and when they asked for help, they realised no-one cared, so
they gave up, sort of retreated. Not retreated from the fight with republicans, but from trying to make anyone listen to their case. That's what
I think about it anyway. At the same time, mind you, we weren't going

to be bullied. I don't mean the type of resilience you saw from Loyalist paramilitaries. As my Uncle said, anyone can pick up a gun and think it makes them some sort of a big man you know? He had been in the war, he knew about fighting, he knew what it did to people. It's the family man, he said, who goes to his work, day after day, come what may, and tries to earn money and do the right thing, that's the brave man. But that's the liberties they were trying to take from us. Our culture. Our way of doing things. And their means, to me, were unforgivable. I'm not sure of the exact timing of it but I remember the year the IRA blew up a wee curtain shop and a bar over in south Belfast. They killed three ordinary, decent people. Three Protestants. So we had the politicians shouting about united Irelands and Paisley and all those characters, and people wonder why the unionist community listened? What were we to do? Those bombs over in south Belfast – a man of nearly 70 years old, and a woman in her fifties. Is that war? Little did we know they would keep that up for 30 years, and that they would do even worse things to ordinary unionist people! Even though the security forces began to get their act together and started to fight back they couldn't stop the IRA killing Protestants, and nobody will persuade me that things like Bloody Friday, or what happened down in your rural areas like Kingsmills or Tullyvallen Orange Hall were not sectarian. I have cousins down in Armagh and they told me 'listen you think it's bad in Belfast these ones down here are really just shooting all the Prods they can'. I'm not naïve, we all know from the mid 70s the British were trying to find a way to get rid of us – that started with Sunningdale until the Loyalists stopped them. There is also that idea some people argue, that the Loyalist gangs gave it to the Provos and that stopped them too, and made it easier for the unionist people. You might hear that a lot. The Loyalists like to think it because it makes them heroes in their own minds, and republicans like to say it because it helps them politically, putting all ordinary unionists as people who were supporters of the UVF or the UDA. I don't believe that at all. Of all the lies they have put about, that's right up there with the worst of them. I lived in an area where the UDA were out every night in the early 70s, and maybe it stopped the IRA coming into our area for a short time, but it just meant the IRA went somewhere else and killed some poor innocent Prod, or blew up a bar or a shop. The ordinary unionist people gave their support to the RUC and the Army. They were law abiding. The majority were far too clever and far too moral to be joining or supporting illegal groups that bullied their own people like the UVF. They knew from seeing the news and reading the papers that these goons weren't going out and killing IRA men. They were knocking on doors of Catholic civilians, some soft targets, men with families, and murdering them, just what the IRA was doing to us. I don't know the numbers, but it's certainly my opinion that if you were to examine it through the course of all the Troubles, the paramilitaries didn't actually kill each other. They had the city carved up – extortion, rackets, and drug dealing. That's what the unionist people never understood. When it came to elections, we never and have never backed Loyalists, and yet for all the IRA did to our community during the Troubles – and especially in those early days when it was just madness – Catholics vote for Sinn Fein time and time again. So if they're going to get into this, looking back at what happened, then you make sure and ask them about the Four Step Inn, about the Red Lion Bar on the Ormeau, about the Bayardo, about Bloody Friday. I'd love to hear their answers.

**('Jonathan', 60, County Antrim)**

Well I lived in a fairly unionist part of Northern Ireland, up in County Antrim. I wasn't in the thick of it in Belfast. Certainly the Troubles touched me in a way like they did with everyone because, because I had been away to university over in England and back, and by the time I returned it had all gone from peace to so called war. My father and mother owned a lovely place in a rural area, so to some extent we were sheltered from it. We would have regarded Belfast as 'our' town, I suppose, if we had to. Given that my parents were from Belfast there was always a big thing in our family that although we lived in a rural area Belfast was 'ours', and we had lots of family there. Maybe a lot of the unionist people of Northern Ireland felt like that. The 'citadel', you know? It was symbolic. It represented us. So when the PIRA started to blow it up it touched all of us, but I think in very different ways. Some people left, many of my friends – first to go to university but a lot of them did not come back. But I loved where I lived, I loved my country and I felt British. I wanted to make sure I felt British in the place I had been born. It might sound silly but that was important to me. I remember there had been a lot of incidents in the autumn and winter of 1971 and 1972. I remember that well. Funny enough I had just returned to Belfast that September and a really good friend – maybe the best friend I ever had, we met at university – he was from West Belfast. I would try and get down to meet up with him almost every weekend, despite how tense it was. There was a series of bombs on the Shankill – a dreadful one I remember in which two wee babies were killed. Too appalling to even contemplate. For me, that was devastating to every unionist in Northern Ireland, that victimised us all as a community, I feel that very strongly.

Anyway, the following summer my friend – and this certainly destroys the myth Protestants walked into jobs back then, because this guy had a degree from a very good English university and he had gone nearly a year without work – he was working in Mackie's, it was a big engineering works in west Belfast, just to try and get enough cash to get a place of his own and some experience under his belt you know? I wasn't exactly doing brilliantly career wise either. I had wanted to become a teacher but I found getting work in the schools really tough. I had done a bit here and there, but my friend, he had said to me 'you should come down they're looking for people here, get a bit of spending money, sure it'll be a good laugh'. I talked it over with my parents and though they were worried about my safety, as old fashioned Belfast people they were proud of Mackie's – it had been the jewel in Northern Ireland's industrial crown at one point – they said they thought as long as I didn't give up on the teaching there would be no harm in doing a summer there and maybe even staying with my friend. I was still a young man. This was about late May, from memory, but I could be wrong. But I remember this – I was due to go down on a Monday and meet one of the bosses, a sort of interview I think, and then the plan was I would stay with my friend and we would catch up.

Well, the day came and I got a bit nervous to be honest. My father had offered me the loan of the car to drive down 'to make a good impression', but it wasn't only the fact that Belfast was unsafe that was putting me off. I couldn't really picture myself labouring in a factory. I had worked my socks off to get a first at university and I badly wanted a good job. I didn't know how I would fit in with the guys in a place like Mackie's. So that morning at the breakfast table I voiced my concerns to my parents. We were talking it over and the phone rang. It was the headmaster of a local school, and he wondered if I could come in that day and fill in until the end of term, which was about a month and half's work, because one of his teachers was sick. That was how it worked in those days, if they knew you or you'd been in and asked about a job they would just phone you up that day. I was ecstatic. I still took the car! I went on into the school and had a great first few days. Of course, there were no mobile phones in those days so I had to telephone my friend's parents and leave a message explaining. I remember his father – he was a real gentleman – answered and he said 'you're just right son – stay you out of this madhouse and get yourself a good career'.

Anyway, after a good day's teaching I returned home with a smile on my face. I felt pretty sure if things went well I might get full time work in this school and as far as the conflict went, I didn't really think about it. I was sure it would be over soon; and anyway, that even though the PIRA had attacked innocent Protestants, they would not be interested in me. A few days later my father got home from work and we put on the television news as we always did. I've never been so shocked, before or since, although that sounds ridiculous in ways because a lot of worse things have happened. The workers at Mackie's had been leaving work as usual when the PIRA machine-gunned them. I was absolutely stunned. I don't even think it was the biggest story of the day. Thankfully, no-one was killed, I think, but I thought about what could have been, and what could have happened to me and what would happen to my friend if he stayed where he was. From that moment on, for some reason it really personalised it for me. I suppose I felt like a victim. I wanted someone to do something about it. They had just opened fire on a crowd of men on the basis that that they were mostly Protestants. A lot, lot worse things were to happen after that throughout the Troubles I know, but I remember that day as one that changed my optimism to a kind of overwhelming pessimism about the whole country. I made a decision if I didn't get full time work in the school I was going back to England. I phoned my friend and he was shaken up badly, and he left Mackie's not long after. He changed. Something inside him changed that day. I never did get the work in the school, and the next year off I went. I stayed in England for 20 years, and I didn't come back here until 1993. I couldn't have timed that worse either, because no sooner was I settled than the PIRA killed those innocent people in that dreadful bomb attack on the Shankill. Nothing had changed. I really questioned my decision to come back, and even now I'm angry about the way history is being rewritten.

Sadly, my friend, he couldn't get work when he left Mackie's. He decided to join the RUC. Before I left for England that summer we talked about it a lot. 'We have a responsibility to do something about this' he would always say. He had really changed. He sounded like a man, if that makes sense, he wasn't a boy anymore. He had a different view of the whole situation to me, he wanted to join the security forces and help end the conflict. I wanted as far away from it as possible. It angers me now to hear people say Protestant civilians joined the RUC because it was a sectarian force. There wasn't a bigoted bone in my friend's body. I watched this guy defend a Catholic friend of ours from a UDA mob in a bar in Belfast, when he could have only been 21. At the start after I left we would write to each other every week and in that autumn of

72 he told me he had joined the RUC. The last straw for him had been Bloody Friday the previous summer. But the whole stress of being in the RUC, and I think he was attacked in a gun battle, he turned to the drink, which was quite common for policemen. He just got worse and worse over the years, you know, he had a really bad problem. He was stationed in a tough area and he was threatened all the time. He was drinking more and more and eventually his wife left and took his kids. I remember I was in England and set to go out for the evening and the telephone rang. His father came on and he just said to me 'He's gone.' I tried to console him but he just said to me 'He made his choice. We'll always be proud of that'. I was in England at the time and I couldn't bring myself to come back for the funeral. I felt too ashamed, like I had escaped and left him behind. I felt guilty. I also felt lucky. And I felt sad. It haunted me for years. I was that upset I had to take leave from school. Why had I not tried harder to persuade him to come to England with me? We were close. There I was, settled, a wife and children, a lovely quiet part of the UK, and trying to protect what he believed in had cost him everything, what we had both believed in at one time. The writing was on the wall that day at Mackie's. I had tried to tell him, but like so many people here, he wouldn't think of himself as a victim – he would say to me 'we can't let ourselves be the victims, we can stop this, we have to do it ourselves.' But I think we can think of ourselves as victims. I think we have to. I visit his grave regularly. I have been back to visit his family. I talk to them and occasionally, we can laugh and think of a young man who was so full of promise. I visit his grave regularly and it gives me comfort. I think of a version of myself I could have been, just like him, fighting for justice but the stress of it breaking me, and I just stand and stare. I don't know why I go. Guilt maybe. If I'm honest, I'm angry. We were just ordinary people trying to get on with things, and they not only created the circumstances that made that impossible, but once they had done that, they blew people up, and shot them, or made their lives so difficult that unionists people just gave up. Not just policemen and soldiers either. That is our truth, or part of it. I would encourage every other unionist to think the same way, to think of those who have been forgotten, and to articulate the same feeling. We cannot forgive those who have no remorse.

**('Claire', 53, County Armagh)**

The year 1974 was a year I remember well. That was the year we thought things might turn. It seems terrible, it's disgusting even, to say it, but we thought if the British people realised what it was like to have the IRA blowing them up, blowing up their towns and their people, on their turf, they would understand what we were going through. I'm ashamed I thought that way because those were ghastly, sickening attacks that the IRA carried out in England. It started with them blowing up that bus on the motorway, killed ten people or maybe more, and continued with those diabolical bombings at the pubs in Guildford and Birmingham. For the first time, we thought there might be more solidarity between us and the English you know? That we were in it together, because it hadn't felt like that before. But it didn't amount to that. I think they blamed us all for creating a conflict that spread to their country. What they didn't realise is we thought of it as our country too – Great Britain, the United Kingdom – we thought we were a part of it. But we weren't, I suppose. Not to them. We were a strange far off place that was just major trouble for them. That's when I realised, anyway, that this was going to be a long struggle, a very long struggle. The IRA had gone into England and shown them they were not afraid to take them on. They knew, just five years into the conflict, that they could carry on murdering Protestants here and that while it might have put pressure on the unionist community, and while it might have satisfied their hatred of us, it wasn't helping their cause as much as they liked. The publicity of bombings on mainland England! That was incredible. We were getting it every day, every single day – but the IRA knew that the big bombs in England, they were worth more. The media flocked to that, it was covered for days. There was a witch-hunt for the IRA men that did it, and even then they didn't get the right people. I had been anti-Sunningdale but I thought there was a middle ground, I thought there was a way that we as a people could communicate the extent of our suffering, what was being done to us. Between 1974 and maybe three years after that, I had given up totally. I was completely disillusioned. No matter what happened to us – and the 70s were really bad you have to understand that, the atrocities that were carried out – we were ignored. Gradually people, although they didn't give in, stopped thinking there was any point in trying to make the world understand it wasn't as simple as the republicans had made it out to be, that our ordinary Protestant and unionist men – and women – were being killed for no reason. I remember my husband he had been active in politics for a short time, he had been a bit of an idealist too, and he would come home and say he was told on the doorsteps 'Good luck to you son but you're wasting your time, sure no-one wants to know'.

It was only a minority – outside Paisley and the like – I mean a minority of the ordinary unionist people, that were prepared to speak out, to try and get justice and truth by telling their stories. And there were lots of stories to tell that never have been told. Then more and more people moved out of Belfast and into what became Protestant unionist towns, and from that moment on – now you would be approaching the 1980s by now – unionist people were not only saying there was no point to their stories being told to the British or the world, but they were starting to say 'look at what has happened through this whole decade, and nothing has been done. If that doesn't change this conflict, nothing will'. So they, I think, began to stop talking about it even amongst themselves.

In the 80s the violence continued but the unionist people just went about their business, they tried to make it normal, because for many of them by then, after ten or more years, it had become normal. So yes, it was very bad in the beginning, and unionist people have been the victims of a dreadful conflict there's no doubt, but for the rest of the Troubles they – we – gave up in ways trying to make people appreciate that. Now I don't mean we gave up in the conflict – but we gave up trying to make people understand what they were experiencing, gave up trying to persuade people we were in the right or that we were victims, and we gave up talking even to each other about the conflict. We adopted that typical Ulster Protestant attitude 'we'll do it ourselves'. And we just got on with it. Terrible things kept happening in the 80s and the 90s but there was a new attitude, one that was maybe based on the idea that the British would sell us out, would give us up, but that the ordinary unionist people of Northern Ireland would not make it easy for republicans, they would not show weakness by talking about being victims or being afraid of terrorists.

Instead, we pulled down the emotional hatches and just got on with it. You could say 'why didn't they keep telling their stories'? In my opinion, no-one wanted to hear, so they just tucked their stories away and they've stayed there ever since. Maybe now, with this truth and reconciliation thing, the truth of what happened to ordinary unionist people will come out, but there's still a big lack of trust there, a fear that republicans and the British and Irish governments will create this false history of what really happened. I think unionist people might be ready to give their side of the thing now, but they'd need a lot of guarantees that it was just not part of some political game to excuse what the IRA did, or to force them into a united Ireland.

# 4
## Untold Stories: Unionist Remembrance of Political Violence and Suffering in Northern Ireland

### Introduction

As evidenced by the histories provided by unionist respondents in the previous two chapters, one of the core socio-political and cultural aspects of contemporary unionist discourse in Northern Ireland is the need to foster and protect a sense of legitimate grievance in respect of the killings and injuries of innocent Protestant civilians (those not affiliated to British state security forces) by the PIRA during the conflict of 1969–1998. This chapter uses particularly memorable illustrative examples – 'Bloody Friday' in 1972; the Kingsmills Massacre in 1976; and the La Mon House Hotel bombing in 1978 – to analyse the ways in which unionists have begun to narrate, remember and attempt to politicise their suffering. This chapter also illuminates the ways in which many unionists feel that the stories of those in their community who were assassinated, blown up or attacked by Irish republican paramilitaries in some of the most grievous and dastardly atrocities of the conflict have remained untold, silenced by their political opponents and ignored by both their fellow British citizens and successive British administrations.

### Background

In this chapter, I have selected those interview extracts from a large amount of data that best represent the despair, futility and sorrow that these particular murderous acts of political violence caused. This was not an easy task. I made a considered and conscious attempt to balance the accounts, attempting to provide the reader with an overall picture, rather than focussing simply on evocative and provocative recollections of what were ghastly terror attacks. I could have opted for interview extracts which stressed much more emphatically condemnation of the perpetrators – that is, angry accounts that made clear demands as to what should have been done in the name of retributive justice. Those, however, were in the minority. More pertinently, and curiously, they were also usually articulated by people who had no direct geographic or temporal connection to the events. Most of those who experienced the traumatic assaults described in this chapter, both directly or from afar, are now beyond anger, and certainly do not seek vengeance. Enervated by decades of grief and feeling ignored, they want explanations and apologies, and the opportunity to tell the world their stories. It is this aspect of the phenomenon of unionist memory that I want to stress in this chapter. It was also important in selecting these extracts that they came from people who experienced the events *at the time*. I wanted to offer, in the best way that I could, rounded perspectives – including those who were directly affected by the attacks and those who happened upon the aftermath or sought to deal with the communal sadness – in order that unionist storytelling would no longer be inaccurately caricatured or dismissed as simply irate, irrational demands for the retrospective punishment of offenders. Rather, the stories in this chapter reflect – in varying forms – the overwhelming sense of lasting melancholy that I discovered during extensive ethnographic research.

## Untold stories

Providing access to these previously 'unheard voices' represents extremely original insights that make this a worthwhile academic exercise in and of itself (Amstutz, 2004). As discussed earlier in this book, it is important to resist the temptation to mask the potency of personal narratives of suffering with overly esoteric argument and/or unnecessary theorising. The numerous unionist narratives of these incidents contained in this chapter reflect the condition of a collection of people who have been left in varying emotional states, and whose recollections fuse fragments of debilitating grief, suffering, loss, anger, nostalgia, fond remembrance allied to episodic and acute melancholia, hope and despair (Das et al., 2001; Boym, 2001). Those extracts which I have chosen to present are a combination of harrowing tales by those who suffered great loss as a consequence of the attacks, and others that are more distant, but no less impassioned, perspectives on the vicarious grief felt by the unionist community. All have one thing in common – they pertain to instances in which paramilitaries in Northern Ireland attacked civilians with callous, unprovoked and malicious intent, with absolutely no regard for the immunity or protection of those who were non-combatants in what the PIRA termed a 'war'. After some deliberation, although the information is already in the public domain I have made an ethical decision in this chapter not to include the names of the victims of these atrocities out of respect to their families and relatives. Should a truth recovery process be instituted in Northern Ireland, it is my view that this will give those relatives ample chance to decide for themselves whether or not they want their details to be disclosed (provided that this is a truth recovery process which allows for individual storytelling, dialogue and communicative rationality). Also, all of those respondents whose testimony is included in this chapter have been given a one-name alias, which is consistent with the approach I have used in the rest of the book. Their age is included to give the reader an indication of how old they were when the attacks took place. No other biographical detail is provided in order to protect their anonymity.

## 'Bloody Friday'

Following political talks with the British Government about a potential settlement to the Northern Ireland conflict that stalled (after absurdly unrealistic demands for complete and immediate British withdrawal by the PIRA), the Belfast Brigade of the PIRA planned and executed a devastating, co-ordinated attack on Belfast city centre on Friday the 21st July of 1972. They detonated a total of 22 bombs in one afternoon, and amid the chaos and confusion, allied to a combination of extremely poorly issued warnings and no-warning explosions, the security services were left bewildered and besieged. Consequently, they made crucial errors in directing people away from areas which had been targeted into areas which were then subsequently attacked, inadvertently exacerbating the toll of casualties. It was a calculated show of terrorist strength. Despite claiming the lives of two British soldiers, the PIRA could not legitimately or credibly argue that this was anything other than a series of random acts of violence and terror directed at ordinary civilians. Nine people were killed, and 130 were seriously injured. Despite the murder of two Catholic women, the event has figured very prominently in unionist political thought and remembrance in Northern Ireland as the first sustained and serious attack of the Troubles upon Protestant civilians by the PIRA. That the atrocities should take place in the centre of Belfast – so long the ethnic marker of Ulster Protestantism and unionist political territoriality (Anderson and Shuttleworth, 1998; Shirlow and Murtagh,

2006) – was especially galling for the unionist community. The Conflict Archive on the Internet (CAIN) – a project run by the University of Ulster – is an enormous and authoritative source of information on all matters pertaining to the Troubles and is routinely used by scholars. It has a section on 'Bloody Friday'. Its introduction is indicative not only of the 'forgotten' nature of that atrocity but of the lack of serious historical attention that has been devoted to even creating a coherent account of what transpired:

> There appears to have been much less material written about what happened on 21 July 1972 in Belfast than on many other events that occurred during 'the Troubles'. This, together with the fact that many of the initial newspaper accounts of the day were confused about the exact sequence of events, means that there are still some discrepancies in accounts of the day.
>
> (CAIN, 2009)

**('Barbara', 56, Belfast)**

I remember it well … that's to say, I do and I don't. I sometimes try to block it out, but it comes back. I'm not going to trot out the same old thing you've heard hundreds of times before – 'scooping up bits of people and putting them in plastic bags'. I didn't do that, thank goodness. I was at work. Without giving too much away, I worked in a tall building right in the city centre. I could see right over the city. I saw the clouds of smoke going up, one by one. It sounds stupid to say it, and maybe I just think this now, but each time one of those bombs went up I'm not sure I was frightened. I think I was just sad. I was sad to my core. I knew someone else had died or been injured. Someone probably, and to me Catholic or Protestant it honestly didn't matter, someone who had nothing to do with any of it, some wee innocent person, you know, just innocent victims. And that's the way it was. I got home and I turned the TV on and it was then – I remember we were all gathered round – it was then we saw the images and we found out … you know … what had happened. I cried that night. All these years later, it still just provokes that in me, terrible sadness. But now … now it's worse in some ways. We're being told as unionists 'it's all your fault', and we have these inquiries into Bloody Sunday and all of that. I'm not against that – those people want the truth too, but why have our people been forgotten? Protestants, unionists, whatever you want to call us. Look at what happened to us! That's just ignored, airbrushed out of history. I tell you, I really do think that they just don't want to hear it. No-one does. We'll be left alone... and in the end all that suffering, all that loss, will have been for nothing. We'll get no truth, no justice. And the people that did it to us run the country! That's what gets called 'justice'. It's a joke. I try not to think about it now, because it just makes me despair. I want people to find out the truth about the past, but we need OUR PAST remembered too. We have that right. I don't think we'll get it though.


**('Billy', 60, Belfast)**

I was there that day. I went into the town for a new jacket. Hopped on a bus – I had the day off work. When the first one [bomb] went off – it seems daft to say it – I didn't think that much about it. I was going to say I was used to it by then but it was only... What...'72? Used to hearing the bullets from them [paramilitaries] maybe, but I suppose not that used to the bombs, not on that level anyway. Soon after the first one I heard another bang. And I got worried. I did. I can admit that. A wee fella I knew from our road by the name of Tommy came past me and he said 'Billy have you heard?' ...he was white. I thought he was pissed [intoxicated] and I couldn't make out the half of what he was saying. I didn't really know what was going on but I thought he meant there had been a bomb, I'd worked that much out you know? He says to me 'we'd better get down there there's people need help'. I honestly don't know what had happened because by this time there must have been bombs going off everywhere. I think I blanked it out a bit, you know? There were peelers [police] all around and they looked to me like they didn't know what they were doing. I saw one of them just stood there, stood still, I think he was crying, though he might have been rubbing dust out of his eyes. It was just complete devastation.

   I thought there and then, and I'm a bit ashamed to admit it: 'I'm doing no good here'. You have to remember we had no idea how many more were going to go off or who might be in danger. I was only young – what was I able to do? So I took off and made my way home. Then I heard they had tried to blow up Prods [Protestants] in the houses up near one of my Uncles, who lived in Agnes Street at that time. I don't really remember getting back, I was panicking by that point. It sort of settled down anyway and a few of my mates called round that night and we all watched the news, tried to take it in you know? I was angry, yeah, I don't deny that – it was like, they were coming now and attacking our people in our city, in the centre of Belfast of all places, killing our innocent civilians, but I wasn't full of hatred the way they [Irish republicans] make out now. Where we lived, you could have gone out and done something about it if you wanted, you know? There was boys, fellas, who went out and done (*sic*) that, and ended up inflicting misery on people, but my family – we were good people. Good people. We didn't believe in that kind of thing. What would be the price of something like that anyway? Some more innocent people? So we moved out of Belfast not long after that. It just wasn't safe anymore. I was getting married and I just thought 'they can have it'. I regret that a bit, it was like, we got pushed out, you know, of our own city? Now I don't think about it that much – or I try not to – but this truth recovery thing has set it all off again. If they want truth they need to come out and say who killed those innocent people that day, and all the other days, or forget it, as far as I'm concerned. As unionists I would have to say I think we have lost the big battle anyway, so why should we co-operate in some process that's going to rub us out of the picture, out of history? I can't think of a reason. At least the way it is now we know, among our own people we know what happened.

### ('Peter', 61, Belfast)

I would say to anyone who says unionist caused the conflict or that we're not innocent victims – were you there?! Did you see what I saw?! 22 bombs?! Over a hundred people injured?! Innocent civilians butchered? I walked those streets and they ran with blood. They ran with blood! I picked up bits of people's bodies, they were scattered everywhere! Bits of limbs, hands and feet! Is that what they want to hear? Of course it's not – they won't let us tell that story – our story! I got no compensa-tion, no counselling, nothing! And I didn't expect it. I did my duty as a citizen of the United Kingdom and as a member of my community. Of course the people killed by the IRA that day were innocent. The IRA with its weasel words says now they killed two soldiers and they were only targeting businesses – well I'd like to know how they knew what would happen? Who works in businesses? People! What about the other people they killed? A wee boy of 15 year old! What about the people injured? Were they not innocent? There were Catholics too, two poor Catholic women … but make no mistake this was an attack on the British state, the British unionist people of Northern Ireland, on our city, to drive us out, there can be no mistake about that. It was a show of strength against the unionist people of Belfast. Are we not entitled to say these were all innocent victims of the conflict? If we're not, then I don't want anything to do with truth recovery, dealing with the past, whatever you want to call it. Sure they might as well go ahead without us anyway, which they probably will. If they admit they did wrong, and that these people that they murdered were innocent, then I think you might get a different take on things. Some unionists – I can't speak for them all – but some might be prepared to get involved in that. But only if that happens. They can't force us to get involved in it if they keep pedalling these lies.

**(Nigel, 64, Belfast)**

What do you want me to say about that? Really, what? You want me to say it's okay, that's it's forgotten now, we should all move on the way the IRA keeps saying we should. I cannot honestly sit here and tell you that as a native of that city – my home town – at that time, even nearly 40 years later, that I would find it easy to forgive anyone for what they did that day to my community. Killing innocent people! It's a sort of sadistic cruelty these IRA boys had, you know, that the ordinary human just cannot comprehend. Pure psychopaths. Or sociopaths, whatever you would call them. I don't know how these people, these terrorists, rationalise it to themselves, or if they even bother to try. It probably doesn't worry those bastards one bit. We get told now it was all part of a 'war'. Well, if it was, Bloody Friday was a war crime, and someone needs to take responsibility for it, so there's the obvious flaw in that argument. For me, there wasn't a Protestant family in Northern Ireland, let alone Belfast, that wouldn't have been touched in some way by what happened that day. It affected us all, emotionally. And unionists don't forget. We remember what was done to us, you'd better believe it, even if non-one else does, and even if no-one else listens. I have friends from abroad and I tried explaining our situation to them. They found it very complicated and I was getting nowhere, so I drew up a list of all the times the IRA had murdered innocent Protestant civilians. They just couldn't believe it. They said they'd never heard any of that before, and that it was just never mentioned in their newspapers or on the TV over there. I don't know if I changed their viewpoint, but it felt for once like at least I was empowered to say 'listen to what was done to us'.

And Bloody Friday was maybe one of the first – but certainly not the last – of that kind of ruthless attack against ordinary Protestants that went on during the Troubles. It was just pure sectarian hatred by the IRA, there's no denying that. Belfast was total rubble. I was a young man at the time of the bombs and I worked in the city. It's not that I actually saw a lot of the terrible things other people did, but I think about what took place and even now it's very upsetting. It makes me angry at times. But I feel too old and too weary to be angry. They [PIRA] wanted to drag the fight out of us, out of our community, and I think to an extent, starting with Bloody Friday, they managed it. For all that, if this situation here continues the way it is, this supposed remembering the past then I'll certainly back anyone in the unionist community who wants to tell their stories, and I'd want to tell mine if the conditions were right. But I'll tell you this – and I know all my friends feel the same way – I'll not have anything to do with it if I'm treated the same way as some terrorist who claims he was a victim of the Troubles too. I think that's absolutely disgusting. We were innocent people targeted by terrorists, there's a clear moral difference there between them and us, for me anyway, and I think the majority of unionists feel that way. Later on in the Troubles I had friends in the police killed, and I saw the devastation that caused to their families and their friends. The IRA says they were so called 'legitimate targets'. But what were the people on Bloody Friday? It's just sickening. A total disgrace. And just so very upsetting and sad. I will not forget hearing the sound of the first bomb that day, and panicking. I was just a junior in our place in those days and it was the boss who said 'everyone get out'. He was quick thinking, because we were quite near Oxford Street where the worst of it was. Had we stayed there another half an hour, we'd have been in big trouble, no doubt about it. I ran down the stairs of our office and I don't think I've ever run so fast! Then I had to try and get home, and believe me that wasn't easy as I had no car. A workmate – a Catholic fella I should say because we in no way blame Catholics and it's important to stress that – gave me a lift home to an area just on the outskirts of the town which was very strongly unionist at that time. That man – who was an elderly guy at the time – showed me that not everyone in the Catholic community, even if they wanted a united Ireland, were murderers and killers like the Provos. He was a very kind, a true gentleman and he just said to me 'this is awful, this is not what we want at all'. When I got in I heard the shudder of the bombs, and this was from about 4 or 5 miles away, as they still went off. My gran lived with us and she was nearly inconsolable – my Dad worked in the town as a bus driver and she was convinced he had been hit when she heard about the Oxford Street bomb, which was the main bus depot at that time. It was a terrible day, a real nightmare to be honest. When my Dad finally arrived home safe and sound I was in a bit of a daze, shocked, and my gran was crying for what seemed like days. She took very ill very soon after because of the stress of that day, and we're all pretty sure she never really recovered. So that's the sort of thing you don't get told either, you know, the way it affected people in so many ways. To me, my gran was an innocent victim of the conflict. Then we watched the TV news that night and tried to take it all in. My Dad was totally silent for a week. I mean silent. Not a word. I never asked him, and he never told me, but I assumed he lost friends or colleagues. I definitely remember him going to a funeral, and after a while he would peak in whispers to my mother. From that moment on almost, there was a deep shock and silence in our house but I remember my father wanting to get straight back out to work. Nowadays that would never happen, it would be post-traumatic stress, and he'd be off for weeks. We were guarded from then on, always on the back foot. Afraid. Of course, in public we had to maintain the whole unionist thing that we would never give up, and I don't doubt for a lot of Protestants the bombs and that stiffened their resolve not to give in, but not us if I'm truthful about it. By the mid 1970s, most of us had left for new developments or towns outside Belfast. So who is going to be brought to account for that? That's another way unionist people were victimised. It makes me laugh, the DUP say what they're going to do, but what have they have done to let people tell their stories? They – I mean Sinn Fein and the British – have it all set up the way they want it to go. A 'war' would excuse both sides, not to mention the Loyalist paramilitaries, who were just as bad – thugs and gangsters. But who gets forgotten? The ordinary Protestant people who got attacked. It's diabolical. My Dad was never able to speak about what he saw that day. The unionist people have been silenced – I mean, I've never even been asked about it before – no-one has come to me from even the unionist parties or the government and said 'how do you feel about that?' And what I feel about it is this: we know no-one is going to be prosecuted for it, that's just the pathetic state we are in now; but remorse and a true apology would be at least be a starting point, an admission from Sinn Fein and the IRA of what they did, to tell the world that what they did was very, very wrong and to tell the unionist people that they are sorry for what they did to us. But I don't think they will do that. They have their story of what happened and why they did it and that's the history of the conflict, as far as they are concerned. Unionists are just ignored.

## The Kingsmills Massacre

Kingsmills is a small village in rural south Armagh, a short distance from the border with the Irish Republic. On 5 January 1976, a minibus carrying workers from the nearby textile factory in Glenanne was stopped en route to its destination of the predominantly Protestant village of

Bessbrook by a group of heavily armed and masked men. Of the 12 occupants at that point in the journey, 11 were Protestants. The armed group (thought to number around a dozen) ordered all of the passengers to disembark. When they did so, they were forced to reveal their religious identity at gunpoint. The one member of the group who made himself known to be a Catholic was told to run from the scene. The remaining men were subsequently made to line up against the bus, and were then shot ruthlessly and systematically. A combination of weapons was used, including automatic rifles, a handgun and a machine gun. Police reports indicated that over 130 rounds of ammunition were discharged in less than a minute. Ten men were killed instantly, although one man survived, despite having been shot 18 times. A previously unknown group claimed responsibility for the killings – the South Armagh Republican Action Force – and though this is widely regarded as a cover name for the PIRA, that organisation has never admitted culpability for the atrocity. The killings were rationalised by the Irish republican paramilitaries involved as retaliation for the murder of six Catholics in the south Armagh area by the Ulster Volunteer Force (UVF) – a Loyalist paramilitary group – the previous evening.

**(Harry, 60, County Armagh)**

What they did at Kingsmills! The mindset of those people! To pull – now you think of it – men doing an honest day's work from their wee minibus, and to line them up, and gun them down. It was extermination! Extermination! 10 Protestants ... just ordinary civilians, slaughtered, there's no other word for it. Just innocent men going home to their families. And we were a close town. We were a tight knit community to that point, Protestant and Catholic. We just couldn't understand it. It came home to us that this was a conflict now in which anyone – or any Protestant anyway – was fair game. Any Protestant, it didn't matter. And it saddened me to say it, but you couldn't trust your neighbours anymore. South Armagh at that time became a really bad place to be. I went round to the houses, each in turn, of all those families that had someone killed. It was the longest day. They use that expression a lot but I tell you, it really was. To go into those houses and to console your friends ... that's an experience you never shake off. Never. Never. I want truth. But I don't want punishment, and more anger, and trouble. I just want people to say to us 'yes, you were innocent people and you were murdered for no good reason'. I want that as part of the history here. I don't think that's too much to ask. If British politicians actually bothered to ask us, they might grasp that. What price is it to the British Government or any of them, that ten fellas were killed in cold blood down some country road 30 years ago? Ten innocent men too! What price? Would it cost them or Sinn Fein or the IRA to even acknowledge us? Why can't they do that? No-one seems to know. Until they tell us why, we can't realistically deal with the past. They can set up all the groups they want but the Protestant people, the unionist people whatever you want to call them, they want the truth.

### ('Ken', 51, County Armagh)

The funerals were bad certainly. The low-point I would say. Can you imagine? Nine funerals in one day, all in Bessbrook, with the other in Mountnorris [a small village nearby]? Boys you knew, men from the village you grew up around? That's a tragedy you just can't comprehend. And it's well known now, but it rained that day. And it rained hard. Those men, one fella going to be a missionary, a Sunday School teacher, a wee fella around the age I was at that time, only 18 ... innocent victims, just civilians, gunned down mercilessly by criminals. Shot in the back, no chance to run. How can you do that? How can someone do that sort of thing? And now our ones [Protestants] try to commemorate it with a wee plaque and from what I hear, because I've moved out of the area now – I wouldn't raise my children there after the abuse we got in the 1980s – they destroy the wee plaque in the road. How much more can they trample on the memory of the Protestant unionist people? I try not to think about it, about the fact the relatives couldn't even get a look at the bodies because they were so badly riddled and totally disfigured with bullets. Because when I think about it, it makes me angry, but more as I get older, it makes me really sad.

I'm sad for those men, a lot of them who were young men now I can see, who would be parents or grand parents now themselves, like I am. Killed by scum, by murderers, in cold blood. I'm sad about that. And so I think now, a lot of miles away and a lot of years away, then maybe all we can expect is an answer as to who did it and why? We're not stupid enough to think anyone will get jailed for it. But we're not going to go into this dealing with the past thing without atrocities like Kingsmills on the table. I'm tempted to say top of the list, because for me, that's the worst of the lot, but there's people on both sides suffered a lot. But definitely on the table, and the republicans and the IRA have to be accountable for that, and this group has to find some way to shame them, publicly. That would be my view. But if we get a situation where unionists and nationalists, the real victims of the thing, have a chance to get... I don't know what you'd call it – closure I suppose – and this group or a commission says, so it's recorded in the history books 'what the IRA did to the Protestant people was immoral, it was illegal and it was wrong', then there's a very good chance the unionist people could be encouraged to participate.

**('Bobby', 47, County Armagh)**

I was just a young fella myself at the time, like, but I do remember it well. The funerals more than anything. One after the other, just a procession. It's a small town, so of course we knew the families. Everyone did. That made it worse. I went down with my parents and we visited the relatives. Even at 15, you know, you're not fully mature and all that, not emotionally. I tried to put a brave face on but I got back to my bedroom that night and I cried for hours. And I remember my Dad came in and he said 'What are you crying for?' He told me not to cry, that the boys that was (*sic*) killed wouldn't have wanted that and that the police would capture who did it and put them in jail. I don't think my Dad was naïve, or that he was lying to me, we all believed that. He never realised I was crying because I was afraid. I was afraid it could have just as easily have been him. He was just a working man too, not army or police. If they killed those ten men on the bus, they could kill any innocent Protestant. Since that day, the fear has always been there. We moved away. But the fear is still there. And now the biggest fear we have is those men will be forgotten. Our innocent victims will all be forgotten. We'll have no place in history. No place at all.

## The La Mon House Hotel bombing

Until February 1978, La Mon House Hotel was not widely known outside Northern Ireland. After that month, it would forever be linked with one of the worst and most brutal atrocities of the conflict. On an evening on which members of an Irish Collies Dogs Club were gathering for their annual dinner, the PIRA planted a devastating napalm-type explosive device at the hotel. Taped to the window of the hotel's 'Peacock Room', indicating (at least as far as unionists were concerned) that the perpetrators would have seen and been aware that their targets were civilians, the RUC later claimed that the bombers had also attached large quantities of flammable liquid to the package. Such a concoction turned the bomb into a formidable incendiary designed to cause maximum damage. Twenty people were killed, including three married couples, and a further 33 were injured. The victims were all Protestants, and also included members of the Northern Ireland Junior Motorcycle Club. Many bodies were burnt beyond recognition. A full day after the explosion, only 6 bodies could be positively identified. The following day, the PIRA issued a statement from Dublin claiming responsibility for the attack and conceding that its warning had given people inadequate time to escape.

**('Terry', 48, County Down)**

Those poor people in that room where the thing went off stood no chance. No chance at all. I don't know how anyone got out. I heard a bang... I mean, I'm not even sure I did. Like a thud maybe. Then I was knocked off my feet. I don't know how, maybe it was the blast or maybe people running by. I have no sense of what order things happened in, you know what I mean? I might have blacked out [fallen unconscious]. I remember my mate, he was dragging me, saying 'your shoe is on fire, your shoe is on fire'. Now I don't recall that. The next thing I knew I was standing outside, just looking... it was surreal, not even shock... just looking at this fireball. I can still hear the crying, the wailing... it stays with you, you know? But it was sort of distant, like it wasn't happening there. Right enough, when I got home later on, I got in the door and my Dad said 'son, your shoes are gone'. He had been asleep and he didn't even know about it! My trousers were all torn and there was my leg was quite badly burned. All that was left of my shoes was a bit of smouldering leather. I was rightly annoyed, as I'd just been down the town to buy a good pair of shoes the week before. My Dad said 'never mind your f-ing shoes, are you okay?' So I said I was. And I maybe thought I was. But I wasn't. That night will haunt me forever. Truth? I don't know about that. I don't know, looking back, what the truth of a night like that was. But I would like to deal with it. I want rid of it. It's eaten me up thinking about it, about those innocent victims – just civilians – people there that had no chance. So let's have a process whereby we can get these IRA boys that did it and get them to tell us why they did it. That's all we need to know – why.

**('Sam', 54, Belfast)**

We lived nearby actually and as soon as we heard about it we knew it was bad. A few of the neighbours came round and we decided we would jump in the motor and go up there and try to find out what was going on. Nothing could have prepared us for it. The place was a mess. We never even got that close, because a lot of people had started to gather and the police were trying to get some kind of order, or at least that's how I remember it anyway. But this one fella came walking past me and he was just covered in blood. Soaked. His clothes were all off him practically. I don't know where he was going. His top was totally ripped off him and he was covered in, it looked to me, like dust, but I think now it could have been like burning skin. No-one was near him. He wasn't shouting, or crying out, he was just wandering. The fella was obviously in shock. The thing I regret the most, I never did anything to help him. I froze, and just watched. He walked on by and then we started to hear things from other people around us that it was ordinary, innocent people had been attacked, that there were no cops [police] there or anything. Then the rumour went about there was (*sic*) kids dead and everything, it was just awful. Absolutely awful. I went on home because I just felt there was nothing else I could do and to be honest I wanted to be near my own kids when I heard that. When you think of what happened there, to have killed 12 innocent people on a night out. It's like you can't take it in at the time, but now, looking back on it, it makes me very angry. Angry at the way the people were treated afterwards, the victims. And angry that in all this talk about the past, all of that, no-one ever mentions La Mon and what happened there. It's just as if nothing ever happened, our people are totally ignored, forgotten, left out. And that's why the unionists are saying 'look, here, you can have all the truth commissions you want but we are not going to help you because you don't want to listen to us anyway!'.

**('Martin', 50, Belfast)**

I mean – that night – it will obviously live long in my memory. There were two big functions on that night. It was packed. Strange thing was, my girlfriend at the time – she and I used to take a drive up that way most week-ends, find out if anything was happening, you know? Kind of bored youngsters but with a car! We almost didn't bother going out at all. It was well into the evening but and the roads round there in the winter are not usually busy you know? But all this traffic, police, ambulance, fire engines, were all going to the hotel. So naturally we followed to find out what was going on. I knew it was bad. And as I arrived I saw the sky lit up before I heard anything. And then what I did hear … well … I don't want to go into it really … I can't. It's strange, but the sounds of people shouting and crying, and at times the strange silence, has affected me more than what I saw. People were just burned so badly … it was pure disbelief. There was nothing I could do. I was worried naturally for those people but I just kept thinking I was glad it wasn't me. I was ashamed how selfish I felt. I think I was relieved. I've had a lot of trouble working that over the years. A lot of trouble. 12 innocent people were killed and a lot more hurt, some of them badly. The IRA planted that to kill as many innocent Protestant civilians as they could, for no reason but sheer evil, and to do so in the most painful and horrific way. We've had people named in Parliament as being responsible, but the laugh of it is they are now in charge of the country. How can we get justice in a situation like that? I'd bet any Protestant or unionist in Northern Ireland feels like I do. We all feel the same – we want the truth, we want to know why, and most of all, we don't want to just be forgotten. The victims need compensated, and not just financially either.

\*   \*   \*

In the aftermath of the La Mon bombing, the PIRA claimed paradoxically (given its concession that the warning was insufficient) that it had not intended to kill anyone in it called 'an IRA military operation' and that the casualties had been due to the RUC's inability to act promptly and efficiently in evacuating people from the scene of the explosion. Such specious rhetoric was commonplace and routine from paramilitary groups on both sides of the divide. By blaming the police service, as it had done on Bloody Friday, the PIRA was attempting to deflect attention away from what was a grotesque, vicious attack on Protestant civilians that seemed to make a mockery of their oft-repeated claim that they were fighting an anti-colonial, non-sectarian war (cf. Dingley, 1998). Blaming the police was also calculated to try and regain the sympathy of the majority of Catholics in Northern Ireland, who found such violence against Protestants totally abhorrent. Rehearsing that debate however, is not the objective of this chapter. There is no desire here to possess or use these histories in an instrumental political fashion, or to frame a distasteful partisan polemic using the suffering of others. Rather, the presentation of these narratives has been an attempt to show the damaging after-effects and the legacy of what were cowardly and tragic atrocities (Antze and Lambek, 1996), and the ways in which they have – in the post-conflict context – become a totem of resistance for unionists who fear the imposition of a distorted, Irish republican-led version of history in which unionist suffering will be erased. La Mon, for example, is an extremely complex case. Its recent 30-year commemoration re-opened old wounds not only between unionists and the republican 'other' (which must be solved as part of a truth recovery process), but also within unionism itself. Democratic Unionist Party (DUP) Leader and First Minister of the Northern Ireland Assembly Ian Paisley, who was previously regarded as infallible by his legion of hardline unionist followers, was publicly shunned in 2008 by the committee organising the 30-year anniversary memorial of the bombing. Following his agreement to share power with Sinn Fein, the political representatives of the Irish republican movement (including its now dismantled armed wing that was responsible for the La Mon bombing), in a devolved administration in Northern Ireland, Paisley's stock was no longer as high as it once was among those directly affected by acts of Irish republican violence. Indeed, shortly afterwards, following this and pressure from within his traditional constituency of voters (reflected in a council by-election defeat by a splinter unionist political party), Paisley announced his resignation as First Minister of the Northern Ireland Assembly and as leader of the DUP. It is suspected that he came under strong pressure from members of his own party – the party he had formed and led for decades – to make this decision.

La Mon, however, is also illustrative of a more important and wider unionist fear in Northern Ireland, which is confined not only to those who were victims of that bomb attack but also to those many others victimised in separate episodes throughout the conflict. Despite the Eames-Bradley process, which has imbued unionists with a small amount of hope, that fear is still manifested and verbalised as a suspicion that it is the intention of the two governments (British and Irish), in co-operation with Sinn Fein, to eradicate unionist suffering and to elide and 'silence' unionist history, and to 're-write' a fabricated version of the Troubles in which unionist grief is not only forgotten, but in which they are stigmatised as oppressors and the causal agents of the conflict (Dawson, 2003; Donnan, 2005; Donnan and Simpson, 2007; Patterson, 2007; Simpson, 2008). Unionists point to La Mon in particular as an instance in which an act of what one respondent described to me as 'pure evil' was perpetrated against Protestant civilians, without anyone 'ever brought to justice'. Many more unionists with whom I have conducted research are dismayed to discover that no attempt to uncover the 'truth' of that attack has ever occurred, and that there is virtually no prospect of retrospective, retributive prosecutions (Booth, 2001). As the conflict moved into the 1980s, there seemed to be no end possible. As Labour Secretary of State for Northern Ireland, Roy Mason had made very appreciable gains in beginning to defeat the PIRA, but the vicissitudes of British politics on the UK mainland meant that Mason's tenure was ended when the Labour government was ousted in the British General Election of 1979. Diplomatic solutions then ran aground, and a new Conservative British government led by Margaret Thatcher – who regarded herself as a tough supporter of unionism – decided it would 'take on' the PIRA, though her period in office would prove to be a retrograde step for Northern Ireland, and for unionism. Her decision to criminalise PIRA prisoners, who had previously enjoyed special category political prisoner status, was widely welcomed by unionists, but it prompted the hunger strikes, which left ten Irish republicans – most notably Bobby Sands, who was the first to die – as martyrs to the PIRA cause, and evoked a well of sympathy for Sands and his comrades among previously moderate Irish nationalist voters. The more sophisticated of unionists recognised that Thatcher's stance was a Pyrrhic victory, in that it mobilised hundreds of young men to join the ranks of the PIRA. It further demonised unionists, who despite having no say in the decision, were regarded as the upholders of an unjust system that was responsible for the deaths of romanticised, mythical Irish republican heroes. In the decade that followed, unionists began to realise that their chances of securing any kind of victory were slim, and that the most they could hope for was to 'hold the line'. Furthermore, and more damagingly, they realised that there was little or no point in attempting to relay their side of the story to an international audience. Although Thatcher professed sympathy, especially after the PIRA tried to kill her in a bomb attack at Brighton in 1985, unionists were outraged when she signed the Anglo-Irish Agreement in 1985, which gave, for the first time, the government of the Irish Republic an official say in the affairs of Northern Ireland. Protestants began to fear that a united Ireland, and victory for the PIRA, was very likely. Unionist stories of loss and suffering consequently almost completely faded, and entered a long period of 'cold storage'.

# 5
## 'Cold Storage': The Disappearance of Unionist Storytelling and the Conflict

This chapter will focus on a collection of retrospective expressions by unionists – in the current post-conflict phase – that detail how during the 1980s and early 1990s, unionists feel that the narratives of their experiences were nearly completely subsumed, silenced or elided. A variety of explanations are offered for this by the respondents. The predominant feeling is that the woes of the unionist community – no matter how dire or callous the attacks upon civilians by terrorist groups – were totally incongruent and contrary to the wishes of British and Irish Government power-brokers and their concomitant, pre-determined plans for political reconstruction in Ireland, North and South (Cunningham, 2001). This chapter, again using a heavy emphasis on detailed and original lengthy narrative extracts, also outlines the ways in which unionists feel that they were totally disenfranchised and disempowered by the political dynamics of this period, and that allied to the fear of 'speaking out' against republican (and Loyalist) paramilitaries; this led to their viewpoints being locked away and hermetically sealed (Humphrey, 2003).

Unionists also arguably, in some small way, conspired in the 'hiding' of their own narratives because of a perceived lack of social, political and communal support – especially cross-communal support from the Catholic community – and their own unwillingness to use their histories in what they would have regarded as any sort of expedient political and instrumental enterprise aimed at ending the conflict (cf. McKay, 2000; Dawson, 2003; 2007). Without a morally normative framework for conflict resolution unionists – then, albeit more forcefully, as now – were not prepared to engage in dialogue which they believed would lead to outcomes that had been cynically engineered by policymakers intent on appeasing the PIRA and contributing to the creation of a 32 county socialist united Ireland (cf. Simpson, 2009).

The stories provided here illustrate the feelings of members of a community that by the 1980s and early 1990s felt utterly exasperated; and who were convinced that even if they did decide to tell their stories, no one wanted to hear (Donnan, 2005; Simpson, 2008). They thought that the graphic and brutal atrocities perpetrated by the PIRA, like those detailed in the previous chapter, would have convinced the 'watching world' (as one interviewee said) 'that we were the victims, not the oppressors. What did we have to do for someone to hear our calls for fairness, for justice, for peace?' This lack of an audience for unionists' suffering forced them to reconsider the value of giving their accounts publicly, or even within their own community, about what happened to them (cf. Parkinson, 1998; 2001). They became increasingly distrustful of the media and all of those whom they regarded as 'outsiders' (and these cleavages occurred even between rural and urban unionists, and between towns and villages). In the absence of sufficient narrative mechanisms for coping with their fear and the continuing conflict, unionists began to conceal their stories. A desire to articulate feelings of victimhood was replaced with an overwhelming sense of underlying despair and futility, which unionists effectively masqueraded as stereotypical and caricatured Protestant stoicism (cf. Mitchell, 2005). In a strategically poor effort to take control of how their image was managed (Goffman, 1990) – although many argue somewhat unconvincingly that they had given up caring how they were portrayed – unionists retreated to a position of cultural familiarity – silence (Donnan and Simpson, 2007). While it had little or no instrumental political value, for unionists it carried moral weight, and as such was a place of some comfort (cf. Margalit, 2004). As the 1980s ended, the evidence of this chapter suggests that many unionists no longer made concerted efforts to articulate their stories, and certainly not beyond the confines of trusted friends of family members; and in this period it is possible to suggest that attempts to do so began to become viewed by other unionists not only as futile, but also as weak, or even reprehensible. Admitting inadequacy was not something that was readily tolerated by many sections of the unionist community – the logic being that conceding any kind of fragility would only give motivation and succour to the PIRA and its allies, and would reinforce the belief that unionists were losing the conflict. This was a message reinforced by the dominant unionist political party at that time, the UUP (cf. Walker, 2004; Farrington, 2006). It was however, in many ways, an enforced silence, the product of dire and threatening circumstances and a belief among unionists that there was a total unwillingness on the part of the British government to offer political, psychological and emotional support that could have helped, at least in part, to ameliorate their grief. It is consequently a curious phenomenon for unionists to try and narrate now that which they did not narrate then (Jedlowski, 2001).

## The evaporation of trust?

In the 1980s, trust had apparently completely evaporated. In an effort to fortify their reputation as those who would not be beaten by terror, some ordinary unionist civilians cultivated and propagated an image of a self-reliant historically courageous people, but this was primarily expressed though iconic imagery, music, marching and other non-narrative methods (Jarman, 1997; Bryan, 2000; Jess, 2007; Kauffmann, 2007). This mythmaking, however, was no substitute for real political assistance, which unionists felt the British Government did not offer, and which many in this research believed was all but removed via a combination of the Anglo-Irish Agreement of 1985 and the announcement in 1990 by then British Secretary of State Peter Brooke that the British Government had 'no selfish, strategic or economic interest in Northern Ireland'. The lack of belief in the British government, in particular, has unconsciously shaped a generation of identities in Northern Ireland. Winning trust back, and convincing unionists that people are now interested in what they have to say, is a fundamental challenge for transitional policymakers in Northern Ireland. In many ways, because of the narrative 'gag' that was in place, the forgotten and untold stories of the 1980s and early 1990s haunt unionist memories of the conflict. As Gordon (1997: 8) noted: 'Being haunted draws us affectively, sometimes against our will ... into the structure of feeling of a reality we come to experience, not as cold knowledge, but as a transformative recognition.' For unionists to feel properly acknowledged in the historical reconstruction that is taking place in Northern Ireland, that 'cold knowledge' must become transformative. It must change doubt, anger and fear into a willingness to speak, to risk swapping the chill of silence for the possibility of acknowledgement and apology that unionists so desperately want.

   The stories in this chapter are less powerful than those contained in the previous chapter. Rather, unionists speak retrospectively not only about the things that happened to them during the conflict (and how attritional and routine such activity had become) but about why they did not speak out at the time. Some of the extracts here describe dramatic and perilous moments, but it is worth noting the change in tone and texture from the previous chapter. The horror of terrorist violence continued, but it was no longer producing the same-level deep-seated shock and disbelief. Instead, there was a disillusioned, defeatist sense that there was going to be no quick end to the violence, and that even the most appalling attacks on unionist civilians were – as unionists perceived it – being dismissed or ignored by the mainstream British, Irish and world politicians and media. The damage to the unionist community that was caused by their attempts to deal with what they believed was intentional violence against them was exacerbated by the perceived indifference and apathy of the rest of the world to PIRA brutality. It would be naïve, therefore, to imagine that the effects of this 'silent' era have not been far-reaching, in both temporal and psychological terms. The consequences of failing to discuss tragedy created deep fracture lines within the boundaries of unionist communities, in both the urban and rural settings. Those who were murdered were often mourned silently, in the privacy of the home of the immediate family. As the extracts below indicate, they were not – and have not – been forgotten, but the communal support which so many families craved dissipated as the battle for the support of the British government slipped away, and on the basis of this research it seems that unionists felt compelled to become increasingly individualistic in their efforts to cope with the depressing reality of the Troubles. Unionists – feeling it was fruitless to highlight their plight – 'held the line' as best they could, despite the omnipresent threat of political violence and the grim apparatus of state security that was necessary to make even the semblance of normality possible (Dewar, 1997; Taylor, P., 2001; Urban, 2001). It is only now, as 'dealing with the past' becomes an issue (Simpson, 2007[a]), that the unionists with whom I spoke have realised that the recovery of their stories and memories of the 1980s is crucial in ensuring that they can be narrated, for the first time, in the post-conflict period. The emotionally destructive aspects of the Troubles in the 1980s and the early 1990s have been long-lasting for many unionists, but they have also been hidden and repressed. There is now a need to deconstruct the social imperative not to talk, to recognise that there was or is no shame in admitting weakness or fear, and to try to bring their experiences – no matter how difficult – into the world of narrative and language that the post-conflict era now demands.

This chapter therefore seeks to offer an analysis of how unionist civilians dealt with the constant threat of violence, and how they now recall those experiences, so that the effects of what was a campaign of

catastrophic terror by the PIRA can be better understood. What unionists remember – or choose to remember – and how that affects them
now is of critical importance. They feel, as evidenced by the extracts
presented in this chapter, that there was little or no public discourse or
discussion of the 1980s and early 1990s in particular. Yet for them the
traces of that trauma penetrate much of how and what they now want to
articulate about the past (Humphrey, 2003; Torpey, 2003). A lot of the
narrative extracts in this chapter allude to how, at the time, unionists
used non-narrative ways of dealing with loss that did not involve direct
dialogue or vocalisation. Their methods of processing tragedy and fear
in the 1980s diverge sharply from traditional methodologies of remembrance, which are largely based on storytelling and oral culture (Felman
and Laub, 1992; Jackson, 2002). Unionist experiences, arguably, are not
easily compartmentalised, compared or contrasted. They are locale and
culturally specific, and influenced by a myriad of factors. These extracts
are not widely known, and their presentation here allows them to find
their way into the public debate about dealing with the past. As in the
other chapters, they are comparatively long and in the style of oral
histories rather than short quotations, because as outlined in the introduction this allows for a much more fine-tuned sense of cultural, social
and political context in which the stories are re-told. It also concen-
trates on the centrality of each person, regarding them not only as part
of an unknown community, but also as an individual who was a victim
of a protracted period of political violence. This is counter-hegemonic
memory, and the challenges it poses to the ways in which contemporary Northern Ireland deals with its past are apparent (Routledge, 2003).
That cannot be a reason, however, for allowing such stories to remain in
'cold storage'.


### ('Stewart', 70, County Tyrone)

You have to remember around that time, now – not being from down
this way you'll probably not know – but the IRA was targeting ordinary Protestant farmers. Ordinary Protestants! Now you make sure you
write that, because that's the part that always gets forgotten. I think that
strategy was twofold – they wanted the land, boy, that's for sure, that's
correct alright – they didn't want any more Protestant people owning
land in the whole area around west Tyrone, and that to me is a fact,
there's no denying it. The Tyrone IRA, they were not be messed with,
that's no secret. They did a lot of damage down round here. A friend
of mine from the church, I think he worked for the British intelligence

boys – he says to me at that time: 'they'll never settle till they drive all the Prods out of this area'. This was about early to mid 1980s. They were stepping it up down here, really giving it to us. We lost a lot of good men down in that police station. And I mean I'll not hide it – I know we have all this now that the IRA says the RUC was not innocent but that's just rubbish. I'm talking about young boys, who were in their 20s, and it wasn't about money for them – they did a job to protect their community. They would go out at night after a full day's work maybe on the farm and do their duty to protect everybody, Catholic and Protestant. And now we're not allowed to say that they were innocent, or we have to accept they were the equivalent of terrorists? That's just ridiculous. There's not a Protestant or a unionist round here would accept that, not a single one. But that aside, what about the ordinary people, the civilians? There was a couple of RUC fellas killed down in this area … it must have been early on that decade, but the IRA started to put it about that all of the Protestant farmers around here were in the RUC or the UDR reserve and were targets. That was a lot of nonsense, just made up lies, because there was only one or two were in it at the time at the most – it was just an excuse for them boys to shoot and blow up ordinary unionist people that had nothing to do with the security forces! And – and – they were killing ordinary Catholics too, a lot of them up in Belfast, saying they were traitors or informers or this or that – that has to recognised too if they are talking about the past. As if the ordinary decent Catholic people didn't have enough to worry about with those Loyalist paramilitaries – and they were indiscriminate boy, and let me tell you there was no support for them here – the IRA was terrorising them too.

So we had to go about our daily business with this threat. Around about 1985 it was, or I think it was, I got this phone call this one day and it was from a friend who was in the know, if you know what I mean. He says to me 'are you alone?' Well I didn't know what was wrong. I thought something had happened to the kids or that you know? I says 'I am'. This was a Sunday night. He says 'Well listen boy when you go out on your Monday morning tractor run, we've info that there will be 2 fellas on a motorbike, and they are going to try and target you, you know for assassination like?'. They were going to try to shoot me, you know? Imagine being told that on the phone – but that was the world we were in then, that's what the young ones these days forget or don't understand. It was quite common at that time to get threats like that, that's what we had to put up with. We had no time to tell our stories and even when we did, who was listening anyway? There they were threatening ordinary decent folk trying to earn a crust and did the news report that? Is that in the history books? They would shoot innocent Protestant people for to get their land and then say 'he was in the RUC'. But this time they had it all wrong, I wasn't in anything, and never had been. Never, not one single day in a uniform for anyone or anything. They were liars, as well as cowards. But you had to take a warning like that seriously, you couldn't sleep or anything. As a farmer I had a shotgun – it was legal like – and I kept it hidden away, I never bothered with it, but I loaded it that night when I got that call. I remember walking out to where I kept it. It kind of unreal. I had it locked up, you know. So I unlocked it and I must have checked the parts over and over, to make sure it was working. But then I had to go and lock it up again in case the kids saw it. So the next day, myself and my wee helper – a good young fella – we met at our usual spot to start our day's work, though I'd been told to vary my time and routine, which was very difficult when animals need tended to you know? So I told this wee lad what was happening – he had no connection to any security forces either by the way – and the colour just drained from his face. I said 'now you can go on home if you want, I know this is not a good thing for to happen to us'. He says to me 'no, I work for you, I'll put a day's work in they'll not bully me, I'm okay, I'll stay and help you'. I admired him for that – he was only a young fella and he needed the work you know? He needed the work so he stayed, even though he knew the danger. Anyway about an hour passed and in my business you don't have time to dwell, there's always something going on, until I noticed a motorbike about 300 yards up the road. It went up the road, stopped, and then just kept its engine on. Well you'd have to be stupid when someone has told you that this might happen to then not realise that this was possibly an IRA hit squad. My helper, he had his car – it was a wee second hand thing, not the most reliable of motors to be truthful – and we had the tractor beside us, but he just lost it. He said 'I'm away here, I'm sorry' – and off he went. Well boy I never saw him run so fast, and I never blamed him for it either. He ran on foot through the fields, through muck and weeds and water, splashing and falling. The only thing I said to him later was 'why didn't you take your car you eejit?' He said 'That pile of junk? I was afraid it would break down.' So we had a good laugh about that. You had to laugh, you know, it was the only way to get through it. Turns out he ran about 3 miles across country and he hid in this barn for another couple of hours.

But I thought to myself if I ran or if I got in my tractor they'd probably follow me and I would be more of a target. So I slipped down the far side of my tractor – it was parked like – and I grabbed my rifle out of the side of the door. I slipped a couple of rounds into it and I bolted the mechanism, so it was ready to fire, but it seemed to take me a really long time to do it, you know? My whole body was shaking, I could hardly hold the thing. From where I was, I thought these boys could no longer see me – they could only see the side of my tractor sticking out on to the road, and I was taking cover down the other side like you know? Hunched up I was. I remember I wanted to shout for help, or even shout at them, just shout out or something like, and that the whole thing seemed like it happened in slow motion. There was a strange calm, like there was no sound. I made my mind up, or at least I think I did: 'if they drive down here and open fire at me, I'll shoot back'. I never had any time for violence but I decided that would be the only thing I could do. At that moment, for a while I didn't care what would have happened to these attackers, all I thought about was my family, my boys, and getting out of there to get back to them. I heard their bike rev and then it sped down the hill towards me. I could just see around the side of the tractor that the passenger on the bike was drawing what looked like a handgun, and then all of a sudden I'm sure I heard these whistling noises, you know the bullets flying by, like a whiz or a whistle, and then a crack. I don't know where I got the courage but I got up and I thought 'I'm not having this'. I went to open the tractor door and grab for my rifle but the thing jammed 'cos I was in that much of a panic you know? They swivelled on their bike to come back but when they looked around – they were close like – I don't think they knew my gun had jammed and to them they might have thought I was armed and they must have thought I had a chance at getting at them. They didn't like that at all. Cowards. So they sped off. Not long after that, though, there were a number of threats, attacks and assaults against police officers in the same area. That's what it was like in the 80s. I was in shock. I came home for tea that night – and you know I was that in much shock I almost forgot to mention it, but I know too I didn't want the kids to know what had happened. Hard to believe. You'd learned to cope with it, daily. As I've said to them, the IRA, many's a time – they know where I live, they can come and try and put me out anytime! I never contacted the police after that day, I don't think. I don't remember. I'd rather not say anyway to be honest with you. I couldn't identify the guys anyway, they had crash helmets on!! I could have passed them in the street half an hour later and not recognised them. So I never bothered chasing it and nothing ever came of it. That's what you had to put up with. They were killing RUC men, UDR men, ordinary Protestants all over Armagh, Tyrone and Enniskillen and sure it was even difficult to get Belfast to notice, let alone London. It was what I would call 'cold storage'. You know how in farming you put the meat in cold storage? That was us. That was our stories. Cold storage. I'm not sure anyone at the political level wants those stories served up to them now, so they got, what would you say, frozen in time, forgotten. And by then, we realised we'd had 15 years of this, and if there was a PR war or whatever going on, we were losing it. Everyone seemed to blame us. We knew that. So, what we had we tried to hold on to, to be good people, good neighbours, good church going people. Upright, you know? Not vengeful or angry. There was no value in that as far as we viewed the Troubles. Some poor Catholic boy having to put up with what people in our community were dealing with. No – there was no support for that at all. That's why you had no Loyalists paramilitaries down here. The people believed in the law, in justice. Now looking back you can say that was foolish, or naïve, but that's what we believed. We talked to each other when something terrible happened and the families helped each other out, but even that was tough because the IRA boys would target funerals. So we tried to support each other by being there – you know, church, sports groups, football teams, activities for the young ones, keeping up our farm. That was our way of saying: 'you're not winning'. But as far as even talking about it, going over all what happened to us – that didn't happen, but I don't doubt it's still very sad and very deep within the Protestant community. I myself was crying for the first time in years the other day about a young friend of mine had just joined the RUC and he was shot and killed not long after. He just came into my memory. It was a dreadful business. The politicians say we can't talk about the RUC or the UDR, but to us a lot of them were just our friends. To say there was the same morality between them and those evil terrorists on either side disgusts me. I couldn't wear that. But, even all that taken into account, I was no policeman, why try to shoot me? The 1980s just went by – you just kept your head down and got on with your work. In a way you were used to it but looking back, it's my view that those were the years the Protestant community forgot how to talk to itself, how to look after itself so that if the conflict did end we would be able to have our say. Our say is totally ignored now, but maybe if we look back that started twenty years ago when we refused to talk about what had happened to our people. And then, in the early 90s, those poor boys at Teebane, just innocent civilians, massacred by the IRA in a car bomb. That was one of the worst ever. One of the worst ever! And sure what have we ever heard about that? That was all part of the IRA stepping up their campaign to include basically anyone who was a Protestant as a target. And what did the British do? Gave in to them, those same murderers – who killed all those men like that? They even had the Secretary of State on some TV show that night – that night! – singing, and it was a TV show down south. Appalling. It's no wonder we all said nothing. There was such despair and exasperation, you know? I mean, in them days, who would you have told your story to?

**('Eddie', 50, County Down)**

The 1980s? That was a strange time. A really strange time. On the one hand, we were setting out, raising a family, trying to get on in our work, you know? All the things normal families do. But then on the other, you turned on the TV or the radio every day and it was always the same, this one or that one had been shot. You began to forget what side you were even on – except that you were against all these scum that were out inflicting misery. Some wee man just going about his business, gunned down by one of these – and excuse my language here – one of these bastards, republican or Loyalist. Evil men. Terrorists. That's what they were. We didn't have time to sit around and examine it and analyse it and tell people about it. We thought the story spoke for itself. We thought it spoke for itself, we really did. How could it not? Look at what was done to us! I can laugh at that now, how naïve it was and how stupid we were to think the world cared about us. But the story didn't speak for itself. It obviously didn't, because here we are now 20 or more years later, 30 even, and there's no proper record of what was done to us as a community. Ordinary Protestant people, town or city, village and country, just lumped in with one side or another in a stupid and bloody political fight no-one could ever win. And my kids, now, well they're grown up and sometimes they annoy me in ways, you know? Don't get me wrong – I love them more than anything but they have no idea of what happened, and what people went through. They were only wee ones when it was going on in the 80s, I suppose. The eldest even, he would still be quite young now, but they do things we would never have done. I'm happy for them – I'm happy they can go about the city centre and not worry about bombs or booby traps or shootings, but a big part of me is envious if I'm honest. Maybe envious is the wrong word. On the one hand I'm worried for them, and on the other I'm jealous that for three decades these IRA terrorist maniacs denied us the opportunity to have some sort of normality. And this normality my kids have – is it really normal? It's not morality, I know that much, and that's maybe where the anger kicks in. I'll not go into details but two of my friends were killed by the IRA, blown up into bits. Two others I know were shot, one was just an innocent civilian, nothing to do with the security forces. Now these IRA men are on TV, or in government, telling us we should forget about the past, or even worse telling us our version of it has no place in history. They just want to brush it out, wipe it away. They don't want to stand up in their fancy suits and say how many people they murdered, with no mercy, how many civilians, how many prison warders, how many policemen. They have an easy get out for that one. This rubbish about 'legitimate targets'. And that's what it is. Rubbish. No-one is a legitimate target, or was. It was not a war. So when my son comes back from his university class – and he loves history, he absolutely loves it – and gives me this version of what supposedly happened I just can't get my head round it. It's republican propaganda. It's not the 1980s I remember. Everyone is sucked in because these people, Sinn Fein and all their allies, they work the system and they have done for years. Their stories are celebrated on TV programmes, books, art, how they broke out of jails, how they mounted 'IRA operations'. What a joke, it's a disgrace. Like they were some sort of army. They were gangsters, and they call themselves 'volunteers'. My recollection of the 1980s is just trying to go about my business – and in the middle of a shocking recession – feed my family while the IRA was out killing people and at the same time taking the dole and sleeping in their beds until lunchtime. They have no shame, in any way. Some of my friends say 'it's our fault, it's our politicians', but that's a lot of nonsense. In all these years, these unionist politicians to be fair to them have done their best, and some of them are very educated, they are respected men and women. It's not that. It's that by the 1980s the British knew Northern Ireland was an embarrassment. We are their dirty secret. They look at us – Protestants and unionists – and they feel repelled. The men in the British army that stuck it out and walked the streets to keep us safe – I'll never forget what they did and they have my gratitude, my sincere gratitude. But otherwise, around the end of the 80s – even after what those vicious, vile scum did at Enniskillen, murdering innocent people who were gathering to remember their war dead – in my opinion the British were helping them, the IRA, create a story about the conflict. And in that story we were the bad guys. We buried our stories and we never went back to them. And boy, we had plenty of stories, more stories than we could handle, but no one to tell them to. I don't think we even told them to each other. That was a major problem – we didn't even talk to each other about it. I tried to tell my children as they were growing up what had happened, but I didn't want them to be bitter. Maybe I didn't tell them as much as I should have. Because now they've almost bought into the IRA's story, and it saddens me, because it was youngsters their ages and even younger who went out to defend ordinary people and were blown up by the IRA.

Now sometimes I pick the eldest up at his university, which is in Northern Ireland, and these boys are running around in GAA and Celtic shirts. One day when I went a crowd of them were sitting, drinking, in the afternoon, singing IRA songs and blocking the road. I wanted to complain to the university but my wife persuaded me not to, she said they would discriminate against us if we complained. I said to my son 'were those people threatening you?' He said 'oh no they're such and such, they're okay, there's much worse than them' – he knew them! I was stunned. I nearly went mad. I stopped the car. I said 'I thought we were past all that – we have peace now, the Troubles are over – those are sectarian songs and maybe you're too young to remember what you're singing about but a lot of good people were killed because of that rubbish you're spouting'. You know what they said to me? 'Fuck away off you Orange bastard, there's no room for your kind here'. I said to my son 'Did you hear that? Do you know what they are singing about?' My son looked embarrassed. I probably made it more difficult for him. I should have kept my mouth shut. But that's been what unionists have done. Just kept their mouth shut. We stopped talking nearly 30 years ago and we don't know how to start now that we need to. I said to my son as we drove away 'Do you know what the IRA did to unionist people, to people we knew as a family, friends, relatives and neighbours?' And in a way his answer told me everything. You know what he said? He said 'No. How would I?' I realised we'd been so worried that they would be exposed to the violence back in the 80s, or that we'd make them bitter or bigoted, we'd sheltered them from it. So no-one wants to know outside our community, and even in our own community or families a lot of people don't know because we were typical unionists – just keep your mouth closed and get on with it.

**('Charles', 42, Belfast)**

In my opinion, since the 80s definitely, our stories are untold, unknown, and unwanted. Nobody spoke about it in the 80s, or the 90s, but at least if they did, they told it how it really was. You can't do that now. As a unionist, you just have to accept that in this theatre, this play if that's what you would call it, you've been cast as the villain. If they try to dig up the past now, and get those unionist stories, they'd better be ready, because there's a lot of people with a lot to say, and I'm not sure the politicians – especially the governments – would be ready for what would come out. It would be a tidal wave. It's too risky for them now. They have the political set-up the way they want it. They didn't listen then, and they won't listen now. Unionist stories will stay hidden in my opinion, unless the British or someone backs us and says: 'let these people give their version what happened, let their history be given all this attention, made into films, TV programmes, books.' But are they interested in dipping into a culture like ours and finding out that really, whatever their ballot boxes say, that a whole generation of unionists will never forget what was done to us in the conflict, and that we want an apology for it at the least? I could go on and on about the attacks the IRA carried out. It's not just shootings and bombings, it was low level stuff, all the time. My wife, who was my girlfriend at the time, used to have to get a bus down into the town and the stop she got off at she was going into a Protestant school to do her A Levels, but it was quite near a nationalist area. They [republicans] stoned the buses most days – that was never reported on the news – and when the girls got off they called them for all the whores and sluts of the day. 'Black Protestant slags f-off back to your own area', all of that carry on. How do you respond to that? These were grown men, not just wee lads, on the dole no doubt, turning up at 8 in the morning to hurl foul mouthed abuse at school girls. My wife was not from a very political family, and she used to say 'what do they mean, why do they hate me, I never did anything to them'. There were boys at her school and one day her cousin – he went to the school too – he had heard this abuse and he'd tried to reason with them, but they told him to f-off. He was actually told he was messing with 'volunteers of the Provisional Irish Republican Army', that he was a 'Brit bastard' and he'd better get out because they knew where he was and where he lived. Now, living up there, we were used to that sort of threat but you just had to get on with it. I remember his Dad was worried so they went down to the station and told the peelers and this cop said 'what do you want us to do?' So much for the RUC being 'our' police force, the way republicans would say. They didn't give a toss. Then one day my wife's cousin was in the town shopping and these characters recognised him. They were well known republicans – and again I'm talking about grown men here – and they set about this lad of 17 year old and his friends. Gave a crowd of wee lads, schoolboys, just a real drubbing, in the full view of passers-by. Clubs and sticks and all from what I was told. Now, in the centre of town in those days you had the peelers at a big security check point right at the end of Royal Avenue [the main shopping street]. What did they do? Nothing. My wife's cousin was bashed up badly, the young lad, they put him in hospital. He had a broken arm, a broken leg where he got hit with a stick, a broken nose and concussion, plus really bad gashes and cuts that needed stitched up. They obviously kicked him in the face when he was knocked out. He wouldn't go out of the house for a year. He was a really smart kid, but he dropped out of school, wouldn't do his exams, and never went to college. His parents were distraught. He had applied to really good universities too, and he would have been the first in his family ever to go. How do they account for that? Is that an IRA mission? His parents got threats to the house for years after that, that the local IRA were after him, that his Dad was an RUC man, and that his family gave information to the British about the IRA. It was a lot of rubbish, he was only a kid, and there wasn't one person in his family even linked to the police. The lad was terrified though, he was on medication – like, you know, sedatives – and everything, and at one point he went to the hospital to stay for a while he was that bad with his nerves. The joke of that is, and what really got me was that when he reported it, he never heard anything back! No compensation, nothing. I think they maybe said no-one could identify who had done it to him. There must have been 100 people had witnessed it, and you would have to say at least half of them would have been unionists. But in those days, people were too frightened to talk, to speak out.

He left Northern Ireland for England and he never came back. He's never been married. He's just a totally different person and he had a nervous breakdown about 5 years after he left. He was isolated over there but he felt too scared to come back because of what had happened. They ruined him the day they gave him that beating. Forced him out of his house, his home, his country, and just destroyed his dreams. Now that's only about the third time in over 20 years I've had a chance to tell that story. Would a truth commission be interested in that? That story goes with the dozens of others I have that no-one has ever been interested in. My wife still never mentions it, she was devastated. As well as being family they were friends and like she would tell you he was the smartest, most outgoing young lad you could have wanted to meet, and now he's just like a shell of a guy you know? One of his mates who was there that day he left school to join the RUC. He had got out of it with only a few cuts and his attitude was he wanted to fight back, but ironically he got quite badly injured in an IRA attack and he had to leave. From what I know he was very depressed too, you know, damaged psychologically? So I'd like to be optimistic, but the reason unionist stories are not told is because unionist people are still afraid, they are terrified. The legacy of that, what would you call it, psychological and physical terror is still there. Why would they trust the IRA? If a wee lad gets pummelled by grown men, who obviously planned it, for trying to be reasonable, why would people whose relatives have been murdered stand up in public and demand to know why? Who would protect them? I'd love it to happen, and if there were some guarantees they'd be safe, I'd be all for it, but those stories have stayed unspoken for a long time because no-one ever wanted to know. Why do they want to know now? So they can fit it into some made-up history they've already decided on? The 1980s was the worst time for that reason, because we never had a chance to get our stories heard, and I'd say we gave up trying to make ourselves heard. It wasn't just the big events like the bombs and the shootings, it was things like that, day to day stuff that made unionist people believe that no-one was interested in listening to what they had to say.

**('Neil', 50, County Londonderry)**

I remember the 1980s well. A terrible time, probably the worst of it all. Things just went on and on, always the same, there was no prospect of peace, or that's what it seemed like. The conflict had been reduced to this sort of attrition. It was just like part of being in Northern Ireland. The checkpoints, the big army bases, the police stations, being searched going into shops, you had just got used to it. Tit for tat, constantly, but it was like people got used to that and accepted it. How? How does that happen? But that's not the important thing as regards why we stopped, as a community, talking about what was being done to us – people know as well as I do what happened during that decade. Among my friends virtually no-one was left untouched by it. A lot of my friends in the security forces killed, broken marriages, very bad drink problems, sui-cides. No-one ever asked me how I felt about that. Standing at funerals, of friends, relatives, grieving silently, ignored by the press, ignored by the British, no help, no sympathy from anyone. Blamed on the televi-sion for causing the conflict every time some Loyalist – and let's get this right, the vast majority of Protestant unionist people had no time for Loyalists, that's not even up for debate. It didn't matter to the media – in fact I think they loved that, you know, the easy hero and bad guys story, and we were the bad guys, certainly by the 1980s. We were stereotyped – 'not an inch', 'intransigent' – every time Paisley came on the TV ranting and raving it gave the English another chance to say that's what we were all like. Republicans hated us, and they loved to watch us suffer – they might not have won the military battle but they won the propaganda one. They say now that the conflict wasn't sectarian, but they have some convincing to do to make unionists buy that. The funny thing is though they think they have won. Maybe they have. A lot of unionists think that they have, there is a lot of people who feel defeated. But their arrogance could be their downfall. Because if, just maybe, the governments do want to listen to all those stories that we locked away in the 1980s – I would want to talk about my experiences for example – if they want our stories 'defrosted' if you like, or taken out of the closet where we had to hide them, then Sinn Fein and the IRA are in a tough position. And that's because they then have to think about what do they do? Do they trot out the usual same old faces who tell us about their heroic freedom fighters? Or do they engage properly and ask their rank and file to come forward and tell their victims why they did what they did and that they recognise it was wrong? Even if they don't mean it, can you imagine some gunman having to squirm and admit – to admit, whether he believed it or not – that their whole seedy 'war' was totally wrong? But unionists would have to go about it very differently. No more Paisley types screaming. We are a proud people, but why does that translate in the minds of so many from outside that we have to shout loudest and longest to get noticed? It just makes us look like dinosaurs, like idiots, and then we can be pigeon-holed for another generation. Don't let any of that DUP crowd near it would be my view. This should be a public thing. Let the people speak, not through their MPs, for themselves. If you do, you'll find among the unionist community some of the most warm, gentle and eloquent people there are. There's no doubt to me that you'll also find anger, hatred even, and you have to allow for that – this has been injustice that has been festering for years. But this is the most important thing – in the right circumstances you'll find forgiveness, and understanding. I really believe that. The Protestant people of Northern Ireland are not just one thing. They can't all be characterised as 'the same'. That's not how it is. There are plenty of unionists I can't stand. Just because someone is a unionist doesn't mean they have to be my friend. But I will support the right of every innocent person that was victimised to be able to come forward and finally have their voices heard. We tried to talk in the 70s and then the paramilitaries took over – UDA men walking the streets, masquerading to the world, on the world's TVs, that they were unionists. Your average American, they don't make the distinction between Loyalists and unionists. But that distinction is crucial, because the ironic thing is those Loyalists, they told their stories. They write books about what they did. They think they are heroes too. And it's all sensational. It's in the papers, people can't wait to hear about how tough these guys were with their stupid nick names, how many people they killed. No wonder the nationalist community and the world does not want to know about us. If they think those Loyalists are representative of the unionist people, they are out of their minds, but why would they want to know anything else about us? If I watch a Mafia film, does that mean I think all Italian-Americans are like Don Corleone? It's almost defamation, you know, it's hard to shake off. So we need a way round that problem.

I think for sure after the 70s when the paramilitaries emerged ordinary unionists kept quiet because no-one listened, but it was because they had to be careful not only about the IRA, but also the UDA and the UVF. If you lived in a working-class unionist area you had more than just one story to tell. Yes, you wanted people to know you felt threatened by the IRA, what they did to people, the explosions, the assassinations. But what you couldn't say either was that it was just ridiculous that the very people you were being mistaken for – Loyalists – were also people you had stories about too. About how they bullied people, about how they extorted businesses, about how they dealt drugs, and ruined whole housing estates. So the 80s are interesting that way too – the UDA got such a grip where I lived that you daren't have said anything about what they were doing; not just to the Catholic people but also to what they would call their 'own' people. They knew they had no support, so they threw their weight about. Just look at the election results in the 80s. Sinn Fein gained and gained votes, and the IRA was still at its height. But the political parties Loyalist paramilitaries tried to put together were just embarrassed. When unionist people could speak in the secrecy of the ballot box, they rejected that whole Loyalist mentality. That story should be told. We might have been quiet but we were sending a message that we were a people under siege, that we were decent people, and that we voted for law abiding democratic parties.

This notion that all Protestants stick together could not be further from the truth in my view. I knew plenty of people in the RUC were as worried about what Loyalists would do to them as what the IRA would. But it's precisely because we never talked to each other about what was happening that we've never been able to transmit the message that we are complex people, that we are diverse, and that we are hurting from what was done to us during the Troubles. If we've never made that distinction within our community, and cast out those people who were perpetrators and wrongdoers, and condemned them, then it gets harder and harder to let the world know we were innocent victims. Protestant people will surprise you – unionists are not all 'no no no'. If we let rabble rousers or thugs control it we might as well never bother taking those stories out of wherever it is they've been kept all these years.

The Enniskillen bomb is just one example – it was 1987 – a Sunday. I remember on work on the Monday no-one talked about it. No-one. It was a small business and the workforce was about 95% Protestant at that time. A few people said how awful it was, and there was real overwhelming sadness and a sense of futility, but there was like this apathy almost. Not that there was not the deepest sympathy for what had happened, and the strong feeling that someone should pay for it, that there should be justice – proper justice, through the courts. But when that didn't happen, that was the clincher. When we realised that nothing was even going to be done about that, that even that story, one so ghastly someone could hardly even make it up, would vanish, we gave up. It's like the stories were tools, and we just packed them all up in bag and put them away. We didn't have the tools to build the stories anymore. We need to get those back, or we'll still be out in the political cold.

# 6
# 'Ready to speak, but will anyone listen?' Truth Recovery, Unionists and Social Memory

## Introduction

In this chapter I retrace my main theoretical argument: namely, that in the absence of agreed processes of truth recovery following the protracted conflict in Northern Ireland, many unionists now increasingly define themselves as oppositional or peripheral, and will attempt to resist anything which they perceive to be the manipulation and distortion of social memory because of the fear of imposed, manufactured history by their political opponents. Unionist resistance to recollections of political violence is primarily influenced by their trepidation about the potential elision of their biographies of suffering (cf. Feldman, 2004). In this chapter – again based on detailed ethnographic research – I argue that unionists in Northern Ireland can be persuaded to participate in truth recovery processes, but that their involvement will be contingent upon the creation of a framework for dealing with the past that can accommodate some form of dialogical, rationally established and morally assessed 'truth' (cf. Ricoeur, 2001).

## Unionists, truth recovery and social memory

As has been evidenced throughout this book, many unionist respondents in this research have indicated that they are anxious about participating in processes of truth recovery. They want their stories to be told, but fear that trying to make their voices count politically could be a futile and enervating process. This is because they believe that historically there has been 'no audience' for their remembrance, even when they were the innocent victims of abhorrent terrorist crimes (Dillon, 1996). It was put to me repeatedly that 'there is no room for our stories of hurt and loss'. This is an enormous challenge for policymakers in Northern Ireland. In many ways, the lack of awareness of just how unique the Northern Ireland conflict was has led to suggestions for facile policymaking by the British and Irish governments, such as the implementation of a Truth and Reconciliation Commission (TRC) akin to – or even an exact replica of – that which was used in South Africa. Elsewhere, I have deconstructed this logic effectively, and have made novel suggestions for other forms of truth recovery processes in Northern Ireland (Simpson, 2007[a]; Simpson, 2007[b]). Indeed, the communicative justice model that I have advocated (Simpson, 2009) is predicated upon rationally established truth via a Habermasian process of inter-subjective interchange, and, eventually, victim–perpetrator dialogue. In this normative framework, it is the force of better (moral) argument between victim and perpetrator that wins – consonant with the Habermasian Ideal Speech Situation (ISS) (Pusey, 1987; Sitton, 2003).

In this chapter, however, my main focus is not to make further recommendations for how truth recovery proceedings should be institutionalised in Northern Ireland, but rather to argue that whatever format they take the importance of including unionist remembrance cannot be understated. This is so that the very possibility of dealing with the past – that is, finding a lasting peaceful solution and something of an agreed history – is not instantly disallowed by an infrastructure that unionists view as skewed in favour of Irish republican mythmaking. In this way, the incorporation of a 'forgotten' group like unionists – who perceive their memories to have been erased (especially in relation to how they might use retrieved memory to be able to offer 'pardon' to those who perpetrated crimes against them) – can be of benefit to other societies in which victims are confronted with the horrific legacy of violence and are required, by the structures and arrangements of new political dispensations, to make some form of accommodation with the past – in many cases with those who were their 'enemies' and who committed gross human rights violations against them (Elster, 1998). The idea of retrieving memory so that it can be used to empower victims by allowing them the opportunity to 'pardon' perpetrators is consistent with the position advocated by both Tavuchis (1991) and Ricoeur (2004). This theoretical dimension is explored later in this chapter.

As has been detailed in the previous four chapters in particular, those unionists in Northern Ireland whom I interviewed believe that in some ways they are intrinsic facets of a historically strong and proud political monolith (Gillespie, 2001; Walker, 2004); yet they also express deep-rooted insecurity about the fragmented nature of their community and their marginal social status; the decreasing coherence of their ideology; and their weakened capacity to have their individual and collective stories of suffering inserted in the 'official' history of the Northern Irish conflict (cf. Wertsch, 2002). Unionist resistance to predominant recollections of the past in Northern Ireland has been influenced by their fear of imposed, manufactured history by Irish republicans (with assistance from the British and/or Irish governments) that would elide unionist biographies of suffering (cf. Caruth, 1996; Paris, 2001). Denied the oppositional and comparatively solid touchstones that previously helped shape the contours of unionist political imaginings – that is, the threat of a united Ireland and the end of British sovereignty, the complete elision of 'Protestant' territoriality (Anderson and Shuttleworth, 1998; Shirlow and Murtagh, 2006); *and most crucially* the political violence of anti-state Irish republican paramilitaries (and to a lesser extent the violence of Loyalist paramilitaries) and its legacy – this research has pointed to a community that is unsure of how it might weave together its disparate threads so that it can formulate an 'acceptable' and validated, morally normative version of the past (cf. Antze and Lambek, 1996).

It is my contention, however, that the attempt to resist the manipulation of history and the formation of counter-hegemonic social memory are now among the fundamental mechanisms that unionists use to provide ideological and communal post-conflict identity (cf. Brubaker and Cooper, 2000). It solidifies their capacity and their desire to retreat to a position of moral and political righteousness when dealing with the past. Putatively, conceding that 'truth' and 'justice' will not be conflated as part of any project of dealing with the past in Northern Ireland has allowed the formation of a 'memory rallying point' around which unionists have attempted to gather, and as such negate the destructive effects of what is arguably a fading, imagined community that has not, as yet, found ways of constructively engaging with its troubled history (Anderson, 1991). The project of re-orienting social memory – involving an uncomfortable confrontation with the violence of the past and a reflexive and introspective departure from their 'traditional' cultural 'wall of silence' – is of enormous value (Caruth, 1995; Ross, 2002). This is because it arguably permits a reconfiguration and reconstitution of 'old' certainties in a rapidly changing transitional environment (Donnan, 2005; Donnan and Simpson, 2007). However, reliance on narratives that totalise unionist perspectives subsume and subjugate the value of individual experiences create damaging simulacra of obsolete unionist socio-political and socio-cultural attitudes, exacerbating the effects of the 'quarantining' of unionist narratives of victimhood and the past (cf. Hamber and Wilson, 2002; Humphrey, 2002).

This is invidious for unionists, because it removes the possibility of erecting socio-political platforms from which they might more accurately remember, articulate and commemorate the complexities of their experiences during the conflict, and impedes their capacity to conceptualise ways in which they might accept the apologies of perpetrators of political violence (Dawson, 2003; Ricoeur, 2004). My research indicates that confused and variegated aspects of the enduring terror of political violence have impacted deeply on the ways in which unionist narratives of the past are framed. In this supposed shared unionist worldview, I found very significant fragments of discourse that highlight the differing and emotionally punishing impact of the legacy of anti-state PIRA political violence and its remembrance at the individual level. It is this which is fundamental in tracing the new dynamics of unionism, especially in relation to truth recovery in Northern Ireland.

Without due recognition of the intricate nature of unionist social memory by governments and policymakers, high levels of dissatisfaction will continue to operate at a subterranean level, and also become a perpetual source of political and legal destabilisation. The uncomfortable reality for opponents of unionism in Northern Ireland and beyond is that in this research a sense of grievance (in its myriad forms) was central to unionist attitudes to dealing with the past. Reductive analyses, however, which frame unionists as part of the 'memory problem', stigmatising and objectifying them as supporters of a repressive government and legal system, or worse, as proxies or ciphers for malevolent agencies who tacitly or actively participated in extra-legal activity, are unhelpful (cf. Jamieson and McEvoy, 2005; Rolston, 2005). They have the unfortunate consequence of inducing and incubating a well-worn cultural reflex ('siege mentality'), thus closing access to unionist narratives for those engaged in research with them as a group, and obfuscating key nuances pertinent to uncovering how unionists position themselves in their quest for 'justice' and 'truth'.

## Ready to speak? Regrouping and the past: Oral histories of suffering

Unionist resistance to truth recovery in Northern Ireland is influenced by the fear of imposed, manufactured history by Irish republicans (real or imagined) that unionists believe could erase their biographies of suffering and create an enduring sense of injustice (cf. Bell, D., 2003). In the post-conflict context, unionists are denied the foundational elements of their previously held anti-paramilitary discourse that was centred on a 'here and now' moral condemnation of PIRA violence. For many, that discourse – as evidenced by the oral histories outlined in previous chapters – pertained and sustained throughout the conflict, but with the political situation in flux, it has had to assume a historical and retrospective quality. My research has shown that unionists are now using stories of the past as a totem of political certainty (interestingly, even those who do not 'possess' the narratives directly, but rather articulate them as a sign of political and ethnic identity and to indicate their 'authenticity' as people with a 'right to speak' [Donnan and Simpson, 2007]) – a marker of a period when the 'other' or the 'enemy' was known and clearly identifiable to unionists as 'evil'. This is in part to contend with the rapid transition, as unionists view it, of republican paramilitaries into political advocates of peace. The empirical material that was collected during this research suggests that truth recovery and its associated problems in Northern Ireland, including perceived and actual resistance by the unionist community, have failed to take account of the ways in which unionists reconstruct privatised memory, and how they attempt to translate it into the public sphere (Mitchell, 2005). In recalling the past – most pertinently in terms of episodes of political violence – unionists in this research articulated a sense of 'injustice', fear and anger that could fundamentally disrupt the possibility of expeditious political transition (cf. Booth, 2001). As noted earlier in this book, the creation of an Independent Consultative Group on Dealing with the Past in Northern Ireland by the British Government to examine the legacy of the past in 2007 was met initially with considerable uneasiness by unionists. Many unionists told me that they thought at first it was another attempt to legitimise the activities of the PIRA and to 'blame' unionists for the conflict.

**('Jeffrey', 40, County Down)**

This new group for 'dealing with the past'. Sure it's another example! I went along and the thing was a joke. They had decided what it was going to be already, talking about amnesty and all that for IRA murderers. What are we going to get from that? As individuals or as a community? They will probably hold more public meetings just like they did about the police and then ignore what unionists want anyway. They'll keep holding meetings and so on until they get the answer they want. It's easy for them to just concentrate on what republicans and the IRA or Sinn Fein say, because everyone in the world knows their story, or the story they tell, that Protestants and unionists were bigots and that they were a 'liberation force' fighting a 'war'. It's just a farce. There is no point in us even trying to get our side of the story across. They will blame us and say it was the unionists that caused the whole thing. Our people will be forgotten.

\*   \*   \*

The suggestion made by the Consultative Group that the conflict be re-termed a 'war' between the British Government and republican and Loyalist paramilitaries did not help ease these tensions, and it was provoked immediate anger from unionists. Ian Paisley Jr, a high-ranking member of the DUP, argued in response that:

> If there was a war fought under the ordinary rules of engagement, they would have a case. Law and order would be turned on its head – it would be sickening and that's why it should be rejected.
> (http://news.bbc.co.uk/1/hi/northern_ireland/7176271.stm)

In the meetings of the Independent Consultative Group that I observed, this had the strange effect of concentrating unionist public speaking on the central importance of disallowing amnesty for what they termed 'terrorists', and also on a coherent and unanimous rejection of the idea that the conflict in Northern Ireland might be re-termed a 'war'. In a number of the Independent Group's public meetings, I heard over 80 people speak, at least 70 of whom, according to my field notes, argued that amnesty and the re-framing of the conflict as a 'war' was utterly unacceptable. The threat was forceful, and it was also both implicit and explicit – if amnesty were to be granted to perpetrators of political violence, or their actions validated in any way, 'ordinary' unionist civilians and unionist victims would refuse to co-operate in the process. Interestingly, Denis Bradley, the co-chair of the group, announced in November 2008 that although the Group had not completed its report or recommendations, there would be definitely be no provision for any kind of amnesty for perpetrators of political violence. This was a very unusual step and it seemed that the sheer force of unionist objection to the idea of amnesty might have been recognised by the Independent Consultative Group. Speaking after Bradley's announcement to some of the unionists who had been so convinced amnesty would be offered, there was evidence of cautious optimism:

**('Arthur', 50, County Fermanagh)**

I do admit it's strange and unexpected that he said that. Maybe he knows now that from those meetings that the unionist people are going to tell their stories now – or they are ready to – whether he or his cronies like it or not, and he certainly would have been aware that we were totally opposed to any idea of amnesty. That just would have made the whole thing a complete nonsense and unionists would not have got involved no matter what the government threatened. The two governments would have looked ridiculous, he knows that. I would still be very suspicious because we have heard all this before. Your man Bradley can say what he wants but when that report comes out that will be when we'll know what they are going to be trying to do. We've been promised a lot of things before and never got them – we have no reason to believe any different yet. And anyway, that's not doing unionists a favour, not giving amnesty, that's doing what is right and moral. There should not ever have even been an argument about that.

*   *   *

This was further evidence of the increased anxiety during this research from unionist respondents that there was some sort of furtive political plot operating at the macro-political level to demonise them (by unspecified clandestine agents). They also viewed demands placed upon them to involve themselves in truth recovery processes as part of an Irish republican project in which they could be unwittingly co-opted. Stories of republican violence against unionists (including security force personnel) are now a cornerstone of unionist political discourse about the past. Ways *can be found* to reconfigure this social memory in a positive way that can contribute to ensuring stable democracy in Northern Ireland (cf. Shriver, 1995). What is it that unionist narratives of the past reveal, in an empirical and theoretical sense? While that is difficult to quantify or qualify, and further in-depth research on this issue would be required (and welcomed) in order to make more definite claims, in the next section I explore some of the key nuances that my research revealed.

## Unionist narratives and the fear of historical manipulation

The core paradoxes of the unionist discourses of 'truth' and 'history' – in the variant forms that I encountered them – are that they are reflective of comparatively poorly managed, amateurish and chimerical attempts at silence and 'closure' that obfuscate deep-needed desires to tell stories of suffering publicly (Bandes, 2000; Donnan, 2005; Donnan and Simpson, 2007; Simpson, 2007[a]). Crucially, truth recovery discourse among unionists as it is currently constituted, and the potential satiation of the objective of 'closure', might only be achieved as long as it is reliant on the notion of the perceived existence and continued threat of the 'evil' ethnic/political 'other' (cf. Tunbridge and Ashworth, 1996). In other words, unionists *want to tell their stories*, but fear that in doing they will subject those stories to critical scrutiny, and that they will potentially become inadvertent participants in truth projects that will elide their histories of suffering. This would be an insupportable threat to their apparently carefully protected hierarchy of social memory. By continuing to re-tell stories within the confines of homogenised political and cultural 'quarantine' (Humphrey, 2002; Jackson, 2002), unionists can free themselves of those burdens, and rationalise their refusal to become involved in formalised processes of truth recovery as unwillingness to conform in what some perceive to be Irish republican political manipulation.

On the basis of the findings of this research and the oral histories provided in this book, the unionist discourse of 'truth', memory and the past – and their new-found desire to articulate it publicly – seems to be motivated by a number of things. They both want and need to escape the horror and abjectness of the legacy of violence and the conflict via a process of public storytelling, but they are also concurrently caught in a position whereby that hierarchical legacy validates their socio-cultural stance and provides symbolic coherence and moral legitimacy that they – as an increasingly disparate community – utilise in a period of political uncertainty (cf. Kristeva, 1982; Das et al., 2000). In that context, truth recovery could be argued to be necessary, but viewed with extreme fear. Unionists recognise that it could – if adequately framed and normatively conceived – provide them with a sense of solidity and solidarity that would negate their anxiety about their suffering being 'removed' from history (Edkins, 2003; Phelps, 2004).

Unionist narratives and memories of the past can also be understood and theorised as a continued attempt to establish a strong emotional and psycho-social constituency that can withstand the deleterious effects of 'manufactured history' that they worry would valorise Irish republican paramilitarism and stigmatise unionists as 'oppressors' (cf. Fentress and Wickham, 1992). The desire that some respondents expressed as part of this research for straightforward 'closure' was not what it first appeared. Instead, it was conceptually and linguistically wrapped in a need for *discursive* closure, which could be applied to both individualistic and collective social experiences (Ricoeur, 1984; 1985; 1988). That is to say, 'drawing a line under the past', as much as it might reflect an anecdotal view of the supposedly stoic Protestant character of Northern Irish unionism (McKay, 2000), camouflages the much greater need that unionists have to articulate their experiences, but to do so in a way that does not threaten the fragile edifice of psychological security that they have erected (cf. Huyssen, 2003). Unionists during this research were not so politically naïve as to think that a widespread process of retributive punishment of what they regard as terrorist offenders was or is an actual political possibility. Nonetheless, as noted, they view unconditional amnesty for former or current paramilitaries (both republican and Loyalist) as totally inimical to a morally normative view of justice, and thus they feel that as part of the democratic reconstruction Irish republican and Loyalist paramilitaries must concede publicly that they were guilty of moral wrongdoing, and apologise unreservedly for it (cf. Amstutz, 2004).

### ('Jane', 58, County Antrim)

I totally condemn paramilitary violence from all sides, both republican and Loyalist. These people wore masks, they were not soldiers fighting a war in any way, they were cowards engaged in illegal activity and criminality. They lingered in the shadows and shot or blew up innocent people, or brutalised and tortured them in acts of pure and total barbarism. Ordinary, good people, just going about their business. They inflicted misery and sadness on untold numbers of families for decades. Are we meant to just forget this slaughter of the innocents? I find the idea that they would simply be cleansed of these sins and offered some sort of an amnesty as totally repugnant. They do not even show remorse! No, no, what we need is a process where we can be heard, and where those evil people admit to what they did and apologise for it.

\*   \*   \*

Unionist attitudes to truth recovery, as discovered in this research, appeared to be centred around an ongoing and re-iterative struggle between the fear of post-conflict political reality and the necessary confrontation with the legacy of violence and the compulsion to reveal the past, which has been buried beneath layers of cultural, political and social stigma and objectification (cf. Huyssen, 1995). The apparently unreachable end-point – the reconciliation or 'squaring' of this circle – is arguably to be found in dialogue, as I have argued forcefully and in considerable depth elsewhere. Yet communication and story-telling, as unionists perceive it, would have to take place in a political climate that was at least somewhat sympathetic to their needs. Dialogue with perpetrators strips them of their mystique or mythic power (Simpson, 2007[b]). To some extent, unionist respondents in this study recognised this:

### ('Barry', 35, County Fermanagh)

We need to confront them, the IRA. We know that. We need to tell our stories but we need people to listen, And will they? We can say 'what you did was wrong, why don't you admit it?' We know now they won't get punished for it. But unionist victims need the truth, they need respect. We need them to admit responsibility, you know? The trouble is that it's just so difficult. How do you tell victims to face those people? If we could be guaranteed a fair outcome, or even a fair chance, I think the unionist people would go for it. I guess some of us are more frightened of facing it finally . . . it's the end of the line for the conflict then, and what are we left with? Maybe some would rather take comfort in the idea that the whole thing can never be solved because these people [Irish Republican paramilitaries] will not face up to the evil that they did. But even to think that people in the unionist community would now be prepared to speak if the situation was right, that's a big thing for us, when you consider that for years people would not even talk about it to their friends or families. But do we get praise for that? Is there anyone out there asking us what we think, wanting to hear us? My parents always said 'there's no point trying to tell them, they don't want to hear'. I used to just think that was an excuse for getting out of debating it with republicans, you know, like accepting defeat? But now I realise that's true, for years no-one wanted to know. Now all of a sudden we have these groups, they are asking questions, wanting to know about the past, but still they're not committed to listening to what unionists have to say. If it's something republicans say, then that's 'history', like accepted facts – but if it's us, then it has to be 'that's how unionists feel'. There's a big difference there that needs sorted out. It's not fair for the thing, any sort of truth process, to be against unionists like that. A lot of people are ready to speak now but they want to make sure when they do that the politicians are listening to them.

\*   \*   \*

This notion of fairness is inherent to the proceduralist and rigorous attitudes of the unionists with whom I spoke. The role of unionist narratives in any truth recovery process is crucial. They must move from a position of denying access to 'outsiders' to allowing their stories to be told and heard (Simpson, 2007[a]). Their participation requires a calculated political gamble given their fear of historical distortion, as discussed by this respondent:

### ('Gordon', 62, County Armagh)

It's all good saying 'why don't you ones just tell your stories?' But they [Irish nationalists] are always going on about their side of the thing. Why would anyone listen to us? It's too late now. Maybe we missed our chance, but probably no-one wants to hear us anyway. Even a lot of other Prods don't care now. They [Irish republicans] have made up their own version of history sure, and that's what it seems to most us will go down in the history books as fact. There's not a lot we can do to change that, unless we take a chance and get involved in asserting our rights to tell our stories, but the British government needs to back us up in doing that, and we all think they won't. That's the problem. The things that happened . . . that some people saw – young men murdered and then left with their testicles cut off and stuffed in their mouth as punishment for being supposed informers. How do you ever get over that? And that was not even the worst thing . . . ordinary civilians – no connection to the police or the Army – blown up on Bloody Friday. I was there, and I helped the police and the army and other volunteers shovel up bits of bodies into plastic bags. How can we be expected to offer any sort of amnesty to the people who did that?

\*   \*   \*

This despairing view of the 'unionist condition' is reflective of the disbelief and defeatist attitude that I encountered among quite a lot of respondents, who thought of Irish republicans not as Lacanian 'vincible' entities (Fink, 1995; Chieza, 2007), there to be challenged in the content of legally mandated dialogic fora; but rather as 'unbeatables', political sophisticates who have won the 'war of words' and the battle for commemorative supremacy. This is consonant with the argument expressed by Margalit, who has noted that the disparity in power between perpetrators and victims emphasises the notion of those who inflict violence as 'invincible' (Margalit, 2004). This indisputably clashes with the growing anecdotal sentiment in Northern Ireland that unionists, and the DUP and its supporters in particular, are on the crest of a 'confidence boom' in which they are re-asserting a cohesive and unified ideology. Unionists in this research widely resisted the idea that they could make republicans accountable for past political violence in any way that would be adaptive to the 'rules' of the transitional 'game' as it is currently constituted. Unionists in this research all but conceded that they will not get 'what they want' from a process of truth recovery, at least not politically. On that basis, it is important to understand that is one of the reasons why they have retreated somewhat from the entire debate, and why their stories have remained hidden for so long. To confront former Irish republican and Loyalist paramilitaries, and to attempt to make them morally or legally 'accountable', requires not only emotional fortitude and courage, but also the recognition that the historical and essentialised 'enemy' is potentially that which is no longer denying unionism as a movement any sense of unity and harmony. Critical truth recovery would require unionists to confront not only the ethnic or political 'other', but also the texture of their own ideology and their own role in the conflict. This is not to cast doubts or to speculate unnecessarily on the veracity of unionist victims' stories of suffering, but rather to suggest that there is a definite lingering doubt among the unionist 'comfortable majority' (the non-affected) that unionists might not be able to always assume a position of moral superiority as regards the history of the conflict.

Unionists in this research articulated varied aspects of a 'discourse of need' – that is, that it is 'necessary' to disengage from truth recovery because it could erase unionist historical consciousness; or that it is 'necessary' to avoid truth recovery because social memory of the conflict is a 'bad' and 'disruptive' thing in a time of prosperous economic transition. Other 'needs' were more overtly political in tone – that it is not 'necessary' to play the truth recovery 'game' because, as unionists perceive it, its ludic dimensions would be invariably loaded in favour of Irish republicans.

**('Tina', 30, County Tyrone)**

Me, personally, I wasn't affected, but I think even the people that were, what do they want? There's no point us trying to remember the past if a lot of other unionists want to forget it anyway. We need to be together as a community for once to make this thing work. Getting into debates with them [republicans] is just too hard and probably pointless, because who in the rest of the UK or in the US wants to listen to our story? Have you seen nationalist and republicans talking on the television and on the radio, and in the papers? We just have to admit that they're far better at that than our ones. They already know their version of history, they have it all set up, and they know how to use the media to tell it too. We don't have films or TV programmes about what happened to us, so we either need to start to try and work out how to do that better, or we just need to go along with it. It's as simple as that.

\*   \*   \*

As evidenced by this extract, some unionists feel that their political adversaries have been far more politically adept in the use of television and others news media outlets in communicating their narratives of the past. 'Tina' feels that the lack of cinematic, media and dramatic representations of unionist suffering has been one of the main reasons for her community's lack of success in having their stories heard domestically and internationally (Boltanski, 1999). Given all of the other inter-penetrating factors analysed in this chapter, this seems to be an over-statement of the capacity of the media – and cinema particularly – to accurately record and reflect the horrors of the past. However, on the basis of this research, it is apparent that unionists feel inadequate and inferior in comparison to Irish republicans, whom they view as having been highly effective in historical mythmaking via the use of films, plays and even literature (both fiction and non-fiction). They also believe that they have been negatively portrayed in the media and that this had had a damaging and lasting effect on how they are perceived (Parkinson, 2001). As such, some now recognise that the media – and in particular television and film – can prove extremely valuable in narrating versions of past that they feel will reveal 'their' story of the conflict (cf. Hoskins, 2004; Hoskins and O'Laughlin, 2007).

In all of this, however, unionists have apparently not countenanced what might be gained (rather than just lost) from entering a process of truth recovery, both instrumentally and emotionally. Truth recovery is seemingly viewed by unionists only in negative terms, as something that will contribute to the destruction of a cherished and keenly protected notion of history. The desire for the truth, however, as complex as it is, requires unionists to enter a process of dealing with the past that demands sustained encounters with troubled histories, and could potentially precipitate widespread individual and collective anxiety (Habermas, 1990; Simpson, 2007[b]). In this context, the complexity of unionist discourse as evidenced by the oral histories in this book is especially perplexing. Nearly all respondents in this research conceded that a 'fair' process of truth recovery, predicated upon a 'just' notion of rational law (even given their distrust of the British Government), would make for sustainable democratic reconstruction (Ricoeur, 2001). This is a search for truth that is predicated upon unionists' perceptions that there are rationally accessible and morally normative, valid versions of the past which have been ignored. This worldview is underpinned by a rather positivistic view of historical knowledge, although in the course of this research I did ascertain that despite the idea among unionists that an 'authentic' past could be discovered (one which debunked the partisan bias of republican history), they recognised that some element of subjectivity was inevitable. They thus accepted that forms of reconciliation that did not subjugate their narratives *were potentially attainable,* but that they might require something akin to a process of Habermasian communicative action and rationality in which victims were able to confront perpetrators in the context of legally established dialogic fora in which the veracity – or even 'objectivity' – of the past could be established (Habermas, 1984; Simpson, 2007[b]). However, many also felt that 'shedding' the cloak of armour that had protected them from metaphorical, emotional and physical disintegration during and after the conflict, in the hope of effective transition, demanded that they maintain critical distance from participation. This notion of critical distance has been important in allowing unionists to conceive of the past as something that has been, or could be, taken or stolen from them by the political 'other', as described by this respondent:

**('Bertie', 49, County Londonderry)**

Dialogue and finding out the truth. It's what our people want. It's what we need. We're ready in ways now to have another go at telling the world our stories. But do we risk it? Why? For what? How can we be sure it's worth it? Will we get there and in the end it's just a whole set-up, and no-one wants to listen to us or accept what they did to us was wrong? You know, that Sinn Fein and the IRA will just hijack it and steal our history? The thing that offers us hope is that the British government would make this a proper legal thing, you know, set the boundaries, get people in, and make it fair. Then it's possible, I think. It could be a good thing for unionists. But there can be no amnesty for terrorists, we must protect the whole community in Northern Ireland, unionists, nationalists, republicans, Protestants, Catholics, by using some sort of commission to find out what these people did wrong.

\*   \*   \*

There is thus some evidence of increasingly positive unionist attitudes towards truth recovery in Northern Ireland. However, they are conditional. Truth recovery, despite the fact that the respondents in this study conceded that some level of political and legal pragmatism would be required, is envisaged by some of those in this research as workable only as something of an idealised process that can eliminate transitional uncertainty (cf. Irwin-Zarecka, 1994). Unionist discourse about truth recovery currently rests to a certain extent upon notions of moral witnessing, thus achieving 'closure' with recourse to some type of legal and political rationality, and without continued insecurity and a festering sense of injustice (cf. Felman and Laub, 1992); or establishing a process whereby the 'other' can be reconstructed, fantastically, as 'conquerable' – a weak political alliance that cannot bear the weight of 'the truth'.

This latter scenario corresponds to a phantasmagorical Northern Ireland in which valorised versions of 'justice' (as perceived by unionists) are realised, and an impervious and subjectively defined 'righteous' version of unionist history can be copper fastened. This, however, is not as depressing a prospect for lasting reconciliation as it seems. While the latter notion is an undoubted impediment to the potential for meaningful communicatively rational dialogue, reliant as it is on a fictitious embodiment and distorted memory of the ethnic or political other and the denial of counter-narratives, the former contains elements of rationality, agency and 'moral witnessing' that would permit unionists to avoid the corrosive effects of historical and emotional disorder, and allow for them to narrow the gap between their fear of revealing and their pervasive trepidation about 'memory theft'. By engaging in rational dialogue unionists can circumnavigate their fear of the unbeatable 'other', re-conceptualising truth recovery as an *equitable process* than can protect history rather than eliminate it (cf. Torpey, 2001; 2003). Unionists can therefore achieve closure discursively and dialogically, and retain control of their capacity to enumerate certain cultural, social, religious and historical imperatives (Habermas, 1984; Borradori, 2004). This was reflected towards the end of an interview with one respondent:

**('Betty', 45, County Fermanagh)**

It's really quite simple. We go on as we are, and we disappear, we fade away, we get forgotten. Or we go with it, we get involved, but we don't go from a position of fear, of weakness. We got to London and Dublin and we say 'Right, we're 25% of the population on the island of Ireland, and we're a majority in Northern Ireland, you can't just pretend we're going to go away. We're not.' And we need to be emphatic about it. As part of that, I'm no fool, they will go on about what part we played in the conflict. They will say there was wrong on both sides – blaming ordinary unionist people for what Loyalist terrorists did – and we have to make sure we remember that. But we have to say to them, the governments, 'use your laws, use what you have, do what you will to find out about the past, but don't palm us off with rubbish and nonsense, or lies like you always have'. Because, ultimately, your average unionist in Northern Ireland just wants the truth now, to know what happened and why. They want to be shown that yes, there is a place for us in history, that people will listen to our stories. In a way, the truth would be justice for us. The law might not punish them [Irish and Loyalist republican paramilitaries] but it will record, in the history books, what they did to our people. And that's, to me anyway, the most important thing.

## Justice, memory and pardon

In conducting this research, I got no sense that unionists *enjoyed* the continued political antipathy that surrounds truth recovery in Northern Ireland. However, as part of a very complex socio-political and cultural stance, they did in part hold on to the notion of historical antagonism against Irish republican paramilitaries in particular, primarily because (as I noted at the beginning of this book) such enmity potentially now offers a 'necessary' rallying 'memory point' for a disaffected and disjointed community that is fundamentally unsure of how to manage the post-conflict transition (cf. Biggar, 2001; Cappelletto, 2003). Unionists in this research, while articulating a clear desire for 'justice' as part of any truth recovery project, also stressed that they did not seek vengeance (cf. Bass, 2000).

**('Jack', 40, Belfast)**

No-one wants vengeance. That's one thing we don't want. We saw enough bloodshed and hurt and loss during 30 years. No more. Never again. We share that view. But at the same time, we can't just let go of those people we lost. We can't be written out of history. We were shot, bombed, threatened, intimidated . . . some horrendous acts of violence were committed against us. As much as I might get criticised for saying this, I feel I have a right to say it as I am a victim. My father was severely injured in a no-warning explosion by the IRA. Yet dealing with the past in lots of ways has to be an individual thing as well as a community thing. We have to at least try to understand why these things happened, or we'll never get to a point where we can reconcile with the other community. Yes, as unionists we think of policemen and the army as innocent victims – and to me they were, they were people who were upholding the law, and who were doing a job to protect the civilian population, and *I mean all civilians*, from paramilitary violence, on both sides. I could just condemn paramilitaries outright, but in my view we need to try to understand what happened and to recognise, however painful, that a lot of the rhetoric and all of that there coming from politicians made young men join these groups. That's very uncomfortable for me to admit, and I'm not sure I'm even certain about admitting it now, but we have to find a way to or we will just be dismissed again as the people who were not willing to compromise.

\*   \*   \*

There was no desire for further violence, or physical retribution, among the people with whom I spoke or observed. Indeed, in the above quotation, Jack's 'never again' trope attempts to mobilise the awfulness of the past in an effort to imagine a much better future. Many did feel, though, that the British and Irish Governments, in line with the wishes of Irish republicans, were prepared to impose a utilitarian mode of truth recovery which would sacrifice the suffering of unionist individuals and the unionist community – as an expendable minority on the island of Ireland and in the United Kingdom – for an ambiguous notion of the 'greater good'. This evoked very negative and emotional feelings, with some respondents expressing the view that a successful political transition in Northern Ireland would inevitably be tainted by the forgotten suffering of unionist victims of political violence.

### ('Paul', 50, County Antrim)

We as a community that was victimised by what we regard as terrorists, we do want justice, yet they tell us that what we actually mean is that we want to go back to the conflict, or some sort of conflict, just because we say we want people to be held accountable for what they did. That's not right, and it's not fair. No-one wants to go back to the way things were. We are prepared to forgive, but not forget. And why should we forget?

*   *   *

This rhetorical question resonated very deeply with all of the respondents in this research. The concept of fairness and justice was inextricably tied to the crucial distinction, in a Ricoeurian sense, between forgiveness and forgetting (cf. Ricoeur, 1988; 2004). Key to this political and moral equation was not only the idea of ensuring a place in history for unionists and the horrors that victims in that community endured, but also the contentious question of amnesty (Zur, 1994). While it has been in place in a *de facto* sense as a consequence of the Northern Ireland Sentences Act of 1998 (NIO, 1998), when those paramilitaries who had been convicted of conflict-related crimes and incarcerated as a result were released early, unionists in this research felt that amnesty as a pre-condition for a legally mandated and formalised process of truth recovery would be totally unacceptable, especially for those cases of political violence for which no perpetrator was ever captured.

This can be theorised with recourse to Tavuchis's (1991) concept of apology and Ricoeurian notions of the 'pardon'. The idea of retrieving memory so that it can be used to empower victims by allowing them the opportunity to 'pardon' perpetrators is consistent with the position advocated by Tavuchis (1991), who has focussed on the importance of the concept of apology in creating the conditions for reconciliation – no matter how difficult the circumstances. Indeed, Tavuchis's notion of the 'apologies of the many' is especially useful. Tavuchis's (1991) contention that an individual perpetrator of wrong can express regret and apology to a collective ('from one to many') would seemingly, on the basis of this research, be welcomed by unionists; as would – indeed perhaps even more so – his idea that the collective can offer an apology to the individual ('many to one').

Unionist individuals in Northern Ireland, on the basis of my empirical research – and whether or not they were directly the victims of political violence – regard themselves as forgotten and liminal, and are dismayed by the aggregation of their narratives into a supposedly homogenous unitary discourse. An apology by a collective of perpetrators of political violence need not be limited just to those who have been directly affected by violence. As Tavuchis (1991: 2) noted, 'the appeal or resort to apology as a way of dealing with normative breaches is not limited to those directly involved.' However, an apology by an immoral collective to an innocent individual – in particular to someone whom they or one of their comrades harmed – would go some way to convincing unionists in Northern Ireland (and arguably sufferers in other post-conflict contexts who are dealing with traumatic pasts) that their stories could and even should be told. A public acknowledgement by Irish republican paramilitaries of this kind – that their campaign of terror was a moral offence – would go some way to satisfying the unionist requests that have been outlined in this book, most notably that evil deeds are 'put on record, to document as a prelude to reconciliation' (Tavuchis, 1991: 109). The failure of wrongdoers to apologise jeopardises the potential for the creation of a new social community in which peripheralised memory is acknowledged. As noted by Tavuchis (1991: 62), there is a 'moral climate required for authentic and effective apologetic discourse'. This connects in a very interesting way with the Ricoeurian concept of 'pardon'. The Tavuchian idea of apology – either 'many to one' or 'one to many' (Amstutz, 2004) – need not be met by unionists with complete forgiveness or amnesty, but it could enable them to offer perpetrators what Ricoeur would term a 'pardon'. This could be crucial in persuading unionists to participate in some process of truth recovery and reconciliation.

'Pardon', according to Ricoeur, could never be *demanded* of victims of political violence (Ricoeur, 2004). In the case of those unionists who either were directly victims of political violence, or regard themselves as representatives of those who were, the perception among some of the respondents was that the effects of some particularly devastating Irish republican paramilitary crimes were simply irreparable. Some were more hopeful, however, articulating the opinion that regardless of the nature of the crime, the conflict had created conditions in which excessive acts of violence were likely, if not ineluctable; and that consequently, forgiveness could be rationalised on this basis. They still, however, drew the distinction between forgiveness and forgetting, and the issue of remembrance is, on the basis of the findings of this research, absolutely fundamental to unionist attitudes to truth recovery.

Not only are unionists anxious because of a perceived fear of being eradicated from history, but they also dread the forgetting of those members of their community who were murdered during the conflict (cf. Young, 1994). Forgiveness bridges this problem, at least for some. It can confer upon the giver a sense of moral righteousness and can be conceptualised as rationally motivated, without conceding the right to retain and possess a morally normative sense of what was 'right' and 'wrong', what was 'good' and what was 'evil', and thus what can be reasonably offered or 'traded' in exchange for political, psychological and emotional peace as part of democratic reconstruction and political compromise (Nytagodien and Neal, 2004). 'Pardon' is an act of political and social benevolence, and as such does not necessarily threaten the veracity of unionist sacrifice during the conflict. It can in some way ameliorate the untold complexities of amnesty (Humphrey, 2005). If the act of 'pardon' is an intrinsic part of the truth recovery process for unionists, as suggested to me by respondents in this research, then it suggests that they might perhaps confront social memory individually and collectively (Halbwachs, 1992). To try to ensure that what union-ists would regard as the unbearable and intolerable price of forgetting would not have to be paid in order to facilitate an expeditious tran-sition in Northern Ireland, they could confront the act of open and public remembrance, no matter how painful and politically risky that might be. 'Pardon' would also be consistent theoretically with a position outlined by Ricoeur, who notably described amnesty as a 'caricature of pardon':

> Amnesty . . . is an institutionalised form of amnesia. . . . in certain cases, public tranquillity can imply amnesty; the slate is wiped clean. But with all the dangers forgetting presents: permanent forgetting, amnesia. Amnesty is a constitutional power which should be used as infrequently as possible.
>
> (Ricoeur, 1998: 126)

The majority of the unionists during this research felt that some formal and rationally, normatively established mechanism that recorded the wrongs of the conflict was necessary, so that 'real' history – or at least *their history* – might be protected.

However, many unionists were concerned that involving themselves in processes of truth recovery would necessitate *too much* political and moral compromise. Many feared that perpetrators would only enter a process of truth recovery for instrumental gain rather than because of genuine remorse, and that the British and Irish govern-ments would entice paramilitaries to participate with promises of legal clemency. This, consonant with arguments outlined by Habermas (1984; 1996) and Simpson (2007[a]) would be an insupportable method of recovering any form of truth in Northern Ireland and would further serve to marginalise unionist social memory. As Tavuchis (1991: 62) argued:

Apology cannot come about and do its work under conditions where the primary function of speech is defensive or purely instrumental and where legalities take precedence over moral imperatives.

The deconstruction of what republicans have argued is a unionist 'hierarchy of victimhood' – that is, that unionists view security force casualties and Protestant civilians as 'innocent' victims but refuse even to countenance that illegal Irish republican or Loyalist paramilitaries were victims in any way – seems, at this stage, to be too much of a price to pay for unionists. However, the notion of 'moral witnessing' (Margalit, 2004) could allow unionists to consider engaging in inclusive, cross-communal dialogue and prospective inter-subjective interchange with other victims, and even perpetrators of political violence, that would certainly test the strength and coherence of their narratives of the past outside their own micro communities for perhaps the first time. This would be a calculated political risk for unionists, but allied to the possibility of forms of forgiveness and remembrance that disallow historical erasure, as discussed earlier in this chapter, it might be that it is one that the majority feel worth taking.

**('Andrew', 54, County Armagh)**

We don't want to be just written off as the people that caused the conflict. So, to me, that means we do need to get involved in some kind of project that sorts it out. It's okay saying we should stay away, but we can't complain then if our suffering gets wiped away from the history books, can we? But to get involved – and I think I speak for a lot of unionists here – we need some kind of thing so that the government or whoever says for definite what was right and what was wrong, and we need them to listen to our stories. Everything can't just be dismissed as 'oh, that was because of the conflict' like in South Africa. So, yeah, morals or morality or whatever you want to call it is very, very important to us, in that way, for sure. And I would think it's especially important for the victims, because wrong and evil things were done to us. But it's like nobody wants to know about that or recognise it. No-one wants to hear our story. We get branded as bigots. No-one is interested, or that's how it seems anyway. Unionist victims have to be offered the chance to forgive. That doesn't mean we have to forget, but if the government and republicans accept that, then to me that says that they also accept we as a community and as individuals need to remember what was done to us, and we need to find a way to commemorate it.

That way, all of us in Northern Ireland can start to try and deal with the past.

\*   \*   \*

Some unionist victims, as is evidenced by the extract below, believe that a truth recovery process – provided it was structured in such a way that it did not appear to have a particularist agenda – would at the very least offer them some chance to tell their story and to have it properly documented for historical purposes.

## ('Elizabeth', 54, County Londonderry)

I just want some respect. I want someone to listen. What happened to my family could have happened anywhere in Northern Ireland to ordinary unionist people. My brother was shot, over and over again. No-one was ever charged. That was a very long time ago. But I still want to know who, when, why, where and what happened to my brother. That would be truth, for me. I want that, and I want people to hear my story. Beyond that, I can't tell people in government what they should or should not do – they'll do what they want anyway, they always have done. But I am not a bigot. I am not against compromise, or reconciliation. I have friends in both communities, Protestant and Catholic. But terrorists murdered my brother and I want answers. Most importantly I want what happened to be known, and I want an opportunity to have my story told.

\*   \*   \*

In seeking to fabricate methods by which unionists, who on the basis of the evidence provided by this research seem to already (and alarmingly) feel somewhat alienated from truth recovery in its abstract or perceived forms, will participate in some form of dealing with the past, the British and Irish Governments should arguably be cognisant of the need to avoid political expediency and essentialism (Rae, 2002). As noted, unionists are threatened enormously by the possibility of being 'erased' from history, but crucially are *not actually completely and actively conceptually resistant* to *some form* of truth recovery in Northern Ireland. The two governments might therefore be sensitive to the anxiety of unionists who dread the possibility of historical mythmaking, the type of which would enable – as unionists perceive it – Irish republicans to monopolise victimhood and truth recovery (cf. Pocock, 1998; Edkins, 2003). Unionists – on the basis of the narratives they articulated in this research – *would accept* meaningful engagement that is predicated on rationality and dialogue, in which *everyone's* entitlement to be acknowledged as victims is not automatically invalidated by the infrastructure of the mechanisms for dealing with the past. For the unionists who participated in this study, paramilitary political violence perpetrated against their community during the Northern Ireland conflict could not, however, be explained by what many regarded as facile structuralist explanations. Respondents in this research felt that these were simply 'get out' clauses for perpetrators:

**('Steven', 61, Belfast)**
It's all right those terrorists saying 'we had nothing, we were underprivileged, we were discriminated against, and we had no choice but to join the IRA and attack the state'. We don't believe that for a second. I came from nothing. My family had no money, and we were Protestants and unionists. A lot of my friends became Loyalist paramilitaries. I didn't. They were scum, thugs, just like the IRA – both are as bad as each other. I had a choice and I made that choice to get out, and they could have done the same. They [Loyalist paramilitaries] came to me and asked me to join, and I told them to clear off. So I don't accept those sorts of explanations at all. If that's what truth recovery is meant to be about, it's a waste of time, because we have heard all that before and we didn't believe it then. They – and I mean all paramilitaries – need to say 'we did this' and it needs to be the truth – even if they're not sorry, it's up to us then if we forgive them or if we don't.

\*   \*   \*

It is potentially only in the 'telling' of unionist experiences that the phenomenological dimensions of their social memory and attitudes to dealing with the past can be properly accessed. The importance of interpretive biographies and the public re-telling of experiences, in combination with the widespread 'reading' of such experience within a truth recovery process – and consequent apologies by perpetrators for the suffering they inflicted – cannot be understated (Rosenwald and Ochberg, 1992; Hamber and Wilson, 2002; Torpey, 2003; Phelps, 2004). Without this, unionist narratives of the past and unionist social memory in Northern Ireland will remain locked in 'cold storage', and meaningful and productive truth recovery will be extremely difficult. Unionists *can be persuaded* to participate in truth recovery processes, but their inclusion in projects of dealing with the past is conditional on their right to remembrance being protected; the willingness of perpetrators to recognise their moral wrongdoing and to apologise for it; and the implementation of a process that does not automatically offer amnesty to perpetrators of political violence as reward for their participation. These are not conditions which – if handled sensitively and appropriately by the two governments – are completely insurmountable. It is a very nuanced and complex position, but it is possible to conclude on the basis of these findings that despite anecdotal and rhetorical evidence suggesting otherwise, there is definite potential for effective truth recovery in Northern Ireland in which unionists can engage meaningfully and positively in an attempt to solidify a cross-community and peaceful democratic administration.

# 7
# Conclusion – Mastering the Past in Northern Ireland

If you can bear to hear the truth you've spoken
Twisted by knaves to make a trap for fools

Rudyard Kipling, 'If', 1895

This book began by outlining its stated intentions: not to underscore the veracity or legitimacy of the narratives that would be provided within it, but to give voice to the dialogically and politically dispossessed during an era of transition in Northern Ireland (cf. Douglass and Vogler, 2003). As noted in the introductory chapter, this was important for a number of reasons, not least because large elements of the majority unionist–Protestant population feel both forgotten and marginalised. Additionally there is an academic necessity to record, for the purposes of accurate and balanced history – and in an effort to begin to 'voice the void' – the stories of those whom I have labelled 'ordinary' unionist civilians. The conflict in Northern Ireland was long and gruesome, and it would be naïve to think that its cessation and its apparently 'settled' aftermath have brought about an easily digestible political or cultural situation for unionists. As has been demonstrated throughout this book, many unionists regard themselves as the victims – directly or indirectly – of a systematised, sustained and co-ordinated campaign of sectarian political violence by the PIRA.

Irish republicans maintain – with what some Protestants regard as expertly affected insincerity – that this was definitely not the case, and that any suggestion to the contrary is merely unionist *perception*. However, as has been shown throughout this book, many ordinary citizens ask very discomforting questions about Bloody Friday, Kingsmills, La Mon House Hotel, Donegall Street, Enniskillen and the 'commercial bombings' of 'Protestant towns', before even beginning to mention the hundreds of RUC and UDR personnel who were ruthlessly assassinated during the Troubles. Policymakers – and more pertinently society – in Northern Ireland must brace themselves for this potential tidal wave of instability, because unless adequate defences are created (in both the legal and metaphorical sense), the edifice of transitional justice and the new devolved government at Stormont which has been so fastidiously pieced together (largely, it must be said, by an astonishing feat of political manoeuvring by Sinn Fein, which has demonstrated its credentials as the party to be reckoned with in Northern Ireland) will eventually crumble.

Now that the 'memory seal' has apparently been broken, no unionist political party – whatever its perceived hardline credibility (Bruce, 2007) – will be able to persist in government if unionist voters awaken to the very real possibility of continued radical historical revisionism in which even the civilian victims of political violence could be eliminated from public remembrance (cf. Kopecek, 2007). Although truth recovery was initially conceptualised by many unionists as a key part of the Irish republican programme for complete political overhaul, and thus originally opposed, republicans – sometimes in co-operation with the British and Irish Governments – have pushed forcibly for extensive and detailed investigations into state wrongs during the conflict (cf. Ní Aoláin, 2000; Hegarty, 2003). This is quite a common strategy in many post-conflict societies (Hayner, 2001). Yet it might have proved to have been a tactical error. Feeling that they were confronted with yet another unstoppable aspect of the transition, some unionists have finally, to some extent, accepted the possibility of a process of truth recovery and examining the past, and decided that if the conditions are right they will make an effort to influence its outcomes (Simpson, 2008). Perhaps banking on the stereotypical 'intransigence' of unionists, this is a development many with vested political interests in Northern Ireland, and who were keen to sponsor a project of historical manipulation which cohered neatly with a republican narrative of the past, might not have anticipated. It is therefore, for them, a potential obstacle that must be overcome. As such, if they wish to protect the new political fiefdoms that they have carved out, the 'conflict about the conflict' is one that Irish republican politicians must now make strenuous efforts to win.

## The republican agenda

In their paramilitary incarnation and latterly in their political guise, though, republicans have never made any secret of such objectives (English, 2003; Alonso, 2006). Indeed, it was only other unionists who dismissed the idea of a republican long-term masterplan to 'green' Northern Ireland from within and/or without as paranoid fantasy, because the PIRA and latterly Sinn Fein publicly committed themselves to the 'long war' time and time again, and often stated that it would require myriad strategies (O'Brien, 1999; Feeney, 2002). At every stage of the conflict – including this, what I have dubbed the 'battle for history' – they have tried to outfox their political opponents. They cannot and should not be blamed for this – it is their core objective. Among the unionist community, as has been shown in this book, republican capabilities have thus unsurprisingly assumed mythical, Lacanian invincible proportions (Chieza, 2007), and as a result many of those unionists who do not want to 'chuck in the towel' (as one respondent said to me) 'are those that are too stupid to realise they have been beaten already, too angry or sad to give in, or too concerned with their houses and their cars and holidays and some vague notion of "peace" than remembering all those poor people that were killed and murdered'. Challenging this respondent as to how he would self-locate in this typology, he replied thus:

**('Christopher', 60, Belfast)**

Me? I'm someone who is just too sad, way too sad, to have come this far and let them [republicans] win this, and for them – all of them up at Stormont now they have agreed to sit round a table – to not even let us have the right to remember the people the IRA killed with dignity. That's what we're reduced to – I know we're beaten, politically, but we want dignity and to tell our truth. And in time, if we get this right, history will record and show just what happened here, unless politicians get hold of it and twist it so that what we say does not really reflect what we mean, you know? I believe that, I really do, and we need more unionist people to believe it. It's like that old thing, you know, in the movies, where the survivors of the battle want someone to go back and try to explain to everyone else just what happened, how people suffered, what they experienced, the loss families here went through and the courage they showed. We want people to know that. We want the world to know. We want our children to know. But it's like they won't let us come and tell that story, they won't even let us come forward and tell the world about the courage and the bravery of the innocent people and families torn apart by the IRA because the IRA is now part of the government of the country.

\*   \*   \*

This impassioned comment cuts right to the very centre of the debate. Unionists know that the politics of remembering the past in Northern Ireland now seems to necessitate an enormous compromise with those whom they view as responsible for killing, bombing and attacking them or members of their community. Acknowledging that many are now beginning to engage and seek strategies for narrating their stories publicly, others simply refuse to countenance this issue, or to frame it in such a way, and not always for the reasons one might suspect (and which have been extensively outlined in this book). When I told one middle-class business man whom I interviewed, for example, that many unionists felt the lure of economic progress and the seduction of prosperity and ostensible tranquillity had allowed republicans to command the historical terrain and shape it accordingly, and that logically this meant that so-called weak unionists had colluded in forgetting victims, he reacted furiously:

**('Arnold', 45, Belfast)**

I've heard all that sort of nonsense before. Same old rubbish. We forget, we don't care, we're not interested. Why should I get involved in debates about the past though? I want to draw a line under it. We have a government in place, the structures for people to go out there and make some money, yet it is our community that is dragging its heels. They are always moaning about the past, calling for justice and all sorts of measures that are just impossible now. Either that or burning bonfires and marching up and down roads. I'm fed up with them. They're an embarrassment to me. If people want to go chasing the past in search of some elusive memory let them, but in my opinion they should get over it and I certainly won't be getting involved in it.

\*   \*   \*

This extract is notable – and is included here – because of its anomalous content. Certainly, I did encounter other unionists who, in various ways, were in a state of denial about the nature of the political process, or who genuinely thought that confronting the past would be a bad idea for their community, but they were in a minority. The somewhat repellent notion – expressed above – that victims of political violence are 'an embarrassment' is an appalling indictment not only of that respondent, but of an attitude of mind that pertains to the excavation of the past in other post-conflict settings (Spain, Chile and Argentina, for example cf. Brown, 1991; Enselaco, 1994, 1999; Taylor, D., 1997; Grandin, 2006). He is, of course, entitled to deviate from the facile notion that as someone from a unionist background, he must subscribe to all aspects of the political historical 'cause' as it now manifests itself, but his tone was risibly indignant and his worldview – essentialising all unionists as people who gather around bonfires or seek to 'march down roads' (presumably meaning members of the Orange Order) – was self-loathing and almost deliberately uninformed. Sadly, if people from within the unionist community are articulating such opinions – so loudly and with the ignorant bombast of the lamentably self-interested – then it is perhaps little wonder that others who have struggled for so long with the burden of grief feel unsupported, disempowered or intimidated, or think that their quest for truth has indeed been fought and lost (cf. Leydesdorff et al., 1999).

On the basis of this research, the unionist community is fractured and fragmented. Those expecting to conduct ethnographic research among the unionist population in Northern Ireland and find total commonality between its many divergent elements should leave their intellectual baggage at the door. Yet in relation to uncovering the past, a curious phenomenon has occurred. Unionists, as the evidence of this book has shown – church-going and not church-going, Anglican, Methodist, Presbyterian and other, victims and those who simply experienced the conflict, working-class and middle-class – have started to form a rallying point that has, at least to an extent, transcended many traditional boundaries and enabled unionists to discuss trauma (cf. Bell, 2006). It has also transcended spatial boundaries, which is crucial given that previously there had been tensions between urban and rural unionists. In particular there was a sense among unionists in Belfast that the city very much belonged to them, and that its destruction by PIRA bombs had victimised the unionist community there disproportionately (cf. Low and Lawrence-Zuniga, 2003; Bevan, 2007). That rallying point is memory: more saliently, the realisation that the telling of unionist stories is now a matter of extreme political, moral and cultural priority (cf. Volf, 2007). Even allowing for the defeatist tone and texture of much of what is recollected and how it might fail to impact upon the politics of remembering the past (at least in institutional terms), the key point to note is that unionists are now ready and prepared to speak about the past. This, many have realised, is not only a valuable political tactic – though one must question how much capital the main unionist parties have sought to make from it given their demonstrably recent poor record of support for victims – but more crucially a matter of historical and moral duty (Rogers et al., 2004; Balfour, 2005).

Paradoxically, the relationship between the erstwhile 'extremes' of the DUP and Sinn Fein has not leant much comfort to unionists, many of whom detect in that arrangement what they regard as traces of elite-level political deals that sully the self-righteous, moralising tone that was adopted by some unionist leaders in the past (Bruce, 2007). Furthermore, many unionists feel that to decry the current settlement on the basis that it has created a warped and partial view of the past would be virtual political and social apostasy, and would provide for critics yet more evidence that unionism would always be undone by its 'backwoodsmen', those supposed bigots in bowler hats who hate Catholics and would never accept anything less than a return to majoritarian rule.

If the oral histories provided in this book have done nothing else, however, they have buried that particularly specious and insidious line of argument. In the course of this research, I encountered the frail, the fragile, the despondent, the self-interested and the disillusioned. I spoke with the hopeful, with the energised and even with some people who had the vitality and sense of purpose to try and negotiate an agreed history in which moral wrongdoing was identified and condemned. These were unionist people who came from all over Northern Ireland, and from various times and places. One should pause long and hard before ever labelling any of them 'backwoodsmen'. This pejorative term of abuse is a stone that is easily thrown, an infantile sound byte that plays well with republicans and their international sympathisers, but one which has no relationship with reality. As with all that republican paramilitaries have done to apply layers of gloss to their record of past violence, unionists believe that it is entirely superficial and easily disproved. To those who enthusiastically embrace and even endorse the faux-Marxist ramblings of former terrorists, especially those who pride themselves as being part of some kind of intellectual vanguard, my experience of actually asking unionists how they felt – especially victims – and outlining their remembrance in this book, surely stands as a firm rebuttal of such simplistic analyses.

Some people, of course, will never be convinced that unionists were not to blame for the conflict, and will continue to argue that all of those who came from a Protestant ethnic-political background were not only responsible for propping up the machinery of an oppressive state that victimised Catholics, but as a consequence were undeserving of any sympathy when the republican 'revolution' came. They, however, should be allowed to fester in the tyranny of their own insupportable universe of thought, which has – or should not have – any influence on how sensible people from across and between the two communities in Northern Ireland go about remembering the past. It is not cowardice on the part of unionists to retreat from debates with such tendentious and irrational partisans.

## Learning from the past?

While it might be edifying to comment that via the collection, reproduction and analysis of unionists' narratives, this book might offer 'lessons from the past' which would lead ineluctably to a stable and reconciled society, such logic would cohere too closely with initiatives aimed at 'healing through remembering' that have not been sufficiently instructive or helpful for the unionist community. This research has shown that many unionists feel that they are, and have been, 'out in the cold'. That is a harsh reality for those who adumbrate a warm, agreed and solid post-conflict Northern Ireland, often from afar, but who also purposefully or unwittingly avert their gaze from the problems still inherent in what remains a deeply conflicted society. If Northern Ireland pre-1969 was an 'Orange state' (Farrell, 1980), in which all unionists were naturally favoured and rewarded as the loyal progeny of the fathers of Ulster (as against rebellious and untrustworthy Catholics) – an absurd notion that is repudiated by large sections of the unionist population in any case – many in this research now feel the balance of power has certainly shifted, and that revenge was more than meted out by the PIRA and its allies during the conflict.

This book is not an authoritative history of the Troubles and was never intended to be, so where possible I have made every attempt not to offer arguments in such a way that they read as objective 'fact'. As a caveat, though, it should be recognised that to couch everything to do with unionists in the language of perception, of subjectivity or of relativity is also something of a moral abrogation. It does little to strengthen the much-needed counter-hegemonic and anti-terrorism voice in Northern Ireland and beyond (Held, 2008). After all, surely it is the perception of more than simply unionists that hideous bomb and gun attacks by political fanatics – on both sides – are and were utterly deplorable?

At what point, one might ask, does perception become reality? Battered and bruised by decades of paramilitary victimisation (as it should be noted, were Catholic civilians), unionist civilians now face a weary and uphill struggle within Northern Ireland to construct any sense of internal cohesion and communitarianism. There is a definite feeling among the unionists with whom I spoke that even though explicit acts of political violence might have ceased, at least on a large scale, a new low-level conflict has emerged, one of political, social and cultural attrition aimed at driving them out of geographic areas, houses and jobs, as described by this respondent:

**('James', 36, Belfast)**
Okay, the violence has stopped, or so they say. But the drug dealing, the punishment beatings, they all carried on. Worse than that is the sense you get now you're a stranger in your own country. I guess if I'm honest we did used to feel this was our country, but what's wrong with that? There's no shame in that. It wasn't like we felt it was ours but no-one else's, or at least I didn't. Now if I travel outside my own particular area I feel lost, I feel empty. I feel like a settler or something you know? I don't know how to describe it. It's a cultural thing. Our culture is vanishing, bit by bit. They stopped their violence, but they've just continued now to try and accomplish what they set out to do in the beginning, by another method. The funny thing is, the politics for them have been more successful. Everything is turning green. Even Belfast is now a republican city, in my view. It seems everyone in any job or position of seniority is not just Catholic, but openly nationalist or republican, and that they deliberately make mention of politics in your work or whatever. To me, that's very uncomfortable and clearly not right because as a unionist you know you're not allowed to say anything about how you feel about the past or the situation here, because you'll get labelled a bigot or sectarian and it just reinforces their notion that we were to blame for it all. It's very depressing. I know of countless of my Protestant friends who feel they are victimised in that new way, discriminated against, in their work because they're unionists. So I've thought about leaving here a lot, and so have they – in fact, a lot of them already have, just decided 'enough is enough'. I really want to go myself. I should have years ago, because in a way we all kind of knew how this was going to go. No-one had listened to us for 30 years, why would they start now? Unionist history is just like any other group that has been deemed to be the bad guys – so we get compared to white

South Africans, Serbians, Israelis, you name it. So yeah, the war by this new method is very effective, because it's driving us out by just making us feel like there's nothing in Northern Ireland for unionists anymore, and that you have no voice at all.

\*   \*   \*

If it is the case that the PIRA and Sinn Fein did not win their 'war' militarily, and certainly they would seem to concede as much themselves (though they are careful to stress that they did not lose it either), then they will surely re-double their efforts to ensure the 'struggle' achieves its aims some other way. That would be the natural political birth child of a failed insurrectionist campaign, and as ever, Sinn Fein and republicans have done little to hide their intentions. What, for example, of the PIRA member quoted by English (2003) who stated that it was his dream to see Ireland wiped clean of 'Orange bastards'? Unionists are surely entitled to wonder if this person – and the strand of thought for which he stands – has simply evaporated? Perhaps so, but republicans continue to openly agitate and strive for a united Ireland, a chimerical 32 county socialist Republic that is true to the fossilised ideals of 1916 (English, 2007). To do this, though, they must at least soften the edges of a history of violence that has now become – in the post-9/11 climate – as much of a hindrance as a help to the furtherance of this goal. Where once it was romanticised, terror is now taboo – this is especially the case in the USA, from where republicans glean a lot of financial and political support. Having wriggled free of the accusation that they were 'terrorists', to label the paramilitary protagonists in Northern Ireland anything other than their favoured and self-created title of 'ex-combatant' is now viewed as heretical by some. The supposed 'transformation' of Northern Ireland's terror groups means that there is a new vernacular and lexicon of the conflict, to which all must apparently subscribe or risk being labelled polemicists bent on re-asserting some draconian concept of unionist supremacy. It is an Orwellian state of affairs that demonstrates how the former men of violence – on both sides – are exerting their influence upon the historical debate, how such spurious semantic argument can seduce professional writers and scholars and how important taxonomy is in this war of ideas. It also demonstrates a profound lack of understanding of unionism, and ironically it grossly overstates the confidence of the unionist community. Unionists with whom I have spent considerable amounts of time do not feel that they have any significant support within the media, and consequently are comparatively unconcerned with trying to disseminate some kind of political 'message' by

proxy. The respondents in this research call the PIRA (and Loyalist terror groups) terrorists, for the most part, because that is what they believe
they were and what they remain, and because they are unafraid of doing
so. In many ways, and for many people, it is no more complicated than
that. If they use the word 'terrorist' conspicuously to assume or retain
the moral high ground, then they view this as their natural right (given
that they self-identify as law-abiding and innocent), rather than as a key
trope in a carefully formulated, community-wide discourse that is aimed
at dismantling a false historical orthodoxy.

Unionists, as this book has shown, have much to say about a lot
that took place, but are deeply frustrated and feel that they have no
forum in which to say it. This – for them – is transitional justice in
Northern Ireland (cf. Campbell and Ní Aoláin, 2003; Ní Aoláin and
Campbell, 2005). For unionists in this book, however, the voices of
the many are efficiently silenced by the political acumen of the few.
Given the rapidity and the texture of the transition in Northern Ireland
thus far, the potential for unionists to enter political, social and cultural quarantine is obvious (Humphrey, 2002). The creation of such a
peripheral, inescapable region of selfhood – both collective and individual – from where no counter-hegemonic stories can be inserted in the
'official' public recollection of the conflict would regrettably be consistent with the logic of formulating exclusionist master narratives of the
past (Simpson, 2007[a]). This, of course, would suit those in Northern
Ireland whose quest is for a process which 'stops' or 'ends' history, and
in its place seek to offer a singular, partisan, commoditised narrative
of the past which excludes all diversity and opposition. Even the kind
of detailed remembrance of unionists as outlined in this book would be
unable to punch through the impervious barriers of cultural and linguis-
tic oblivion (Augé, 2004). Indeed, the distortion of history in Northern
Ireland has in many ways relied on semantics and the reconfiguration
of language (Simpson, 2007[a]). The euphemisms of past violence have
become absolutely integral to a process of moral disengagement by
former terrorists. Indeed, euphemistic labelling is a deliberate and calculated process by which ex-paramilitaries internalise the legitimisation
of their illegal and criminal activities, and also a method by which they
can externalise and vocalise it at the macro-political level, where they
can use subtle (or not so subtle) shifts in the ongoing political discourse
to self-exonerate. Language in post-conflict societies shapes thought pat-
terns on which governments base their decisions, and also contributes
seamlessly to the processes of cultural estrangement to which unionists
in this research referred. Irish republicans, certainly as far as unionists

in this research are concerned, have cynically used euphemistic language to make their insupportable campaign of violence respectable, and also to relocate all individual responsibility for acts of murder, robbery, kidnapping assault and torture into a collective paradigm of remembrance. This paradigm frees those terrorists who each possessed personal agency and unleashed brutal acts upon their 'enemies' from any moral opprobrium, and instead frames such activity as a community 'struggle' against 'oppressors' in which a supposedly subjugated minority were forced to resort to violent means to secure equality and freedom from oppression (Shanahan, 2009). Despite being patently worthless logic, it has proved to have been a major success for Irish republicans, who have managed to ensure that for many, especially in their own community, the Troubles are now viewed as a liberation war against an occupying British force, and in which not a single member of the PIRA is held accountable for their actions, especially in relation to the malicious attacks on unionist civilians.

For politicians at the elite level intent on securing some ambiguously defined notion of peace at all costs in Northern Ireland, euphemistic labelling is also extremely useful. In re-creating a sanitised history, even the morally unpalatable activities of terrorists lose much of their repugnant potency. Post-conflict society is encouraged to view PIRA killings as part of a wider desire for freedom from the British, and as such rather than the terms 'murder', 'terror', 'torture' or 'attack', there are instead vacuous phrases such as 'targeted military operation'. Ex-paramilitaries have stolen the lexicon of legitimate, legal fighting forces and used it to their advantage. According to this new vernacular of the conflict, they were not murderers – they were volunteers or 'operatives', on duty and on a justified mission to shake off the shackles imposed by the British/unionist tyrannical administration (Toolis, 1996).

Unionists are dismayed by this and it is certainly no coincidence that after the Eames-Bradley public meetings the unionists with whom I spoke were furious, most of all, at the idea that the British Government would consent to the reclassification of the Northern Ireland conflict as a 'war' (with all of the concomitant legitimacy that would confer). Although the British Government seemed to initially panic, caught unaware by the strength of unionist feeling, it seems that it simply waited for the clamour to fade away, without any guarantee that some form of unscrupulous euphemistic labelling would occur, and which would once again mute the voices of unionist dissent. Expedient forms of comparative analysis with other geopolitical contexts in which armed resistance to actual tyranny and dictatorship (such as was directed against the Nazi Regime) has taken place and enforces the notion of historical exoneration by terrorists, who self-romanticise and liken themselves to heroic 'resistance movements'. Violent PIRA perpetrators and their supporters and apologists in Northern Ireland pointed to the alleged transgressions of previous Unionist governments as 'just cause' for armed, illegal, immoral insurrection and programmatic violence which was – as far as unionists were concerned – directed against civilians on the basis of their differing ethno-political background. Attributing constant blame to 'adversaries' underscores a weak structuralist argument that is used instrumentally by former terrorists to justify or excuse their actions (cf. White, 1992). Terrorists were victims of economic or social circumstance, they claim, and as such had no option but to become involved in the conflict in order that they might 'defend their people' or 'win cherished freedom for the Irish people'.

Within this framework, it is unionist victims who are re-traumatised, blamed for bringing despair and suffering on themselves because they were essentialised as active supporters of the security forces and all of the policies designed to halt PIRA violence. By concentrating the blame on the 'targets', ex-terrorists retrospectively legitimise their dastardly actions using the same logic that they did at the time of the crime – furthermore, in the current political climate in which former paramilitaries are celebrated as statesmen and bringers of peace, they have even begun not only to excuse their misdeeds but to become angrily self-righteous about their entitlement to pursue 'armed struggle' during the Northern Ireland conflict. Some unionists, especially unionist victims, have started to almost accept that this is the case. Trapped in a position of ontological and psychological insecurity, the sheer force of the political process and its associated outworkings has convinced some whom I spoke to that they were deserving the degradation to which they were subjected. By allowing if not sponsoring historical revisionism in which perpetrators of political violence can excuse themselves for their former acts, the British Government is permitting a distasteful and destructive narrative to emerge, and some of the unionist victims – because of this – have been bullied into submission by the glib, self-serving and unapologetic words of the terrorists who victimised them. Consequently, some unionist civilians have begun to articulate notions of self-contempt, and have blamed themselves for the tragedy that destroyed their lives. This, in turn, allows other disinterested unionists to hold victims in some form of contempt, viewing them as self-pitying. This is an explosive concoction of social and political phenomena that actually enables further, rather than lesser, mistreatment and marginalisation of the unionist civilian victims of the Northern Ireland Troubles. Unsure of whether or not they have the emotional fortitude to move towards telling their stories in the first place, the pernicious political wind of radical historical distortion has left many unionists feeling totally unable to verbalise their suffering (cf. Pillemer, 1998). The process of silencing has thus continued, as noted by this respondent:

**('Vicky', 45, County Armagh)**

You hear all the way things are going, with this truth and reconciliation and all, and you do start to think to yourself: were we to blame? Could we have done more? What did we do wrong? I know those are all ridiculous questions because we were law-abiding people that never wanted to do anyone any harm at all, and we got attacked for no reason, but the way the politics are now, it's like republicans and Sinn Fein are totally content with what they did. They have no remorse, they are certain what they did – in their twisted heads – was right. That does shake you, it gets you wondering: who is supporting us? Who is making our voices heard? I know some unionists are starting to speak out but I think now that we have devolution and Sinn Fein in government – though I accept that's better than the conflict – it's just going to be more of the same. They are gaining confidence all the time and the way the thing is now, there is no place for unionist stories or voices, they're totally silenced.

\*   \*   \*

To continue to silence people in this fashion is not only despicable, but it is also entirely undemocratic. It invites discontent, anger, despondency and disempowerment among a large section of the majority population in Northern Ireland. As noted in this book, however, some unionist respondents have *already alluded* to a scenario in which they feel regional and national policymakers will never listen to them, and that they have been consigned to total defeat in the battle for history. This is very discouraging for those who want to secure feasible stability for a new political dispensation in Northern Ireland, and threatens the prospects of ensuring any form of lasting consensus about the past between unionists and Irish republicans. The lessons that might be learned therefore are that the apparent appeasement of terrorism, political violence and its proponents – in all of their iterations, and even after the violence has finished – can lead, whatever the apparent short-term benefits, to a deeply unsettled state of historical affairs in the longer term (cf. Biggar, 2001). Some scholars are hopeful that recent legal developments in countries where victims experienced brutality and execution at the hands of autocratic, terrorist regimes – in Latin America and Spain for example – are important signs that there is a movement away from what I label the 'traditions of transition' (McEvoy, 2007). Such traditions have typically included forms of political and legal mimesis that facilitate expedient 'solutions' – masquerading as democratic state building – and are depressingly dystopian. These traditions have meant that all too often post-conflict regimes have merely selected elements that 'fit' their own geopolitical context from the conventional dealing with the past 'package', rather than devising new consensual dialogical mechanisms that ensure that all voices are heard. Seemingly bold steps that have witnessed the overturning of blanket amnesty laws, for example, (which were part of the grubby process of deal making during the 'handover' of power from fascist military juntas to 'democratic states', and that arguably should never have taken place in the first instance) which created a loathsome climate of impunity for perpetrators of human rights abuses in Argentina in particular, have been encouraging, but are yet to yield the sorts of results that render them effective critical processes of enabling all of the silenced to have their stories heard.

The latest example of a country struggling with empowering the previously oppressed and unheard is Spain (De Brito et al., 2001; Beevor, 2004). The decision of the Spanish government in the immediate post-Franco era to 'bury' the past (both metaphorically and literally) merely forced individual and collective memories and experiences of violence into interstitial, liminal social and cultural spaces. Such a strategy was viewed as the best method of effecting a rapid political transmutation from a right-wing dictatorship guilty of gross human rights crimes to an inviting tourist-friendly democracy (as it had been in the immediate aftermath of the Second World War in both West Germany and France) (Boyd, 2008). Discontent and grief, though, continued to rumble in the nation's collective subconscious. In 2006, after being confronted with a series of exhumations of the remains of those who were murdered and buried in mass graves by the terror squads of the Franco regime, the new socialist Spanish government, after much deliberation, announced its plans to formulate a new 'memory law' (Historical Memory Bill), which would ostensibly allow for a puncturing of the pretence of historical forgetting that had hung uneasily over Spanish society for nearly three decades (Ferrándiz, 2006). The Spanish are now committed (at least rhetorically) – after the law was passed in 2007 by the Spanish Parliament – to finding out more about what happened during the Franco era and deconstructing the apparatus of silence, no matter how 'destabilising' that might be in the short term. The current Spanish government has recognised that complete consensus on a process of remembering is all but impossible, as the right wrestles with its own complicity in systematic violations of acceptable moral codes. Zapareto, the incumbent left-wing Prime Minister and leader of the Spanish Socialists Workers' Party (PSOE), took the decision knowing the competing memory claims of the right (principally the Popular Party [PP]) and the left would potentially threaten his own position. While such an apparently brave decision might be commended, it is unclear how the initiative will eventually unfold and the idea that it might provide a template for Northern Ireland is misinformed and erroneous. There is no direct comparison at all with the Northern Ireland situation, and in any case the aims of the Spanish law are relatively modest, especially given Zapareto's pre-election commitment to ensure that complete justice would be secured for the victims of the Franco regime. They do not include demands for a truth process, for example, and the summary judgements that were dispensed by military tribunals during the Franco dictatorship have not been nullified, but instead declared 'illegitimate', which means that although those who were arbitrarily convicted of crimes against the state are exonerated, they are not entitled to automatic financial reparation. Rather, the onus is on them – many of them old people – to go to specially convened courts to make their case for recompense. This smacks of unwieldy political compromise as the 'two Spains', the left and the right, continue to struggle for historical supremacy and cater for their core supporters. Rather than tearing down the hideous symbolism of the Franco regime – most notably the 'Valley of the Fallen', a monument to the Francoist 'war dead' – the Zapareto administration has suggested that it be reconfigured so that it becomes a memorial to all the victims of the conflict in Spain, to which even the PP has agreed. This coheres with an absurd and reformulated master narrative of 'shared responsibility' dating back to the Spanish Civil War, thus failing to underline and illuminate the consequent misery inflicted by the Franco regime when it was in power, and more perniciously suggesting there is somehow some kind of equivalence between assassin or torturer and victim.

Some might lionise this as a pragmatic effort to address the past after years of censure, but presented with a chance to enable and empower victims, the traces of moral failure are regrettably all too evident, as the opportunity for widespread condemnation of a regime that some have estimated to have murdered up to 200,000 of its political opponents has been lost. It is not, therefore, recommended here in any way as a prototype for Northern Ireland. All of that criticism noted, the Spanish process does at least crucially provide each citizen with the right to 'personal and family memory'; and permits those who feel they were victimised for their political or cultural identity in the past to seek a 'Declaration of Reparations and Personal Recognition'. Local administrative units have also been ordered to facilitate the continued location and exhumation of those victims of the Franco regime who were executed and remain in hidden graves.

While the 'traditions of transition' – even those that are being refashioned – do not seem to provide unionists in Northern Ireland with the belief that their stories will be told publicly and their victimhood acknowledged, it is important to recognise therefore that it is *the moral principles* rather than the actual political outworkings (which are often tainted by elite-level negotiations) of any project of historical excavation that represent a key that can potentially unlock the customary barriers of dealing with the past and smash the legal architecture of transitions that have tended to obscure rather than illuminate historical wrongdoing. This is the extremely awkward truth that unionists feel the key political players in Northern Ireland do not want to confront. This is the spoke in the turning wheel of pre-determined reform. To give voice to it is to risk being regarded as a troublemaker, sifting through the emotional detritus of pain and grief in order to find something durable enough to oppose the pace and the content of political and cultural change.

Any advocate of such a critically oriented enterprise is often easily (yet totally erroneously) derided as an 'opponent of the peace process' by those seeking to maintain the status quo. Even worse, they risk being labelled part of an irrelevant, lunatic fringe – a bigoted relic of the 'bad old days'. This nefarious and constant compartmentalisation is partly why ordinary unionists are not comfortable articulating their stories. In many cases, people who spoke to me told me that they had approached their own unionist political representatives time and again and asked them to try and stop what they viewed as the apparently irresistible force of republican revisionism. Some, they said, were promised that detailed plans were in place to ensure the suffering of unionists would never be forgotten. Appallingly, others were simply thanked for their time and turned away, having been briefed that the realpolitik of the new political dispensation meant their stories were unwanted, and if anything posed a discrete threat to the delicate compromises that had been made at the highest political level. In Northern Ireland and beyond people are searching desperately hard for proof that the 'recipe' for peace can be replicated in other conflict zones; but if the silenced unionist voices in this book are anything to go by, they are searching in vain (cf. Samuel, 1996). All of the initiatives, including Eames-Bradley, that have been tasked with 'dealing with the past' are for unionists transmitting on the same frequency and rehearsing the same narrative – republican experience of state violence is *fact* and must be thoroughly investigated and commemorated, but unionist experience of terrorist victimisation is mere *perception*.

The notion that no one side can 'win', or has won, is arguably the essence of diplomatic political–legal fudge rather than the reality of successful conflict resolution. Unionists in this research argued that violence has won in forcing negotiations with terrorists. Many believe that it will win again, until such times as the British and Irish governments are prepared to adopt a universal moral bottom line that states clearly and unambiguously that in the absence of a complete cessation of terrorist activity and a retributive or restorative truth process founded on sound legal and moral principles rather than political expediency, there will be complete refusal to engage with or amnesty those who have perpetrated acts of illegal political violence. For his suggestion that the British Government will or should one day negotiate with Al-Qaeda, the British media and the British Government ferociously lambasted Sir Hugh Orde, the Chief Constable of the Police Service of Northern Ireland (PSNI). Yet if Orde made his calculations on his experiences in Northern Ireland, then his logic was flawless, and the condemnation of politicians was predictably hollow and nonsensical. Regardless of how this moral dilemma of dealing with violent agents of terror is dressed up, the fudge that has been evident in Northern Ireland has become the very sustenance of the post-conflict government. It has traded feverishly in search of deals (that cement isolated locales of influence) on the basis of the confidence it has acquired that the discordant tones of the disenchanted have been effectively muffled. Many ordinary unionists in this research believe that some of those charged with leadership have become bedazzled by power and its attendant privileges.

If challenged, as noted previously, the new Northern Ireland regime points to its universally lauded success, but this is a gag that mutes the unwelcome noise of dissent that is crucial to any democracy (Lapham, 2005). Many believe that the politicians in the unionist community have failed their people. They have failed to reach ordinary unionist civilians and reassure them that the place in history of all those who endured protracted misery will be recognised. Though unionist politicians now gladly work the levers of governmental power in co-operation with their former political opponents, there has been no 'happily ever after' for those who were victimised during the conflict, and who continue to suffer and struggle with their memories of the past. This must be addressed, and as one respondent argued:

### ('Tom', 41, County Down)

It's okay for them, sitting up in government, getting big fat salaries – but what about us? To even say you are a unionist now is getting more and more difficult. The UUP and then the DUP, they all promised us great things, but they never deliver. What we're saying now is, if it's going to be a united Ireland or even if Northern Ireland is going to be dominated by republicans – and it certainly appears that is going to be the case – then let us at least get our version of history written down, get it out there. Let people know. It's urgent, it really is. Yet the unionist parties, they don't seem to be doing anything about this. We hear about these initiatives for dealing with the past and all of a sudden a unionist is on the TV shouting about how it's not right and 'his people' won't stand for it, or they say nothing at all. So how do they know what we want? When do they listen to the ordinary unionist and what they have to say? Since this Eames-Bradley thing, and the Victims' Commissioners, they've done nothing. They're not pro-active at all.

They haven't come up with their own plans for any sort of dealing with the past programme. If I had a chance what I would say is 'let us tell our stories'. That's all we want. Find a way to let us do that that doesn't mean we have to accept that terrorists were just the same as us and have the same rights as those poor innocent people they murdered during the conflict. They don't, and we'll never accept that. Never. We've had to accept them in government, their prisoners getting out, their supposed decommissioning, all of that, and we have done. But this is our Alamo, I really think that. If they don't let unionist people tell their stories now, and find a way of getting some sort of truth process, then they are really storing up trouble for themselves. They can go off all around the world telling everyone how they sorted the conflict out, but of they don't let unionists speak soon, the same old thing will happen – the settlement will fall apart. A new unionist party will emerge that will say 'no', and it will promise these forgotten people what they want. The DUP will be knocked off its perch just the way the UUP was. They don't learn their lesson. They can't – just can't – ignore the ordinary unionist people and expect to carry on getting support. Politically, it's a catastrophe, and morally it's disgraceful. We do need a truth process, but it has to be one that will allow unionist voices to come out and be heard and not another thing in which we get blamed and we have to agree to give ex-terrorists amnesty just for them to even get involved.

## Truth and the politics of remembering the past

The stories in this book show that for unionists, the memory 'process' has been drastically stultified, and that the articulation of personal narratives has been disbarred firstly by the dynamics of the conflict, and latterly by the political and historical demands of the 'conflict about the conflict'. Without any sense of memory – that is, the actualisation of symbolic or mnemonic practices, memorialisation and storytelling – unionists are denied a framework via which they can locate themselves in time and space, and are unable to make sense of their current feelings of cultural and emotional dislocation (Olick, 2007). Consequently, they feel rather hopeless about the future, consigned to the margins of social and political activity. Some fear that if they are not *actively* persecuted in terms of their total inability to express and remember their suffering and their truth, they will be the *passive victims* of an 'official' history of the past in Northern Ireland which identifies them as caricatured villains. They need to be offered sufficient opportunity to actively fashion and configure their memories through dialogue and a process of public 'telling', and allowed to reconstruct some sort of selfhood from the fractured experience of the Troubles.

The idea of the republican master narrative, in its most politicised and partisan form, that unionists were to blame – or more likely the subtle continuance of a paradigm of remembrance in which innocent unionist civilians are forced to concede that the conflict was one of 'co-responsibility' in which 'all were guilty' (which for unionists – especially victims of terrorism – is a reprehensible notion) – is a very dangerous form of active forgetting and historical distortion. If unionist politicians sign up to this 'pact of oblivion' – arguing that sealing off the past is a better way to deal with the political present – the transition to ostensibly workable democracy will be facilitated. The moral imperative to recount and recall the past as it was, though, will be surrendered.

As unionists have indicated throughout this book, such a strategy would not be acceptable to them; furthermore, to 'wipe' a group from history in the apparent pursuit of a synthetic form of democracy built on lies, manipulations and mistruths would be a catastrophic means of 'solving' any conflict. The revision of official memory so that it includes all of the individual memories that were previously muted is a crucial aspect of reconciliation and the creation of a genuinely democratic system. The politics of remembering the past in Northern Ireland should not hinge upon the ability of politicians to repress unionists' recollections of the past, or on enforced collective amnesia. This 'disremembering' could only damage any democracy that it would be designed to fortify (Boyd, 2008).

It is also clear from the evidence of this book that the politics of remembering the past in Northern Ireland now demand that unionist voices be heard. The key question is thus: how best to ensure that this happens, and that it happens in a timely and efficacious fashion? The priority for those within the main unionist political parties and the British government – to whom ordinary unionists still turn to for support despite their criticisms – should be to build trust in the unionist community via the construction and implementation of a process of morally normative and dialogical truth recovery, so that all of those unionists who self-identify as victims of the conflict can be afforded the chance to narrate their stories publicly, even if those do not cohere with the prevailing political atmosphere (Simpson, 2007[b]; Simpson, 2009). While such trust might not be viewed as politically necessary by instrumentalist power-brokers, truth is a crucial demand of all of the unionists I have spoken to.

Without the required sensitivity from the British government in particular, unionist narratives of the past will in all likelihood remain unaired and unknown, except within the homogenised 'quarantine' of their own community (Humphrey, 2002; 2005). This will make the politics of remembering the past in Northern Ireland potentially chaotic, disruptive and all but impossible (cf. Biggar, 2001). It should be noted, as has been evidenced throughout this book, that unionists are firmly opposed to forms of moral relativism and equivalence in which perpetrators of political violence would be afforded equal status with victims (cf. Moser and Carson, 2000). At this stage of the transition, such an idea remains particularly unpalatable for the majority of unionist civilians, and it is therefore highly problematic for them – as noted earlier – that one of the four Victims' Commissioners in Northern Ireland had a brother who was an active member of the PIRA (Borradori, 2004; Simpson, 2007[a]). Although unionist participation in any project that seeks to deal with the past might appear highly conditional, however, it is still nonetheless feasible.

From the research that I have conducted it is apparent that one of the main problems for unionists is that they now fear that 'their past' is in danger of being obliterated (Caruth, 1996). Many have told me that they are convinced that the political rhetoric surrounding dealing with the past is a malicious effort to blame unionists for the conflict and to 'demonise' those in their community who were killed during the Troubles; worse still, some view it as a project of dangerous palingenesis by their political opponents. One of the most difficult and unsettling aspects of this process for unionists is the idea that Protestant civilian victims of the conflict – 'all of the lost souls' as one unionist put it to me during my research – will be 'forever forgotten'. For many unionists, history is now of fundamental importance. Widows, husbands, siblings, sons and daughters – indeed all those who yearn for a dead loved one – are terrified that their stories will be denied, degraded or ignored (cf. Felman and Laub, 1992). Many simply long for what one respondent told me was: 'just a name and a place in history'. Given the scriptural focus of much of Ulster Protestantism, it is not surprising that this desire has biblical significance – most notably, the Old Testament Book of Isaiah, chapter 26, verse 5: 'And even unto them will I give in mine house and within my walls a place and a name better than of sons and of daughters: I will give them an everlasting name, that shall not be cut off'.

Yet this objective, to 'just be remembered', cannot be satiated in the current political climate in Northern Ireland. This is because the union-ists with whom I have conducted research have told me that they believe there has been a sustained and deliberate attempt by Irish republi-cans to destroy their cherished individual and collective memories; and concurrently a legitimisation of the vicious activities of those whom they regard as 'evil'. In many unionist households and in many other contexts, I have observed first hand scenes of extreme pathos as aged women (and men too), some of whom have been widowed longer than they were married, dust and polish with pride decades-old photos of husbands or sons 'as they once were'; others tend to graves fastidiously and routinely, a curious mixture of retrospective pride and crushing sorrow. Parents of those who loved and lost congregate in graveyards, sombre and silent, totally unable to comprehend the sheer senseless-ness of their loss (Kristeva, 1982; Caruth, 1995; Huyssen, 1995). Those who were killed are frozen in time – age has not wearied them – but their departure is felt with aching and agonising pain on a daily basis by those left behind, some of whom struggle to simply 'get through' each day. Of course the phenomenology of grief is not particular to Northern Ireland, or to unionists there, but the notion that they should be dis-allowed – in the interests of social and political 'closure' – the right to mourn and to ask searching questions of those who inflicted misery is both unjust and absolutely inimical to any form of political, social or cultural compassion (Ricoeur, 2004).

Furthermore, the notion of unconditional amnesty for those who committed acts of political violence in exchange for truth-telling is – as far as unionists are concerned – simply morally and politically impossible. The dissonance between the realities of post-conflict politics in Northern Ireland and such individualistic, micro-level acts could not be more emphatic. Many unionists are trapped at a point of trauma – a disastrous moment of despair in their personal history – and the idea that they can be forced to relinquish these acts of commemoration in the name of the 'greater good', which translates to many unionist as political expediency, is deeply unethical (cf. Caruth, 1995; Pillemer, 1998). Yet an overwhelming number of those unionists with whom I have spoken hope that some method of facing the past can be found that will reassure them that they will not be 'wiped out' of history, and that their sacrifice was not wasted. This is not a complete rejection of confronting the legacy of the conflict in Northern Ireland. Encouragingly, therefore, unionists are not opposed to truth recovery as an idea. Rather, they are concerned that in its current form, it will result in the creation of a distorted, synthetic version of history that they feel they cannot accept. Lacking clear leadership at the top political level, unionists in the course of my research have issued a clear and loud call to the British government, and all those who desire lasting peace in Northern Ireland, to help bring silenced unionist voices in from the political wilderness, and to 'remember all the lost souls'.

Much of the testimony in this book has been stark, and in places the tone is unmistakably angry and also despairing. It is also reflective of the way many of the victims of brutal republican paramilitary attacks attempt to make sense of the past. Furthermore, it is indicative of the way that many sections of the wider unionist community with whom I have spoken feel. The stories in this book are high-profile examples of what unionists believe is a widespread social and political phenomenon – namely, their marginalisation and the refusal of the British and Irish governments and Irish republicans to accept that unionists were often *innocent victims of the conflict in Northern Ireland*. The repetition of this phrase in variant forms penetrates all of the unionist stories that I have provided in this book. I have collected many, many more that hinge on that same phrase. If there is a 'hierarchy of victimhood', in which unionists still regard former RUC and UDR personnel as innocent victims while nationalists and republicans do not – and this is, in the majority of cases, true – then that debate should be postponed until a point has been reached where sufficient confidence-building has taken place among unionists. It is they who historically have felt alienated and isolated from the very idea of truth recovery.

If all parties involved in the politics of remembering the past can demonstrate good faith by accepting, without reservation, the condemnation of *all illegal paramilitary activity perpetrated against civilians* during the conflict it stands as a clear symbol of a moral commitment to truth (Simpson, 2007[b]; Borradori, 2004). Unionists fear and resistance of becoming involved in projects of dealing with the past that they feel will not acknowledge their suffering can at least in part be ameliorated by this sort of strategic political move. Unionists will not and cannot, however, subscribe to a process that does not include in some form a morally normative framework that renders the killing of civilians as irrefutably wrong, or one which seeks to muffle their attempts to speak of atrocities carried out against innocent civilians (cf. Habermas, quoted in Borradori, 2004). In seeking to better comprehend unionism, therefore, Northern Ireland as a society is provided with greater potential for effectively mastering its violent past.

As these anthropologies 'of the near' become increasingly important, the need for a close-up examination of this unheard community has arguably never been more pressing (Augé, 1995). Even as someone indigenous to Northern Ireland, however, this ethnology of mine presupposes, as all do, the 'authentic' witnessing of actualised and remembered experience (Bloch, 1998). Accessing that experience was methodologically difficult, undeniably, and in this research odyssey I was certainly confronted with many problems – not least gaining the trust of those with whom I spoke. As noted, the charge of naïvety cannot be ignored, and while I believe I have addressed that issue capably, it is worth noting that research respondents, as Augé (1995: 9) noted, often 'tell us less about the past than what he knows he thinks about the past'. All of these caveats aside, there are practical political imperatives for taking note of the findings of this research. Unionists are still something of an unknown entity, but they form the majority of the population in a post-conflict locale that is now being used (in an unseemly hasty fashion) as a paradigmatic example of conflict resolution throughout the world. This notion of Northern Ireland's transferability is founded upon a temporal error (Ricoeur, 1984) – that is, the idea that since there has been ostensible peace in Northern Ireland for a decade, its transition is complete. As the extracts throughout this book have shown, however, that is demonstrably not the case. Conflicts that last for 40 years cannot be 'forgotten' (much as governments and the unaffected might like them to) in 10 years.

The legacy of violence is arguably more lasting than its perpetration. It leaves in its wake political, cultural, emotional and psychological detritus – fragments of a cohesive society, and in metaphorical terms, victims as fragments of their former selves (Torpey, 2001; 2003). This cannot be simply ignored. The quest and the struggle for truth is the key element in an effective post-conflict settlement in Northern Ireland, yet for all the macro-level initiatives, it is being trivialised and side-lined, not least because unionists feel that their collective and individual voices are not being heard. It could be the case that a politically feasible (though ideologically dysfunctional) inter-group political dispensation – such as that which currently exists between the DUP and Sinn Fein – could continue to function at the macro level for a period of time without any serious attempt to confront or master the past. That, unfortunately, is the nature of elite-level deals that purport to have 'resolved the conflict'. However, for all the reasons noted in this book, it is absolutely crucial to re-emphasise the point that the micro-level hyper-individuated perspectives of unionists are fundamental to any effort to resolve the Northern Ireland conflict and solidify workable democracy.

In this book, the respondents' accounts say as much about the present as they do about the past, and as ethnographers and as citizens, we are in the privileged position of being contemporary with both the narrative and the narrator. There is a myriad of intersecting and interpenetrating phenomena that can arise from such stories which remain obliterated from what has become a sanitised and manufactured history of Northern Ireland. Government, politicians, policy-makers and crucially, the citizenry must attempt to piece together a cosmology of meaning in Northern Ireland that is reflective of competing perceptions, and not the vaguely Orwellian impositions to which unionists in particular feel they have been subjected (and expected to subscribe to). The 'near contemporaneousness' of violence in Northern Ireland means that there have been shifting centres of interest, but as has been argued, those centres have rarely shifted to ordinary unionist civilians. What is therefore required is a political anthropology of the here and now with regard to unionism, but which also factors in episodes of memory and the past.

For this reason, an inventory of accounts of suffering is required, lest terrorist violence be erased from history, with the perpetrators venerated as 'successful revolutionaries' and the victims demonised as integral parts of the discriminatory machinery of an oppressive regime. This inventory, though, must not be a grand narrative established by political elites. The new social order in Northern Ireland must begin with the individual. The idea of essentialised government-sponsored totality of political memory in Northern Ireland mutilates the notion of the centrality of the individual and continues the regrettable process of 'othering' unionist as a monolithic population. Unionists distrust absolutist and restrictive ideas of collective identity – they have already been falsely homogenised from outside the barriers of their own communities (Rae, 2002). This has allowed their voices to be silenced (Donnan and Simpson, 2007). Of course, unionist individuals will express political memory from a particular angle – as noted there is no suggestion here that in the mere re-telling of past suffering the veracity of any account can be measured. To paraphrase Pierre Nora, unionists need to decipher what and who they are in the context of what they are no longer (Nora, 1984). It is an extremely poor reflection of the condition of the politics of remembering the past in Northern Ireland, however, that they feel that they have not been given this opportunity. Unionists need to give meaning to the consequences of what was an overabundance of traumatic events and the resultant narratives can offer a chance to provide this, if they are given the political space to be articulated.

Post-conflict Northern Ireland is apparently united in its supposedly new and shared political diversity, but the evidence of this book suggests that the unionist universe of political memory is increasingly discordant with the tone of the new arrangements, and consequently increasingly marginalised and silenced. Large sections of the unionist community have found themselves in a politically anthropological 'non-place', their narratives becoming subterranean and absurdly, regarded as somewhat subversive because they do not cohere with the texture of memory as dictated by Irish republicans and transitional power-brokers. For peace to last in Northern Ireland, and for genuine and effective truth recovery to take place, governments, politicians and citizens must allow for the individual and collective production and articulation of memory from within the unionist community. This book has been an attempt to make that point in a way that is divorced from polemic and partisan arguments, and which has focussed instead on allowing the reader to access previously silenced or unknown narratives of the past (cf. Trouillot, 1995; West, 2003). In that way, it is hoped that not only has this proved a worthy project for that very reason, but also that it has contributed towards furthering the debate about the politics of the past in Northern Ireland that allows more nuanced understandings of individual unionist perspectives to emerge.

# References

Abell, J., Stokoe, E. and Billig, M. (2004) 'Narrative and the Discursive (Re)construction of Events'. In *The Uses of Narrative*, Andrews, M.D., Sclater, S.D., Squire, C. and Treacher, A. (eds). London: Routledge.

Adams, G. (2001) *Before the Dawn: An Autobiography*. County Kerry, Ireland: Mount Eagle Publications.

Adams, G. (2004) *Hope and History: Making Peace in Ireland*. County Kerry, Ireland: Mount Eagle Publications.

Alonso, R. (2006) *The IRA and Armed Struggle*. London: Routledge.

Amstutz, M. (2004) *The Healing of Nations: The Promise and Limits of Political Forgiveness*. London: Rowman and Littlefield.

Anderson, B. (1991) *Imagined Communities: Reflections on the Origin and Spread of Nationalism*. London: Verso.

Anderson, C. (2004) *The Billy Boy: The Life and Death of LVF Leader Billy Wright*. Edinburgh: Mainstream Publishing.

Anderson, J. and Shuttleworth, I. (1998) 'Sectarian Demography, Territoriality and Political Development in Northern Ireland'. *Political Geography*, 17(2): 187–208.

Andrews, M.D., Sclater, S.D., Squire, C. and Treacher, A. (eds) (2000) *The Uses of Narrative*. London: Routledge.

Ankersmit, F.R. (2002) Historical Representation (Cultural Memory in the Present). Stanford: Stanford University Press.

Antze, P. and Lambek, M. (eds) (1996) *Tense Past: Cultural Essays in Trauma and Memory*. London: Routledge.

Appy, C.G. (2006) *Vietnam: The Definitive Oral History, Told from All Sides*. London: Ebury Press.

Augé, M. (1995) *Non-places: Introduction to an Anthropology of Supermodernity*. London: Verso.

Augé, M. (2004) *Oblivion*. Minnesota: University of Minnesota Press.

Bal, M. (1999) *Acts of Memory: Cultural Recall in the Present*. Dartmouth: Dartmouth College Press.

Balfour, L. (2005) 'Reparations after Identity Politics'. *Political Theory*, 33(6): 786–811.

Bandes, S. (2000) 'When Victims Seek Closure'. *Fordham Urban Law Journal*, 27: 1599.

Bar-On, D. (1999) *The Indescribable and the Undiscussable: Reconstructing Human Discourse after Trauma*. Budapest: Central European University Press.

Bass, G.J. (2000) *Stay the Hand of Vengeance: The Politics of War Crimes Tribunals*. Princeton: Princeton University Press.

Beattie, G. (1992) *We Are the People: Journeys through the Heart of Protestant Ulster*. London: Heinemann.

Beattie, G. (2004) *Protestant Boy*. London: Granta.

Beevor, A. (2004) *The Battle for Spain: The Spanish Civil War 1936–1939*. London: Cassell.

Bell, C. (2003) 'Dealing with the Past in Northern Ireland'. *Fordham International Law Journal*, 26(4): 1095–1148.

Bell, C. (2004) *Peace Agreements and Human Rights*. (2nd edition). Oxford: Oxford University Press.

Bell, D. (2003) 'Mythscapes: Memory, Mythology, and National Identity'. *British Journal of Sociology*, 54(1): 63–81.

Bell, D. (2006) *Memory, Trauma and World Politics: Reflections on the Relationship between Past and Present*. London: Palgrave Macmillan.

Bevan, R. (2007) *The Destruction of Memory: Architecture at War*. Chicago: University of Chicago Press.

Bew, P. and Gillespie, G. (1999) *Northern Ireland: A Chronology, 1968–1999*. Dublin: Gill and Macmillan.

Bew, P., Gibbon, P. and Patterson, H. (2001) *Northern Ireland: 1921–2001*. (2nd edition). London: Serif.

Biggar, N. (ed.) (2001) *Burying the Past: Making Peace and Doing Justice after Civil Conflict*. Washington, DC: Georgetown University Press.

Bloch, M. (1998) 'Autobiographical Memory and the Historical Memory of the More Distant Past'. In *How We Think They Think: Anthropological Approaches to Cognition, Memory and Literacy*, 114–127. Bloch, M. (ed.). Boulder: Westview Press.

Boltanski, L. (1999) *Distant Suffering: Morality, Media and Politics*. Cambridge: Cambridge University Press.

Booth, W.J. (2001) 'The Unforgotten: Memories of Justice'. *American Political Science Review*, 95: 777–791.

Borneman, J. (1997) *Settling Accounts: Violence, Justice and Accountability in Postsocialist Europe*. Princeton: Princeton University Press.

Borradori, G. (2004) *Philosophy in a Time of Terror: Dialogues with Jurgen Habermas and Jacques Derrida*. Chicago: University of Chicago Press.

Boyarin, D. (1995) *Remapping Memory: The Politics of Timespace*. Minnesota: University of Minnesota Press.

Boyd, C.P. (2008) 'The Politics of History and Memory in Democratic Spain'. *The Annals of the American Academy of Political and Social Science*, 617(1): 133–148.

Boym, S. (2001) *The Future of Nostalgia*. New York: Basic Books.

British Broadcasting Corporation (BBC). 'Anger at Idea Troubles Was a War', available at http://news.bbc.co.uk/1/hi/northern_ireland/7176271.stm, last accessed January 2009.

Brown, C. (1991) *Human Rights and the Politics of Agreement: Chile during President Alwyn's First Year*. New York: Americas Watch.

Brubaker, R. and Cooper, F. (2000) 'Beyond Identity'. *Theory and Society*, 29(1): 1–47.

Bruce, S. (1994) *The Edge of the Union: The Ulster Loyalist Political Vision*. Oxford: Oxford University Press.

Bruce, S. (2007) *Paisley: Religion and Politics in Northern Ireland*. Oxford: Oxford University Press.

Bryan, D. (2000) *Orange Parades: The Politics of Ritual, Tradition and Control*. London: Pluto Press.

Buckland, P. (1981) *A History of Northern Ireland*. Dublin: Gill and Macmillan.

Burleigh, M. (2007) *Sacred Causes: Religion and Politics from the European Dictators to Al Qaeda*. London: Harper.

Burleigh, M. (2008) *Blood and Rage: A Cultural History of Terrorism*. London: Harper.

CAIN Web Service (Conflict Archive on the Internet), University of Ulster. (2009) Available online at http://cain.ulst.ac.uk.

Campbell, C. and Connolly, I. (2006) 'Making War on Terror? Global Lessons from Northern Ireland'. *Modern Law Review*, 69(6): 935–957.

Campbell, C. and Ní Aoláin, F. (2003) 'Local Meets Global: Transitional Justice in Northern Ireland'. *Fordham International Law Journal*, 26(4): 871–893.

Cappelletto, F. (2003) 'Long-term Memory of Extreme Events: From Autobiography to History'. *Journal of Royal Anthropological Institute*, 9: 241–260.

Caruth, C. (1995) *Trauma: Explorations in Memory*. Baltimore: Johns Hopkins University Press.

Caruth, C. (1996) *Unclaimed Experience: Trauma, Narrative and History*. Baltimore: Johns Hopkins University Press.

Chieza, L. (2007) *Subjectivity and Otherness: A Philosophical Reading of Lacan*. Boston, MA: MIT Press.

Coogan, T. (2002) *The IRA*. London: Harper Collins.

Crawford, C. (2003) *Inside the UDA: Volunteers and Violence – The Ulster Defence Association, 1971–2003*. London: Pluto Press.

Crawford, R.G. (1987) *Loyal to King Billy: A Portrait of the Ulster Protestants*. Dublin: Gill and Macmillan.

Crossley, M. (2000) *Introducing Narrative Psychology: Self, Trauma and the Construction of Meaning*. Buckinghamshire: Open University Press.

Cubitt, G. (2007) *History and Memory*. Manchester: Manchester University Press.

Cunningham, M. (2001) *British Policy in Northern Ireland 1969–2000*. Manchester: Manchester University Press.

Daniel, E. Valentine (1996) *Charred Lullabies: Chapters in an Anthropology of Violence*. Princeton: Princeton University Press.

Das, V., Kleiman, A., Lock, M., Ramphele, M. and Reynolds, P. (eds) (2000) *Violence and Subjectivity*. Berkeley: University of California Press.

Das, V., Kleiman, A., Lock, M., Ramphele, M. and Reynolds, P. (eds) (2001) *Remaking a World: Violence, Social Suffering, and Recovery*. Berkeley: University of California Press.

Dawson, G. (2003) 'Mobilising Memories: Protestant and Unionist Victims' Groups and the Politics of Victimhood in the Irish Peace Process'. In *Political Transition: Politics and Cultures*, Gready, P. (ed.). London: Pluto Press.

Dawson, G. (2007) *Making Peace with the Past: Memories, Trauma and the Irish Troubles*. Manchester: Manchester University Press.

De Brito, A., Gonzalez-Enriquez, C. and Aguilar, P. (2001) *The Politics of Memory: Transitional Justice in Democratizing Societies*. Oxford: Oxford University Press.

Dewar, M. (1997) *British Army in Northern Ireland*. London: Weidenfeld and Nicolson.

Dillon, M. (1989) *The Shankill Butchers*. London: Hutchinson.

Dillon, M. (1991) *The Dirty War*. London: Arrow Books.

Dillon, M. (1996) *Twenty Five Years of Terror: The IRA's War against the British*. London: Bantam.

Dingley, J. (1998) 'A Reply to White's Non-Sectarian Thesis of PIRA Targeting'. *Terrorism and Political Violence*, 10(2): 106–117.

Dixon, P. (2001) 'British Policy towards Northern Ireland 1969–2000: Continuity, Tactical Adjustment and Consistent "Inconsistencies" '. *Journal of Politics and International Relations*, 3(3): 340–368.

Donnan, H. (2005) 'Material Identities: Fixing Ethnicity in the Irish Borderlands'. *Identities: Global Studies in Culture and Power*, 12(1): 69–105.

Donnan, H. and Simpson, K. (2007) 'Silence and Violence among Northern Ireland Border Protestants'. *Ethnos*, 72(1): 5–28.

Douglass, A. and Vogler, T.A. (2003) *Witness and Memory: The Discourse of Trauma*. London: Routledge.

Dudley-Edwards, R. (1999) *The Faithful Tribe*. London: Harper Collins.

Edkins, J. (2003) *Trauma and the Memory of Politics*. Cambridge: Cambridge University Press.

Elster, J. (1998) 'Coming to Terms with the Past'. *European Journal of Sociology*, 39: 7–48.

English, R. (2003) *Armed Struggle: A History of the IRA*. London: Macmillan.

English, R. (2007) *Irish Freedom: The History of Nationalism in Ireland*. London: Pan.

Enselaco, M. (1994) 'Truth Commissions for Chile and El Salvador: A Report and Assessment'. *Human Rights Quarterly*, 16(4): 656–675.

Enselaco, M. (1999) *Chile under Pinochet: Recovering* the Truth. Pennsylvania: University of Pennsylvania Press.

Families Acting for Innocent Relatives (FAIR), available at www.victims.org.uk/news.html, last accessed January 2009.

Farrell, M. (1980) *Northern Ireland: The Orange State*. London: Pluto Press.

Farrington, C. (2006) 'Unionism and the Peace Process'. *British Journal of Political and International Relations*, 8(2): 277–294.

Feeney, B. (2002) *Sinn Fein: A Hundred Turbulent Years*. Dublin: O'Brien Press.

Feldman, A. (2004) 'Memory Theatres, Virtual Witnessing, and the Trauma-Aesthetic'. *Biography*, 27(1): 163–202.

Felman, S. and Laub, D. (1992) *Testimony: Crises of Witnessing in Literature, Psychoanalysis and History*. London and New York: Routledge.

Fentress, J. and Wickham, C. (1992) *Social Memory*. Oxford: Blackwell.

Ferguson, N. (2006) *The War of the World*. London: Penguin.

Ferrándiz, F. (2006) 'The Return of Civil War Ghosts: The Ethnography of Exhumations in Contemporary Spain'. *Anthropology Today*, 22(3): 7–13.

Fink, B. (1995) *The Lacanian Subject*. Princeton: Princeton University Press.

Foster, R.F. (1990) *Modern Ireland, 1600–1972*. London: Penguin.

Ganiel, G. (2006) 'Ulster Says Maybe: The Restructuring of Evangelical Politics in Northern Ireland'. *Irish Political Studies*, 21(2): 137–155.

Gillespie, G. (2001) 'Loyalists since 1972'. In *Defenders of the Union: A Survey of British and Irish Unionism since 1801*, Boyce, G.D. and O'Day, A. (eds). London: Routledge.

Gillis, J. (ed.) (1996) *Commemoration: The Politics of National Identity*. Princeton: Princeton University Press.

Goffman, E. (1990) *The Presentation of Self in Everyday Life*. London: Penguin.

Gordon, A. (1997) *Ghostly Matters: Haunting and the Sociological Imagination*. Minnesota: University of Minnesota Press.

Graham, B. and Shirlow, P. (2002) 'The Battle of the Somme in Ulster Memory and Identity'. *Political Geography*, 21(7): 881–904.

Grandin, G. (2006) 'The Instruction of Great Catastrophe: Truth Commissions, National History and State Formation in Argentina, Chile and Guatemala'. *The American Historical Review*, 110(1): 46–68.

Grayling, A.C. (2007) *Among the Dead Cities: Is the Targeting of Civilians in War Ever Justified?* London: Bloomsbury.

Habermas, J. (1984) *The Theory of Communicative Action (English) – Vol. 1: Reason and the Rationalization of Society*. London: Heinemann.

Habermas, J. (1990) 'Discourse Ethics: Notes on Philosophical Justification'. In *Moral Consciousness and Communicative Action*, 43–115. Cambridge, MA: MIT Press.

Habermas, J. (1996) *Between Facts and Norms: Contributions to a Discourse Theory of Law and Democracy*. Cambridge, MA: MIT Press.

Halbwachs, M. (1992) *On Collective Memory*. Chicago: University of Chicago Press.

Hamber, B. and Wilson, R. (2002) 'Symbolic Closure through Memory, Reparation and Revenge in Post-Conflict Societies'. *Journal of Human Rights*, 1(1): 35–53.

Harnden, T. (1999) *Bandit Country: The IRA and South Armagh*. London: Hodder and Stoughton.

Hass, K. (1998) *Carried to the Wall: American Memory and the Vietnam Veterans Memorial*. Berkeley: University of California Press.

Hastrup, K. (2003) 'Violence, Suffering and Human Rights: Anthropological Reflections'. *Anthropological Theory*, 3: 309–323.

Hayner, P.B. (2001) *Unspeakable Truths: Confronting State Terror and Atrocity*. New York: Routledge.

Hegarty, A. (2003) 'The Government of Memory: Public Inquiries and the Limits of Justice in Northern Ireland'. *Fordham International Law Journal*, 26(4): 1148–1193.

Held, V. (2008) *How Terrorism Is Wrong: Morality and Political Violence*. New York: Oxford University Press.

Hennessey, T. (1997) *A History of Northern Ireland, 1920–1996*. Dublin: Gill and Macmillan.

Hinton, A. (ed.) (2002) *Annihilating Difference: The Anthropology of Genocide*. Berkeley: University of California Press.

Holland, J. and McDonald, H. (1994) *INLA: Deadly Divisions*. Dublin: Poolbeg.

Hoskins, A. (2004) 'Television and the Collapse of Memory'. *Time and Society*, 13(1): 109–127.

Hoskins, A. and O'Laughlin, B. (2007) *Television and Terror: Conflicting Times and the Crisis of News Discourse*. Basingstoke: Palgrave Macmillan.

Hughes, M. (1994) *Ireland Divided*. Wales: University of Wales Press.

Humphrey, M. (2002) *The Politics of Atrocity and Reconciliation: From Terror to Trauma*. London: Routledge.

Humphrey, M. (2003) 'From Victim to Victimhood: Truth Commissions and Trials as Rituals of Political Transition and Individual Healing'. *Australian Journal of Anthropology*, 14: 171–187.

Humphrey, M. (2005) 'Reconciliation and the Therapeutic State'. *Journal of Intercultural Studies*, 26(3): 203–220.

Huyssen, A. (1995) *Twilight Memories: Marking Time in a Culture of Amnesia*. New York: Routledge.

Huyssen, A. (2003) *Present Pasts: Urban Palimpsests and the Politics of Memory (Cultural Memory in the Present)*. Stanford: Stanford University Press.

Irwin-Zarecka, I. (1994) *Frames of Remembrance: The Dynamics of Collective Memory*. New Brunswick: Transaction Books.

Jackson, M. (2002) *The Politics of Storytelling: Violence, Transgression and Intersubjectivity*. Copenhagen: Museum Tusculanum Press.

Jamieson, R. and McEvoy, K. (2005) 'State Crime by Proxy and Judicial Othering'. *British Journal of Criminology*, 45(4): 504–527.

Jarman, N. (1997) *Material Conflicts: Parades and Visual Displays in Northern Ireland*. London: Berg.

Jedlowski, P. (2001) 'Memory and Sociology: Themes and Issues'. *Time and Society*, 10(1): 29–44.

Jess, M. (2007) *The Orange Order*. Dublin: O'Brien Press.

Kauffmann, E.P. (2007) *The Orange Order: A Contemporary History*. Oxford: Oxford University Press.

Kopecek, M. (2007) *Past in the Making: Historical Revisionism in Central Europe after 1989*. Budapest: Central European University Press.

Kristeva, J. (1982) *Powers of Horror: An Essay in Abjection*. New York: Columbia University Press.

Lapham, L. (2005) *Gag Rule: On the Suppression of Dissent and the Stifling of Democracy*. London: Penguin.

Leydesdorff, S., Dawson, G., Butchardt, N. and Ashplant, T. (1999) 'Introduction'. In *Trauma and Life Stories: International Perspectives*, Rogers, K., Leydesdorff, S. and Dawson, G. (eds). London: Routledge.

Lister, D. and Jordan, H. (2004) *Mad Dog: The Rise and Fall of Johnny Adair*. Edinburgh: Mainstream.

Low, S. and Lawrence-Zuniga, D. (eds) (2003) *The Anthropology of Space and Place*. Oxford: Blackwell.

Luckmann, T. and Berger, P.L. (1991) *The Social Construction of Reality: A Treatise in the Sociology of Knowledge*. London: Penguin.

Lundy, P. and McGovern, M. (2001) 'The Politics of Memory in Post-Conflict Northern Ireland'. *Peace Review*, 13(1): 27–33.

Margalit, A. (2004) *The Ethics of Memory*. Harvard: Harvard University Press.

McDonald, H. and Cusack, J. (1997) *UVF*. Dublin: Poolbeg.

McDonald, H. and Cusack, J. (2004) *UDA: Inside the Heart of Loyalist Terror*. Dublin: Penguin Ireland.

McEvoy, K. (2007) 'Beyond Legalism: Towards a Thicker Understanding of Transitional Justice'. *Journal of Law and Society*, 34(4): 411–440.

McGarry, J. and O'Leary, B. (2004) *The Northern Ireland Conflict: Consociational Engagements*. Oxford: Oxford University Press.

McGladdery, G. (2006) *The Provisional IRA in England: The Bombing Campaign 1973–1997*. Dublin: Irish Academic Press.

McKay, S. (2000) *Northern Protestants: An Unsettled People*. Belfast: Blackstaff Press.

Miller, M. and Tougaw, J. (2003) *Extremities: Trauma, Testimony and Community*. Illinois: University of Illinois Press.

Mitchell, C. (2003) 'Protestant Identification and Political Change in Northern Ireland'. *Ethnic and Racial Studies*, 26(4): 612–631.

Mitchell, C. (2005) *Religion, Identity and Politics in Northern Ireland: Boundaries of Belonging and Belief*. Aldershot: Ashgate Publishing.

Mitscherlich, A. and Mitscherlich, M. (1975) *Inability to Mourn: Principles of Collective Behaviour*. New York: Grove/Atlantic Publishers.

Moloney, E. (2007) *A Secret History of the IRA*. London: Penguin.

Moser, P.K. and Carson, T.L. (eds) (2000) *Moral Relativism: A Reader*. New York: Oxford University Press.

Mulholland, M. (2002) *The Longest War: Northern Ireland's Troubled History*. Oxford: Oxford University Press.

Nelson, S. (1984) *Ulster's Uncertain Defenders: Protestant Political, Paramilitary, and Community Groups and the Northern Ireland Conflict*. Belfast: Appletree.

Neumann, P.G. (2003) *Britain's Long War: British Strategy in the Northern Ireland Conflict 1969–1998*. London: Palgrave Macmillan.

Ní Aoláin, F. (2000) *The Politics of Force – Conflict Management and State Violence in Northern Ireland*. Belfast: Blackstaff Press.

Ní Aoláin, F. and Campbell, C. (2005) 'The Paradox of Transition in Conflicted Democracies'. *Human Rights Quarterly*, 27(1): 172–213.

Nora, P. (ed.) (1984) *Les Lieux de mémoire* (7 vols). Paris: Edition Gallimard.

Northern Ireland Office (NIO). (1998) *The Agreement, Text of the Agreement Reached in the Multi-Party Negotiations on Northern Ireland* (Cmnd. 3883), [Good Friday Agreement; Belfast Agreement]. Belfast: HMSO.

Nytagodien, R. and Neal, A. (2004) 'Collective Trauma, Apologies, and the Politics of Memory'. *Journal of Human Rights*, 3(4): 465–475.

O'Brien, B. (1999) *The Long War: The IRA and Sinn Fein*. Dublin: O'Brien Books.

Olick, J.K. (ed.) (2003) *States of Memory: Continuities, Conflicts and Transformations in National Retrospection*. Durham: Duke University Press.

Olick, J.K. (2007) *The Politics of Regret: On Collective Memory and Historical Responsibility*. London: Routledge.

Oppenheimer, A.R. (2008) *IRA: The Bombs and the Bullets: A History of Deadly Ingenuity*. Dublin: Irish Academic Press.

O'Reilly, K. (2004) *Ethnographic Methods*. London: Routledge.

Orr, P. (2008) *The Road to the Somme: Men of the Ulster Division Tell Their Story*. Belfast: Blackstaff Press.

Paris, E. (2001) *Long Shadows: Truth, Lies and History*. New York: Bloomsbury.

Parkinson, A. (1998) *Ulster Loyalism and the British Media*. Dublin: Four Courts Press.

Parkinson, A. (2001) 'Bigots in Bowler Hats? The Presentation and Reception of the Loyalist Case in Great Britain'. In *Defenders of the Union: A Survey of British and Irish Unionism since 1801*, Boyce, G.D. and O'Day, A. (eds). London: Routledge.

Patterson, H. (2007) *Ireland since 1939: The Persistence of Conflict*. Dublin: Penguin.

Patterson, H. and Kauffman, E.P. (2007) *Unionism and Orangeism in Northern Ireland since 1945: The Decline of the Loyal Family*. Manchester: Manchester University Press.

Phelps, T.G. (2004) *Shattered Voices: Language, Violence and the Work of Truth Commissions*. Pennsylvania: University of Pennsylvania Press.

Pillemer, D.B. (1998) *Momentous Events, Vivid Memories: How Unforgettable Moments Help Us Understand the Meaning of Our Lives*. Cambridge, MA: Harvard University Press.

Pocock, J. (1998) 'The Politics of History: The Subaltern and the Subversive'. *Journal of Political Philosophy*, 6(3): 219–234.

Potter, J. (2001) *A Testimony to Courage: The History of the Ulster Defence Regiment 1969–1992*. Barnsley: Pen and Sword Books.

Pusey, M. (1987) *Jurgen Habermas*. London: Routledge.

Rae, H. (2002) *State Identities and the Homogenisation of Peoples* (Cambridge Studies in International Relations). Cambridge: Cambridge University Press.

Ricoeur, P. (1984) *Time and Narrative, Volume 1*. Chicago: University of Chicago Press.

Ricoeur, P. (1985) *Time and Narrative, Volume 2*. Chicago: University of Chicago Press.

Ricoeur, P. (1988) *Time and Narrative, Volume 3*. Chicago: University of Chicago Press.

Ricoeur, P. (1998) *Critique and Conviction: Conversations with Francois Azouri and Marc de Launay, trans. Kathleen Blamey*. Cambridge: Polity.

Ricoeur, P. (2001) *The Just*. Chicago: University of Chicago Press.

Ricoeur, P. (2004) *Memory, History, Forgetting*. Chicago: University of Chicago Press.

Robben, A.C.G.M. and Suarez-Orozoco, M.M. (2008) *Cultures under Siege: Collective Violence and Trauma*. Cambridge: Cambridge University Press.

Rolston, B. (2005) 'An Effective Mask for Terror: Democracy, Death Squads and Northern Ireland'. *Crime, Law and Social Change*, 44(2): 181–203.

Rogers, K.L., Leydesdorff, S. and Dawson, G. (eds) (2004) *Trauma: Life Stories of Survivors*. New Brunswick: Transaction Publishers.

Rosenwald, G. and Ochberg, R. (eds) (1992) *Storied Lives: The Cultural Politics of Self-Understanding*. New Haven: Yale University Press.

Ross, F. (2002) *Bearing Witness: Women and the Truth and Reconciliation Commission in South Africa*. London: Pluto Press.

Rossington, M. and Whitehead, A. (eds) (2007) *Theories of Memory: A Reader*. Edinburgh: Edinburgh University Press.

Rotberg, R. and Thompson, D. (eds) (2000) *Truth v. Justice: The Morality of Truth Commissions*. Princeton: Princeton University Press.

Routledge, P. (2003) 'Anti-Geopolitics'. In *A Companion to Political Geography*, 236–248. Agnew, J., Mitchell, K. and Toal, G. (eds). Oxford: Blackwell.

Ryder, C. (1989) *The RUC: A Force under Fire*. London: Methuen.

Ryder, C. (2001) *Inside the Maze: The Untold Story of the Northern Ireland Prison Service*. London: Methuen.

Samuel, R. (1996) *Theatres of Memory: Past and Present in Contemporary Culture*. London: Verso.

Scarry, E. (1985) *The Body in Pain*. New York: Oxford University Press.

Searle, J.R. (1970) *Speech Acts*. Cambridge: Cambridge University Press.

Shanahan, T. (2009) *The Provisional Irish Republican Army and the Morality of Terrorism*. Edinburgh: Edinburgh University Press.

Shirlow, P. and Murtagh, B. (2006) *Belfast: Segregation, Violence and the City*. London: Pluto Press.

Shriver, D.W. (1995) *An Ethic for Enemies: Forgiveness in Politics*. New York: Oxford University Press.

Simpson, K. (2007a) 'Voices Silenced, Voices Rediscovered: Victims of Violence and the Reclamation of Language in Transitional Societies'. *International Journal of Law in Context*, 3(2): 89–103.

Simpson, K. (2007b) 'Victims of Political Violence: A Habermasian Model of Truth Recovery'. *Journal of Human Rights*, 6(3): 325–343.

Simpson, K. (2008) 'Untold Stories: Unionist Remembrance of Political Violence and Suffering'. *British Politics*, 3(4): 465–489.

Simpson, K. (2009) *Truth Recovery in Northern Ireland: Critically Interpreting the Past.* Manchester: Manchester University Press.

Simpson, K. and Donnan, H. (2006) 'Changing Relationships in the Irish Borderlands'. *Anthropology in Action*, 13(1–2): 69–77.

Sitton, J. (2003) *Habermas and Contemporary Society.* New York: Palgrave Macmillan.

Sluka, J. (1989) *Hearts and Minds, Water and Fish: Support for the IRA and INLA in a Northern Irish Ghetto.* Greenwich: Jai Press.

Sluka, J. (1999) *Death Squad: The Anthropology of State Terror.* Philadelphia: University of Pennsylvania Press.

Squire, C. (2005) 'Reading Narratives'. *Group Analysis*, 38(1): 91–107.

Switzer, C. (2007) *Unionists and Great War Commemoration in the North of Ireland, 1914–1939: People, Places and Politics.* Dublin: Irish Academic Press.

Tavuchis, N. (1991) *Mea Culpa: A Sociology of Apology and Reconciliation.* Stanford: Stanford University Press.

Taylor, D. (1997) *Disappearing Acts: Spectacles of Gender and Nationalism in Argentina's Dirty War.* Durham: Duke University Press.

Taylor, P. (1997) *Provos: The IRA and Sinn Fein.* London: Bloomsbury.

Taylor, P. (1999) *Loyalists.* London: Bloomsbury.

Taylor, P. (2001) *Brits.* London: Bloomsbury.

Taylor, S. (2001) *Ethnographic Research: A Reader.* London: Sage.

Terdiman, R. (1993) *Present Past: Modernity and the Memory Crisis.* New York: Cornell University Press.

The Billy Wright Inquiry, available at http://www.billywrightinquiry.org/, last accessed January 2009.

The Bloody Sunday Inquiry, available at http://www.bloody-sunday-inquiry.org.uk/, last accessed January 2009.

Tonge, J. (1999) *Northern Ireland: Conflict and Change.* London: Prentice Hall.

Toolis, K. (1996) *Rebel Hearts: Journeys within the IRA's Soul.* London: Picador.

Torpey, J. (2001) 'Making Whole What Has Been Smashed: Reflections on Reparations'. *The Journal of Modern History*, 73: 333–358.

Torpey, J. (2003) *Making Whole What Has Been Smashed: On Reparation Politics.* Cambridge, MA: Harvard University Press.

Townshend, C. (1998) *Ireland: The Twentieth Century.* London: Arnold Publishing.

Trouillot, M-R. (1995) *Silencing the Past: Power and the Production of History.* Boston: Beacon Press.

Tunbridge, J. and Ashworth, G. (1996) *Dissonant Heritage: The Management of the Past as a Resource in Conflict.* Chichester: John Wiley and Sons.

Urban, M. (2001) *Big Boys' Rules.* London: Faber and Faber.

Volf, M. (2007) *The End of Memory: Remembering Rightly in a Violent World.* Cambridge: William B. Eerdmans Publishing Company.

Walker, G. (2004) *A History of the Ulster Unionist Party: Protestant, Pragmatism and Pessimism.* Manchester: Manchester University Press.

Walzer, M. (2006) *Just and Unjust Wars: A Moral Argument with Historical Illustrations.* New York: Basic Books.

Wertsch, J. (2002) *Voices of Collective Remembering*. Cambridge: Cambridge University Press.

West, H. (2003) 'Voices Twice Silenced'. *Anthropological Theory*, 3(3): 343–365.

Wharton, K. (2008) *A Long Long War: Voices from the British Army in Northern Ireland, 1969–1998*. Solihull: Helion and Company Ltd.

White, H. (1987) *The Content of the Form: Narrative Discourse and Historical Representation*. Baltimore: Johns Hopkins University Press.

White, H. (1992) *Identity and Control: A Structural Theory of Social Action*. Princeton: Princeton University Press.

Wilson, R. (2001) *The Politics of Truth and Reconciliation in South Africa: Legitimizing the Post-Apartheid State*. Cambridge: Cambridge University Press.

Wilson, R. (2003) 'Anthropological Studies of National Reconciliation Processes'. *Anthropological Theory*, 3(3): 367–387.

Young, J. (1994) *The Texture of Memory: Holocaust Memorials and Meaning*. New Haven: Yale University Press.

Zur, J. (1994) 'The Psychological Impact of Impunity'. *Anthropology Today*, 10(3): 12–17.

# Index